NATO before the Korean War

NEW STUDIES IN U.S. FOREIGN RELATIONS
Mary Ann Heiss, editor

NATO before
the Korean War

April 1949–June 1950

∽

Lawrence S. Kaplan

The Kent State University Press
Kent, Ohio

© 2013 by The Kent State University Press, Kent, Ohio 44242
ALL RIGHTS RESERVED
Library of Congress Catalog Card Number 2012043645
ISBN 978-1-60635-169-7
Manufactured in the United States of America

Library of Congress Cataloging-in-Publication Data
Kaplan, Lawrence S.
NATO before the Korean War : April 1949–June 1950 / Lawrence S. Kaplan
pages cm.—(New studies in U.S. foreign relations)
Includes bibliographical references.
ISBN 978-1-60635-169-7
1. North Atlantic Treaty Organization—History—20th century.
2. World politics—1945–1989. I. Title.
UA646.3.k3652 2013
355'.03109182109044—dc23   2012043645

17 16 15 14 13   5 4 3 2 1

To Morris Honick
NATO's Institutional Memory

Contents

Preface

Conventional wisdom has the Korean War putting the "O" in NATO. Prior to that time, from the signing of the treaty on April 4, 1949 to the North Korean invasion on June 25, 1950, the treaty allies were just going through the motions of establishing an organization. The alliance spawned a host of committees in this period that pretended to develop a credible defense posture for the United States and its European partners, partly to appease congressional critics in Washington, partly to prop up the morale of vulnerable European members, and partly to envelop West Germany in the transatlantic fold. The Soviet menace was the glue that held the alliance together.

In reality, little was accomplished in that first year beyond promises that were not being fulfilled. Like the Western Union Defense Organization (WUDO), NATO could be compared to a Potemkin village, all show and no substance. Only the sudden onset of the Korean War could shock the alliance into fashioning an effective military organization. Such is the image that NATO projected before the Korean War. It still informs most students of NATO's history.

This book aspires to provide a detailed examination of the state of NATO in its first fourteen months to judge if the image is accurate. It is a period I have touched on in other studies, particularly in *A Community of Interests: NATO and the Military History Program, 1948–1951* (Washington, D.C.: Office of the Secretary of Defense, Historical Office, 1980) and in *The United States and NATO: The Formative Years* (Lexington: University Press of Kentucky, 1984). Essentially the book is a sequel to *NATO 1948: The Birth of the Transatlantic Alliance* (Lanham, Md.: Rowman & Littlefield Publishers, Inc., 2007), in which I examined the fifteen months in which the alliance germinated.

While there are a few documents in the NATO archives and some useful material in the archives of the Western European Union, both in Brussels, the bulk of the unpublished primary sources for this volume are in the National Archives II in College Park, Maryland. These are clustered in Record Group 59, contain-

ing records of the U.S. State Department and, to a lesser extent, Record Groups
330 and 218, the Defense Department and Joint Chiefs of Staff, respectively. The
British National Archives in Kew provided supplemental documents. The most
valuable contributions from the European allies derived from memoirs of leading
statesmen and diplomats. Major British and French newspapers complemented
the *New York Times* for insights as well as sources. My bibliography covers only
those primary and secondary materials used in the preparation of this book.

This was a time of American domination of the alliance, evidenced by the events
of the fourteen months of NATO's history before the Korean War. Limits of American authority were also evident in this period. The U.S. archives not only provided
the most detailed information about NATO's development but frequently opened a
window permitting access to the views of most of the allies in this period.

As usual, this author needed help from scholars and librarians. It was available
in abundance. Without exception the requests I made of archivists at home and
abroad were honored quickly and positively. My first acknowledgment is to the
Harry S. Truman Library Institute for the travel grant that permitted me to spend a
week at the Harry S. Truman Library in Independence, Missouri, in May 2010. Archivist Randy Sowell anticipated many of my queries, while Lisa Sullivan did much
more than discharge her responsibilities as financial officer. An old friend from my
Ohio days, Mike Devine, director of the library, made my stay particularly pleasant.

Through correspondence with Malgosia Myc, assistant reference librarian at
the Bentley Historical Library of the University of Michigan, I was able to locate
important correspondence of Senator Vandenberg in 1949. Similarly, Christine A.
Lutz, assistant university archivist at the Seeley G. Mudd Manuscript Library of
Princeton University, and Vera Ekechukwu, Fulbright Papers research assistant at
the University of Arkansas Library, provided useful documents from the Kennan/
Dulles and Fulbright collections, respectively. I am grateful for their help. In conversations with Ineke Deserno, NATO archivist, and her colleague, Anna-Marie
Smith, I discovered that there were materials in Brussels before the Korean War.
Those documents were made available to me, and I am grateful for their coop-
eration. As with *NATO 1948*, I was able to take advantage of the archives at the
Western European Union in Brussels. Visits to Britain's National Archives in Kew
gave me an opportunity to consult its NATO materials from this period.

I owe a continuing debt of gratitude for the support the Georgetown University
librarians have given me in this project, most notably Maura Seale. The government
documents librarians Kristina Bobe and her successor, Jason D. Phillips, have been
particularly helpful, as have Meaghan Corbett and her successor, Shane Hickey, of
the Interlibrary Loan office. I also thank the staff of the National Archives in College
Park, Maryland, for facilitating my explorations of the rich resources of NARA II.

Once again, I have benefited from the advice of knowledgeable friends, particularly Stanley Kober, Diego Ruiz Palmer, Steven L. Rearden, and Stanley R. Sloan.

I am pleased to express my appreciation for the support of Will Underwood and Joyce Harrison, director and acquiring editor, respectively, of the Kent State University Press, and to Mary Ann Heiss, editor of *New Studies in U.S. Foreign Relations,* for her perceptive commentary on the manuscript. It has been twenty years since I last had an opportunity to publish with the KSU Press, and I am happy to return with this contribution. My wife Janice was always helpful with her advice on choice of words. This is also an opportunity for me to recognize the important effort that Morris Honick has made on behalf of this book as collaborator in this project from his presence in Brussels. I am pleased to dedicate this volume to him.

Abbreviations

APP	Additional Military Production Program
CIA	Central Intelligence Agency
DC	Defense Committee
DELWU	U.S. Delegate to the WU
DFEC	Defense Financial and Economic Committee
DoD	Department of Defense
ECA	European Cooperation Administration
ECC	European Coordinating Committee
FACC	Foreign Assistance Correlation Committee
FASC	Foreign Assistance Steering Committee
FMACC	Foreign Military Assistance Coordinating Committee
	(replaced the FACC in June 1949; the change is only in title, not functions)
FRUS	Foreign Relations of the United States series
IWG	International Working Group
JAMAG	Joint American Military Advisory Group
JCS	Joint Chiefs of Staff
MAAG	Military Assistance Advisory Group
MAP	Military Assistance Program
MB	Munitions Board
MDAP	Mutual Defense Assistance Program
MPP	Military Production Program
MPSB	Military Production and Supply Board
MTDP	Medium-Term Defense Plan
NAC	North Atlantic Council
NARA	National Archives and Records Administration
NME	National Military Establishment (predecessor of DoD)
NSC	National Security Council
OEEC	Organisation for European Economic Co-operation
OSD	Office of Secretary of Defense
PPS	Policy Planning Staff (State Department)
RA	Office of European Regional Affairs (State Department)
RG	Record Group-National Archives
SG	Standing Group
STOP	Short-Term Defense Plan
UNP	Office of UN Political and Security Affairs (State Department)
WU	Western Union
WUDO	Western Union Defense Organization

1949 General view of April 4 signing. Interdepartmental Auditorium, Washington, D.C.

Close-up view of Acheson signing.

1

Origins of the Alliance

The Nervous Celebration

President Truman, Secretary of State Dean Acheson, and the foreign ministers of the eleven nations that signed the North Atlantic Treaty on April 4, 1949 were well aware of the significance of the occasion. For the United States it marked the termination of a tradition of non-entanglement with the political and military affairs of the Old World, notably the powers of Western Europe that had colonized North America. The one and only entangling alliance that the United States had made had been with France in 1778, which ended in 1800 in mutual dissatisfaction. For the European allies the treaty was a major step toward ensuring an American guarantee of their security in the face of internal and external Communist challenges. The economic revival of Europe after the devastation of World War II required the psychological comfort that the new transatlantic bond would create, without which the Marshall Plan aid would fail in its effort to rebuild a unified Europe freed from the destructive rivalries of the past.

The U.S. organizers, conscious of the historic moment, made every effort to mark the event as special without excessive pomp. The customary diplomatic dress was replaced by ordinary street clothes, although almost half of the signatories showed up in striped pants in spite of the State Department's advice. The speeches were brief, with each foreign minister emulating Secretary Acheson's short address. And President Truman's equally brief support of the treaty won a standing ovation from the 1,080 invited guests seated on the auditorium floor and 245 more in the balcony.[1]

Granted that the magnificence of the stately Interdepartmental Auditorium in Washington militated against excessive modesty, as did the gold chairs where the foreign ministers and ambassadors of the eleven members sat in alphabetical order, nevertheless the use of plain black dip pens to sign the treaty, as each minister solemnly signed the document, underscored the atmosphere of informality the chief of protocol tried to instill in the hall. Worrying that fountain pens might run dry, as had happened in the past, a State Department official stood by and wiped the pens clean after each signing, and then returned the pens as souvenirs.[2]

The president did his best to foster this spirit by his homely identification of the treaty as "a neighborly act. We are like a group of householders, living in the same locality, who decide to express their community of interests by entering into a formal association for their mutual self-protection." But the treaty was intended to be more than "a simple document" that would have prevented two world wars if it had existed in 1914 and 1939.[3] The president was echoing the text of the treaty, with its wording that, as Theodore A. Achilles, chief of the State Department's Division of Western European Affairs, put it, would be understood by an Omaha milkman.[4] Unlike the flowery pretentious terms used in the Brussels Pact, the "High Contracting" was removed from the text; the plain language of "the Parties" would be more appealing to the common man. Conceivably, according to the Jesuit magazine, *America,* the extravagant promises of the failed Locarno Pact of the 1920s was an inhibiting factor.[5] Yet members of all the delegations were aware that potentially they were opening a new chapter in transatlantic history and perhaps in European history as well.

The schizophrenic element in the ceremony has often been noted in the Marine Corps band playing two irreverent songs from George Gershwin's *Porgy and Bess*—"I've Got Plenty of Nothin'" and "It Ain't Necessarily So"—at the start of the ceremonies.[6] Much more embarrassing, however, was the failure of the State Department to respect the delicate sensitivities of U.S. senators at this critical moment. The problem was the list of invitations. The State Department initially failed to invite any of the rank and file in the Senate. Its assumption had been that the presence of the vice president, the speaker of the House of Representatives, and the entire membership of the Senate Foreign Relations Committee and the House Foreign Affairs Committee would suffice. That both Democrats and Republicans were represented should have been perceived as a triumph of bipartisanship. If this was the intention, it did not work. Senators of both parties felt insulted by their exclusion. Tom Connally of Texas, chairman of the Senate Foreign Relations Committee, was embarrassed. He criticized the State Department for "poor taste and bad finesse." Connally said he understood that any senator "can get in if he cares to go. I had nothing to do with the arrangements, and neither did our committee." The Democratic leader in the Senate, Scott W. Lucas of Illinois, was more specific in his complaints: "The State Department has been very lax. Certainly this has been something of a blunder. After all, they have got to depend on the United States Senate for ratification of the pact. They might better have looked out after the Senate than someone else."[7]

The small squall over the invitation began at 11 A.M. when the Senate convened on the morning of April 4, but had blown over by 2 P.M. when Senator Lucas announced on the floor that "a slight misunderstanding" had been corrected. All senators were welcome. Most, but not all, accepted the belated and somewhat begrudging invitation. While disclaiming any involvement with the original plan, Senator Connally made a point of noting that the seating capacity of the auditorium was limited. Still, the feelings the "misunderstanding" aroused were to be reflected in what was to be an extended debate before the treaty would be ratified.[8]

Background of the "Atlantic" Treaty

That the ratification of the treaty in the U.S. Senate would be a long and complicated process should not have come as a surprise to any of the participants. The American hosts had a right to be nervous about the prospects of the treaty, given the complicated negotiations that preceded the signing of the document. Nor had they forgotten that the weight of the tradition of non-entanglement may not have been fully lifted. While the new European partners had their own reservations about the alliance, they were more concerned with how the senior partner would manage the process than they were about the reactions of their legislatures. Admittedly, Communist-led protests would mark debates in Italy and France, but the protesters were marginalized in those countries. The leaders of the many factions were as anxious to secure the treaty as were the more unified governments of Northern Europe.

The initiative for the alliance, after all, was European, not American. The desperate economic plight of Western Europe in the wake of World War II seemingly led such vulnerable countries as France and Italy into the arms of Communist parties supported by the Soviet Union. Only the United States had the resources to cope with this challenge, and in 1945 it was not clear that Americans, victorious over the Axis powers but tired of international obligations, would rise to the Communist challenge, or would revert to its familiar isolationist positions of the past.

The untried Truman administration did not offer a clear answer in 1945 and 1946. It veered between efforts at accommodation with Stalin's USSR and refusal to accept the Communist actions bringing Central and Eastern Europe into the Soviet orbit. None of the meetings of the foreign ministers of the victors of World War II yielded any concessions from the Soviet leadership. On the contrary, sensing weakness in Washington and impotence in London and Paris, the Soviets not only consolidated their control of Poland and Hungary, but increased their demands for more authority over divided Berlin.

Not until George Kennan, a Soviet specialist and minister-counselor at the U.S. embassy in Moscow, sent his famous long telegram in 1946, urging containment of Soviet expansion, was the Truman administration able to forge a consistent policy toward the Soviet Union. It assumed the impossibility of dealing with the Soviets in customary diplomatic terms, and recommended a firm support of forces in Europe and elsewhere that would counter the attractions of Communism. Kennan's

assumption included an expectation that patient application of political and economic pressure would expose its flaws and ultimately lead to its demise. Conventional diplomacy was irrelevant to the relations between the United States and the
Soviet Union.

Guided by Kennan's advice, the Truman administration issued in the following
year the Truman Doctrine, which promised U.S. military support of nations un-
der Communist threat, and the Marshall Plan, which promised economic help to
Western European economies in their resistance to Communist blandishments.
Greece and Turkey were the initial beneficiaries of the Truman Doctrine. Western
Europe would be restored to economic health through the implementation of the
Marshall Plan.[9]

While Europeans applauded the renewed engagement of the United States
with the outside world, and particularly with the plight of their economies, their
leaders were convinced that the new face of American foreign policy was insufficient either to protect them from the USSR's external pressures or from internal
subversion by domestic Communists. Economic aid, massive though it would be,
was not sufficient to revive the economies of the West if Europeans lacked a sense
of security in the face of the Soviet adversary in the East, and of parties devoted
to the Soviet Union in their midst. Nor would military aid instill the confidence
Europe needed to recover and revive. Much more was needed in 1947. It would
require a guarantee of American commitment to the defense of Europe, a commitment that was not present in the two world wars of the twentieth century.
The isolationist tradition that dominated America's history even into the mid-
twentieth century would have to be terminated before Europe could be assured
that America would be at its side. Had the United States been there in 1914 instead
of 1917, or in 1939 instead of 1941, both world wars might have been avoided. Such
was the thinking that circulated among Western European leaders.

In many respects the Marshall Plan pointed the way. In exchange for the economic reconstruction of shattered Europe, the United States expected Europeans
to abandon the divisive policies that fostered wars in the past, and replace them
with a path toward the economic and potentially political integration of Western
Europe. The spirit informing the Marshall Plan spoke to the missionary impulse
in American history that had inspired the liberation of Cuba and the Philippines
in 1898. It also fed into a national sense of self-interest in which a prosperous
West would not only be a bulwark against Communist expansion but also bestow
advantages on the United States as a trading partner. None of these considerations
was lost on European leaders, along with the danger of becoming victims of an
American imperial presence in Europe. But that future was far less intimidating
than the immediate threat of a Communist Europe that U.S. power could counteract. The Europeans responded with the establishment of the Committee (later
the Organisation) of European Economic Co-operation in July 1947 to implement

the aims of the Marshall Plan. The Council of Europe, which emerged two years later, was a product not only of American encouragement for political as well as economic integration of Europe but also of movements in Western Europe nourished during the war to create a new order in the West.[10]

But in 1947 the prospect of a united Europe, backed economically by a supportive United States, was only a vision. The reality was that the Atlantic Ocean separated America from Europe while the Soviet Union was a close neighbor. Together, British Foreign Minister Ernest Bevin and his French counterpart, Georges Bidault, agreed that the United States must be persuaded to participate in a military alliance with Britain and France as the guarantor of Europe's survival. Once America participated in a European defense arrangement, the confidence Western Europe needed to promote integration and rebuild their economic and social systems would be in place.

Making an entangling alliance with the United States would require Americans to abandon a tradition of non-entanglement with Europe that went back to the founding of the republic. The only alliance the United States made with a European power was in 1778 with France in order to secure independence from Britain. The alliance fitted a typical eighteenth-century model, a temporary arrangement wherein a weaker party enlists a stronger partner to win a specific objective without intending France to replace Britain as controller of its destiny. For its part France sought to use the colonial rebellion to weaken Britain, but only to the extent of inducing it to join an Anglo-French common front against Eastern European powers. The new nation was an instrument for France to achieve that goal. Both parties achieved their objectives. This classical European alliance of convenience became irrelevant immediately after the war and dissolved in mutual discontent in 1800. The aggressive behavior of France appeared to threaten the stability of the new nation. When the Convention of Mortefontaine was signed with Bonaparte's consulate, the memory of the alliance deepened American distrust of the Old World that would require 150 years to erase.[11]

The collapse of the foreign ministers' meeting in December 1947 over the status of occupied Germany provided the incentive to set in motion the Anglo-French grand design. This was the beginning of a long and arduous process of convincing the United States to accept a military alliance with Europe that was to consume the entire year of 1948 and the first few months of 1949. To assure the United States that Europe had turned a new leaf, Britain and France formed the Brussels Pact with the Low Countries in March 1948, creating a Western Union in keeping with the premise of the Marshall Plan—to collaborate in the economic rebuilding of Europe. This was an earnest of their good intentions. While the language of the pact centered on economic issues, an important article promised that "if any of the High Contracting parties should be the object of an armed attack in Europe, the other High Contracting Parties, will, in accordance with the provisions of

Article 51 of the Charter of the United Nations, afford the party so attacked all the military and other aid and assistance in their power."

Their hope was that the United States would become one of the "High Contracting Parties," and they had some grounds for optimism in the winter and spring of 1948. Soviet behavior had become more aggressive, as Czechoslovakia fell under complete Communist domination and Norway came under pressure to sign a non-aggression pact with the USSR, an invitation reminiscent of Hitler's overtures on the eve of World War II. Over Germany, the relations between the former allies had become so toxic that by summer the Soviets had instituted a blockade denying the West ground access to Berlin. Moreover, the British and French had won over influential U.S. diplomatic officials to the need for an alliance with Western Europe, if not membership in the Brussels Pact. It is noteworthy that immediately after the Brussels Pact was signed, the United States, Britain, and Canada sent delegates to a secret meeting in the Pentagon who recommended the creation of an Atlantic security pact to cope with potential Soviet aggression against Western Europe.[12]

But the operative word in the Pentagon negotiations was "secret." The Truman administration was not prepared to support such a radical departure from the American tradition of political and military non-entanglement with Western Europe. It had to deal with the remnant of the isolationists whose size and influence had shrunk in World War II but who included such powerful members as Sen. Robert Taft (R-OH). Additionally, the U.S. military, disturbed as they were over the administration's low ceiling for the defense budget, worried that a military alliance would open the floodgates to Europe's demand for arms and equipment. The military was skeptical that Europe, even with U.S. aid, could stop a Soviet invasion. But the most daunting challenge to the State Department was the negative reaction of former isolationists, now fervent internationalist supporters of the United Nations. Would a European–American alliance undercut the role of the UN as the world's peacekeeper? If so, the European allies would give a low priority to the putative incompatibility between the North Atlantic Treaty and the United Nations Charter, a conflict that disturbed their American colleagues.

Terms of the Treaty

The Truman administration inched toward accommodation with the Europe's demands, first by promising military aid to the new Western Union but without participating in the organization, and then agreeing to a conference in Washington in the summer of 1948 that would work out, again in secret, the terms of U.S. engagement. The key requirement, from the U.S. perspective, was to win the backing of Sen. Arthur Vandenberg (R-MI), the powerful chairman of the Foreign Relations Committee. His overriding concern before he would support an alliance was to ensure that a treaty would accord with the terms of the UN Charter, and that the military component, particularly military assistance, would be minimized.

The Europeans were willing enough to accommodate the Americans by paying obeisance to the United Nations in linking the Atlantic Pact to the charter. They were less comfortable with the Truman administration's insistence on expanding the membership of the alliance by encompassing the Scandinavian countries and Portugal, and they were most uncomfortable with the terms the United States required for responding to an attack on members of the alliance. The Western Europeans wanted to include the clear language of the Brussels Pact's Article IV, making an attack against one member the equivalent of an attack against all. This guarantee was at the heart of the alliance from the European perspective. But the most they could extract from the United States was Article 5, a seemingly evasive promise that "if such an armed attack occurs, each of them . . . will assist the Party or Parties so attacked by taking forthwith, individually and in concert with the other Parties, such action as it deems necessary, including the use of armed force, to restore and maintain the security of the North Atlantic area." In deference to the Senate's fears about infringement of its power to commit the United States to war, the wording of the article was designed to ensure that its constitutional prerogatives would be safeguarded. The Europeans did manage to insert "the use of armed force" into the text. They were comforted by the understanding that should a crisis arise, the United States would have no choice but to accept the obligations the treaty imposed on it. Bevin felt that the language of Article 5 would not matter in the event of war, despite the exclusive constitutional right of the Congress to declare war. The treaty would have set up the machinery of entanglement.[13]

Concern over Article 5 pushed into the background the Western Union's reluctance to extend membership to peripheral nations with the probable negative impact on its own central role in the alliance Although the military aid anticipated from the alliance would have to be shared by too many other parties to the treaty, this shortcoming could be corrected in negotiations with the United States after the treaty was signed. Moreover, the Western Union leaders understood that bringing Denmark or Portugal into the alliance provided stepping-stones needed for air or sea military assistance to Europe. Lost on many of the allies, however, was the significance that the inclusion of Canada and Iceland in the alliance had for the American psyche. Their presence emphasized the "Atlantic" as opposed to the "European" character of NATO, which was vital for the treaty's acceptance in the United States.[14]

What particularly captivated the European allies was an illusion that should American membership in the alliance fail to deter Soviet aggression, the United States was capable of dispatching B-29s, equipped with atom bombs from their base in Nebraska, to cope with any emergency. They were unaware just how few bombs the U.S. Strategic Air Command possessed and how limited its capabilities were without access to bases that future allies could supply.[15] The importance of Iceland, Norway, Denmark, and Portugal in the alliance for the facilities their territories would afford aircraft-carrying military assistance took time before it registered with the Western Union.

From a European perspective, the next step after the signing of the treaty was quick ratification of the treaty in order to secure substantial U.S. military aid. The path to ratification, like the path to the signing ceremony, would be longer than the allies assumed, and for much the same reason that the negotiations in 1948 were so protracted. American hesitation over abandoning its 150-year-old tradition of non-entanglement with European political and military affairs had to be overcome.[16]

2

Toward Ratification

April–July 1949

The Treaty in the UN

Before the treaty could undergo scrutiny by the Senate, it had to meet a more immediate challenge in the UN General Assembly. By unhappy timing, the Assembly convened on April 5, the day after the treaty was signed where it could expect attack not only from the Soviet bloc but from U.S. friends worried about the treaty's compatibility with the UN Charter.

The framers of the treaty were well aware of its vulnerabilities, and took steps to thwart criticism. It was no coincidence that four of the fourteen articles of the treaty invoked the name of the UN Charter and either implied or directly asserted that its purposes were to serve, as the preamble stated, the purposes and principles of the United Nations. Article 7 was entirely an expression of devotion to the UN: "This Treaty does not affect, and shall not be interpreted as affecting in any way the rights and obligations under the Charter of the Parties which are members of the United Nations, or the primary responsibility of the Security Council for the maintenance of international peace and security." Article 5 specified that "any such armed attack and all measures taken as a result thereof shall immediately be reported to the Security Council. Such measures shall be terminated when the Security Council has taken the measures necessary to reassure and maintain international peace and security." The linkage between treaty and charter seemingly could not be more intimate. Yet only one article of the charter, Article 51, was identified—the right of individual and collective self-defense, embedded in the treaty's Article 5, without observing that the right of self-defense was independent of any of the charter's articles.

What was missing in the text of the treaty were the key passages in the charter's articles 52, 53, and 54, which defined the obligations of a regional organization in the service of the UN and which was the treaty's stated objective. These articles required reporting all activities to the Security Council where the Soviet Union had a seat and a veto. Since NATO came into existence to circumvent the Soviet veto that had rendered the UN impotent to maintain peace and international security, there was no way of fitting the treaty legally into the charter as a regional organization in support of its objectives.

It required, then, an exercise in casuistry—and an element of hypocrisy—to fit the two documents together. The United States, no more than its adversary, had any intention of giving up its veto power, or of allowing the smaller nations to remove the constitutional authority of Congress to declare war. This had been a critical factor in the Senate's defeat of the League of Nations a generation before. The veto power in this context was as much appreciated in the Pentagon as in the Kremlin.

There was still another dimension to the veto issue: namely, the Soviet recognition that its voice would not be heard in a Western-dominated General Assembly, or even in the Security Council, where the other members would be in the Western European or Latin American camps, hostile to Soviet interests. The USSR could count only on the three votes in the General Assembly it had been allotted at the Yalta conference in 1945 and three from Communist Poland, Czechoslovakia, and—less reliably—Yugoslavia. It was understandable that Communist nations regarded any deviation from the understandings of 1945 to be a subversion of the UN. Without the veto power, the Soviet Union, like the United States, would not have approved the charter.[1]

But the veto became the symbol, in the eyes of the West, of Soviet obstructionism and, even more, as an instrument for advancing Communism worldwide. Frustration over Soviet policies in Iran, Greece, and Germany accounted for the recognition that the UN was an insufficient bulwark against Soviet-led Communism. The formation of a military alliance in the form of the North Atlantic Treaty was the end product of this understanding. The mission of this action was to embrace the goals of the charter without the constraints imposed by the veto power of the four victors of World War II. The text of the treaty itself implied that the pact not only shared the purposes of the charter but that it also conformed to the letter of the charter.

These objectives confronted some serious obstacles. In the international community two key leaders—UN Secretary-General Trygve Lie and General Assembly President Herbert V. Evatt—were skeptical about NATO's claims of conformity with the UN Charter. Not that either of them was in sympathy with the Soviet Union or with Communist ideology. Lie had been Norway's foreign minister in London during World War II and was concerned with protecting the integrity of the UN. Two days before the signing of the treaty he warned that "no regional arrangement can ever be a satisfactory substitute for the United Nations." Lie despaired of a lasting peace "if alliances were regarded as a path to genuine collective security."[2]

Like Lie, Evatt was a veteran of the San Francisco conference in 1945 and a fervent champion of the UN. The Australian statesman spoke for the smaller nations in asserting at the General Assembly on April 5 that "nearly all the difficulties of the United Nations have been caused by one factor: great power disagreement outside the United Nations and completely independent of the United Nations."

He went on to remind his listeners that "world-wide security, and surely that is our goal can only be secured in a world-wide organization."[3]

There was no doubt that NATO was the target of Evatt's speech. Yet it was not the unhappiness of internationalists that distressed the advocates of NATO. It was the anticipated attack from the Soviet adversary that they assumed would burst forth at the meeting of the General Assembly in New York the day after the treaty was signed. The Soviets gave enough signals in advance of the General Assembly session to suggest that they would strike hard at the West's new alliance. The Kremlin's pressure on Norway in January 1949 and its subsequent harsh dismissal of that country's promise not to permit military bases on its territory was a particular indication of the USSR's position.[4]

Soviet charges of violation of the charter picked up steam as the allies concluded their negotiations. The Soviet press printed the full text of the treaty on March 29 to expose the hollowness of NATO's claim of harmony with the charter. On March 31, just five days before the official signing, the Soviets issued a formal protest. It mocked the assertion that NATO was a regional agreement under the charter's Article 52 in light of the location of its members "in both hemispheres of the globe." Moreover, the Soviets noted that "Article 5 of the North Atlantic Treaty envisages the application of armed forces by parties to the Treaty without any authority whatsoever from the Security Council. Thus even if the North Atlantic treaty were considered a regional agreement, Article 5 of the Treaty is incompatible with the UNO Charter."[5] It seemed that the Kremlin was preparing to zero in all the vulnerabilities in the treaty, and the meeting of the General Assembly just after the Western foreign ministers had signed the treaty would be the scene of the Soviet challenge.

In preparation for the Soviet onslaught at the General Assembly, the staff of the U.S. delegation at the UN General Assembly produced a position paper on March 30, suggesting ways of coping with its polemics. First, the United States should not oppose putting the issue of the treaty's incompatibility on the agenda; rather, it should accept the challenge and then immediately send it into a committee for discussion if possible without prior debate in the plenary session. The U.S. delegation should "content itself with a moderate and straightforward exposition in general terms of the true meaning of the Pact within the framework of the Charter." If the Soviet delegates become excessively abusive, then turn the tables on them by emphasizing how the Soviet exploitation of the veto has paralyzed the Security Council. Contrast the constructive role played by Western democracies with the repressive behavior of the Soviets toward their satellites.[6]

Notwithstanding this advice, the U.S. delegation became increasingly agitated as the third session of the General Assembly was about to open. It was divided over whether the United States should take a reactive position, as the position paper recommended, and as Warren R. Austin, chairman of the U.S. delegation, supported. Other delegates preferred that the United States take the initiative in explaining and justifying the treaty instead of waiting for a Soviet denunciation. Why not use, as delegate Benjamin V. Cohen suggested, the platform of the General Assembly to explain to the world just how the treaty reinforced rather than subverted its obligations under the UN Charter? The delegation, decided, however, to keep the issue out of the Assembly unless the Soviets introduced it.[7]

Soviet efforts to condemn the treaty in advance of the meeting of the General Assembly failed. Their verbal assaults had to be toned down in light of the extensive pains the Soviets were taking to show a peaceful face to the world as they tried to portray the West, by contrast, as the aggressive enemy of both the UN and the Soviet Union. A Soviet-inspired Cultural and Scientific Confederation for World Peace had convened at New York's Waldorf-Astoria hotel in late March to alert the world to the danger of war that the United States was creating. Violent protests against the newly signed North Atlantic Treaty could undo the effect they were seeking.[8]

When the UN General Assembly convened on April 5, the day after the treaty was signed, there was no echo of Soviet outrage against the Atlantic alliance from Asian or African members, conscious though they were of the prominence of colonial powers among the signatories of the treaty. And when the Soviet delegates tried to present themselves to Africans as enemies of colonialism, their own recent approval of Italian claims on Italy's former African territories, presumably to bolster the fortunes of the Italian Communist Party, undermined their efforts. This schizophrenic behavior spoiled the image the Soviets were seeking to polish in the UN. The thirty vetoes cast by the Soviets in the four years of the UN's history was another source of unhappiness among the smaller members of the organization.

It should have come as no surprise to the U.S. delegation that the Soviets would introduce the treaty into the proceedings to divert the Assembly's displeasure with their stance on Italian colonies and the excessive use of their veto power, even though the new North Atlantic Treaty was not on the agenda. On April 13 Deputy Foreign Minister Andrei Gromyko charged that the treaty was only a device to wreck the UN by forming an aggressive bloc that would lead to a new world war: "The USSR deemed it necessary," Gromyko asserted, "to draw the attention of the General Assembly to the aggressive policy of the ruling circles in the United States and the United Kingdom. . . . The North Atlantic group of countries was being set up as an instrument to enforce United States and United Kingdom domination over other countries and peoples." Gromyko evoked familiar accusations of the West's isolating the Soviet Union, much as it had done in collaboration with "Hitlerite Germany" in the 1930s. The West's efforts to curb the exercise of the veto were part of a plot to attack both the Soviet Union and the UN. In this context, Soviet vetoes were in support of the charter against the attempt of the militaristic West to undermine it.[9]

There was no doubt why Gromyko ignored the agenda in launching his assault against the United States. The U.S. delegates were taken by surprise by the absence of a formal notice about Soviet intentions. But should they have been surprised? They had anticipated just such an attack at the time the treaty was signed. Given the hostility they encountered in the Assembly, the Soviets needed an excuse to move to an offensive position, and the Atlantic Pact was just the instrument to serve this purpose. Over the next few days the Soviets had assistance from Polish and Czech delegates insisting that NATO was nothing more than a refinement of the Dunkirk and Brussels pacts in preparing for war against the Communist nations. Why else, they asked, would the United States consider providing military assistance to its allies if it were not for "receiving in return air bases and vital staging areas for the offensive?"[10]

If U.S. Ambassador Austin was genuinely upset by the Soviet effort to change the subject, he recovered sufficiently to point out that the Soviets should accept the will of the majority in the UN and agree to voluntary moderation of the use of the veto. Austin then warned that "if a permanent member attempts to destroy through force the political independence of his neighbor . . . the responsibility for the violation cannot be avoided or obscured through the casting of a negative vote when the victim takes the aggression to the Security Council."[11]

Gladwyn Jebb, head of the British delegation, observed that while Austin had "a considerable capacity for indignation . . . he was a little old-fashioned in his oratory and his outlook and therefore was not entirely suitable to represent the USA." Jebb's colleague, Hector McNeil, spoke contemptuously of Gromyko's introduction of the North Atlantic Treaty into a debate on the veto, "in spite of the fact that it was not on the agenda." He wanted to "remind the Soviet Union delegation and the other delegations which supported its view on the North Atlantic treaty . . . that they could request the inclusion of the question in the agenda of the General Assembly in accordance with the established procedure." He doubted, however, that the USSR delegation would follow such a procedure. He expected, on the contrary, that "it would prefer to make repeated attacks on the North Atlantic Treaty every time it should find itself in a political tight corner." McNeil dismissed the Soviet case as he elaborated on the differences between the military agreements it has concluded with its satellites and the free association of the Atlantic countries.[12]

At the end of the day the failure of the Soviets to put the United States on the defensive was manifested in the defeat of its draft resolution (A793) by a vote of six in favor and forty against. By contrast, the draft resolution (A792), approved by the Ad Hoc Political Committee, was adopted by a vote of forty-three to six.[13] Although the practical results of the votes were slight, they were sufficient to puncture any illusions the Soviets may have had about the credibility of their pose as champions of the charter. Mounting resentment against Soviet behavior undoubtedly accounted for the majority's tolerance of the treaty's putative infractions of the charter's obligations. For the balance of this session the Soviets ignored the treaty. Defense of their veto power was more important than a continued attack against the NATO allies. It was that power alone in the Security Council that served as a brake against the apparent automatic majority in the UN General Assembly.

The Treaty and the U.S. Senate—the UN

Of all the obstacles in the way of ratification of the treaty in the U.S. Senate, the military character of the pact was more serious than the protests of the weakened isolationists or of the Joint Chiefs of Staff concerned both with potential damage to their budgets and with commitments they could not honor. The question of the UN inevitably emerged as an integral part of this problem. The administration had to allay the qualms of the many friends of the UN in the Senate and in the country who feared that an Atlantic security pact would alter the direction the nation had taken since World War II. Instead of an organization dedicated to the abolition of the balance-of-power structure that had characterized the West over the past three hundred years, NATO could be identified with the alliance structure that inflicted so much damage in the past.

Many of the American supporters of the UN were converts from isolationism to internationalism and were imbued with the enthusiasm of true believers in a new cause. For them World War II had provided the lesson that withdrawal from the responsibilities of a great power had opened the path to war. The United Nations was the instrument to achieve a new world order and American power should be used to further this objective.

The most articulate advocate of the UN in the Senate was Arthur H. Vandenberg (R-MI) whose influence was reflected in the frequent references to the charter in the articles of the treaty. A passionate internationalist since the Japanese attack on Pearl Harbor, he had been equally passionate as an isolationist candidate seeking the Republican presidential candidacy in 1940. Vandenberg looked the part of a senator, a big man with a big ego who required appropriate attention from the State Department at all times. Accordingly, Undersecretary of State Robert A. Lovett was deferential as negotiations for the treaty proceeded in 1948. He stopped by regularly at Vandenberg's suite in the Wardman Park Hotel for a drink and conversation. By contrast, Kennan was bemused by the senator's preening over his actions and professed not to understand the rationale for the elaborate deference paid to him at that time. Acheson did know the reason even if he disliked participating in the courtship of the senator. But all the leaders of the Truman administration recognized that Vandenberg was the key to the Senate's acceptance of the North Atlantic Treaty.[14]

Despite his success in appearing to make the treaty a partner of the charter, Vandenberg was worried about the obvious military elements in the alliance. Respond-

ing to a pacifist history professor two weeks after the treaty was signed, he insisted
that he, too, would disapprove of a "military alliance in the historic pattern. But in
my humble opinion the North Atlantic Pact is *fundamentally* of an entirely different character. It is a *peace* Pact. It is written scrupulously within the structure of the
United Nations Charter and is directly authorized by the U.N. charter."[15] According
to Vandenberg, neither he nor the American public would accept a commitment that
would undo the change in America's outlook on the world symbolized by the UN.

U.S. officials responsible for the ratification process had some justification for
their worries about the linkage between the treaty and traditional alliances. Objections were raised not only from the usual sources—the surviving isolationists
mostly from the Right and Soviet sympathizers from the Left—but also from uncomfortable religious leaders. Twenty-two ministers and theologians from such
institutions as the Harvard Divinity School and the Union Theological Seminary
declared on April 15 that the treaty "means a continuation of the Cold War in a
divided world." They insisted that it was time to act against such provocative measures, "instead of supinely underwriting national policy."[16] These were sentiments
that would be raised repeatedly before the treaty was ratified.

Although the treaty emerged from the UN debates relatively unscarred, the vulnerabilities that the Soviet bloc was unable to exploit did not go unnoticed in the
Senate. From April 27 intermittently to May 18, 1949, the Senate Committee on
Foreign Relations listened to ninety-six witnesses air their views about the treaty.
Of this number more than fifty spoke in opposition. It took courage for the Truman administration to give a platform to public and private witnesses, ranging
over the entire ideological spectrum, many of whom would assail the treaty as a
violation of the basic traditions of American foreign policy. The Senate leadership
invited the most hostile Republican senators—Forrest C. Donnell (R-MO) and Arthur V. Watkins (R-UT)—to the hearings even though they were not members of
the Foreign Relations Committee.

The result was a full-scale assault on the treaty on more counts than the Soviets
were able to find—its rejection of an isolationist tradition that stretched back to
the termination of the Franco-American alliance in 1800, its ludicrous attempts to
equate it with the Monroe Doctrine, its embrace of an alliance system Americans
had always condemned, and its flouting of the UN Charter. No one spoke more
passionately against the treaty than Curtis. P. Nettels, a distinguished professor of
American colonial history at Cornell University. By joining the alliance, he judged,
the United States would "abandon the historic policies of the Nation and substitute
therefore a new policy alien to our traditions. We are asked to forsake the unbroken
practice of 149 years—the practice of abstaining from peacetime military alliances.
We are asked to reject the wisest counsel of the farewell address. . . ."[17]

None of these charges fazed Acheson, who seemed to relish the challenge. With
his guardsman's mustache he looked every bit the part of an aristocrat who, in the

words of journalist Robert Donovan, "would have looked as much at home at 10 Downing Street as in Foggy Bottom."[18] Son of an Episcopal bishop and the product of Yale and Harvard Law School, he displayed an air of arrogant authority that was bound to antagonize most congressmen, even if they were inclined to agree with his arguments. Instead of avoiding elements in the treaty that did not fit American traditions, Acheson made a point of showing how the treaty accorded with the spirit of isolationism. He proclaimed an elastic interpretation of the Monroe Doctrine by citing the Inter-American Treaty of Reciprocal Assistance, signed at Rio de Janeiro in 1947, as the multilateralization of the isolationist doctrine. And if the Rio Pact did not constitute a break with the past, it followed that the Atlantic Pact was just a variation of the Rio Pact. Substantially the same language was used in both documents. Both spoke of fulfilling democratic ideals; both pledged loyalty to the UN Charter; and both contained clauses providing responses to armed attack. It was Tom Connally, chairman of the Foreign Relations Committee in the eighty-first Congress, who stated specifically that "The treaty which the Committee on Foreign Relations now presents for favorable Senate action is but the logical extension of the principle of the Monroe Doctrine to the North Atlantic area."[19]

Acheson's lofty manner allowed him to get away with including Western Europe within the boundaries of the Monroe Doctrine. U.S. ambassador to the UN, Warren R. Austin, shared these sentiments but lacked enough of Acheson's brio to make an effective case for the treaty's harmonization with the charter. His trouble was less with the literal relationship between the two documents than with the images opponents of the treaty were able to project. These centered on the military aspects of the alliance that appeared to be contrary to the spirit of the charter, particularly the military assistance that the United States intended to supply its allies. This was a connection the State Department had worried about at the meeting of the General Assembly in April. The veto issue, where the Americans were on the popular side from the perspective of most of the delegates, prevented the Soviets from making an effective case against the alliance as a belligerent instrument of American imperialism. But the issue of militarism was a problem for the administration at the hearings on the treaty. Communists railed against its hostility to the Soviet Union, and the various supporters of Henry Wallace's Progressive Party condemned the treaty as a divisive force in the relationship between the wartime allies. To Wallace, the treaty represented the failure of Truman's foreign policy, especially since the Marshall Plan's objective had been to preclude the need for a military program for Europe.[20]

Arguably, more damaging to the treaty's prospects were pacifists who spoke out against it because of the perceived militarism inherent in the alliance. Halting the arms race was their priority. NATO appeared to be directly opposed to those who believed in the possibility of permanent peace between nations. They feared that the treaty strengthened military influence on U.S. policy that would counteract the benign influence of the United Nations. Mrs. Clifford A. Bender, an active member of the Women's Division of Christian Service of the Methodist Church, could have spoken for the Society of Friends and the Church of the Brethren when she declared that "the most that can be achieved by military alliances is a temporary balance of power, while they eventually give rise to increasing insecurity and a menacing armaments race, ending in war."[21]

Austin tried homespun language to exorcise the notion that the treaty created an alliance of the kind associated with European balance-of-power policies. "I have been asked," he noted, "whether the North Atlantic Treaty is not the resumption of the practice of setting up a power equilibrium. . . . My answer is 'No'. The ancient theory of balance of power was given a blue discharge when the United Nations was formed. The undertaking of the peoples of the United Nations to combine their efforts through the international organization . . . introduced formally the element of preponderance of power. And out went old man balance of power."[22] There was a comedic element in Austin's artless attempt to banish "old man balance of power" by calling the new relationship between the United Nations and aggressor nations "preponderance of power." That NATO was fulfilling the purposes of the UN Charter by contributing to that preponderance was never a question in Austin's mind. In fact, he was saying nothing that Acheson had not stated more eloquently—and probably more cynically.

The sharpest attacks against the administration's defense of the treaty were delivered by the isolationist remnant rather than by the larger group of pacifists. Senator Donnell took full advantage of the invitation to participate in the Senate hearing, and made himself as annoying as possible to Acheson. The secretary of state put it mildly in saying that Donnell was not his "favorite senator. He combined the courtliness of Mr. Pickwick and the suavity of an experienced waiter with the manner of a prosecuting attorney in the movies—the gimlet eye, the piercing question. In administering the *coup de grace* he would do so with a napkin over his arm and his ears sticking out like an alert elephant."[23]

Acheson was more than a match for Donnell. When the senator pressed him on whether the treaty's justification "would at least in part be in that portion of the United Nations Charter that refers to regional arrangements," Acheson flatly said, "No. It lies in Article 51."[24] Donnell then moved on to another topic even though Acheson had not really responded to his query.

Ambassador Austin was an easier target for Donnell's gimlet eye. He first forced Austin to admit that he did call the North Atlantic Treaty a regional arrangement, and then to waltz around the definition by saying that "It is not necessary to define the organization of the North Atlantic community as exclusively a regional arrangement, or as exclusively a group for collective self-defense, since activities under both article 51 and chapter VIII [regional organizations] are comprehended in the treaty." Donnell reminded him that Article 54 of Chapter VIII required that the Security

Council be fully informed of activities under regional arrangements. Badgered by Donnell, Austin lapsed into incoherence, saying that "I do not regard this treaty as making a regional arrangement, a fully panoplied regional arrangement . . . but it comprehends some activities that may get in there, and when you try those activities then you come under the restrictions in chapter VIII."[25]

Austin never did get out of the corner Donnell had backed him into, but it did not matter. The administration's team had the upper hand and the majority of votes. Acheson allowed critics from the Senate and the public at large to express their opinions firm in the knowledge that the treaty would survive the hearings. The administration had additional help from the gavel of committee chairman Tom Connally, who regularly and often rudely cut off comments of critics from the Left.[26] He was no more accommodating to critics from the Right. Senator Watkins walked out of the committee room claiming to have been insulted by the chairman's discourteous refusal to allow persistent questioning of supporters of the pact.[27] No matter how logical the arguments against the treaty, they had no more chance of success at the hearings in May than did the Soviets at the UN General Assembly debates in April.

The Treaty and Military Assistance

Compatibility between treaty and charter was legally the most difficult hurdle the U.S. supporters of the pact had to confront, and to some degree it was also the most emotional for converts to internationalism. But as the debate played out in the United States, it was not the most controversial. The question of military assistance drew more argument in and out of Congress. In fact, some of the emotions expressed over the UN were ignited by the close association both friends and opponents of the treaty made between the military implications of an alliance and the military aid sought by the new allies. When W. Averell Harriman, roving ambassador for the European Recovery Program, testified before the Senate Foreign Relations Committee that to give the pact "real meaning," Congress must pass promptly the $1,130 billion military assistance program that the administration was preparing, he upset Vandenberg, who was uncomfortable with the linkage. Given his antipathy to the military component of the Atlantic Pact, which he had hoped to deflect in the Vandenberg Resolution of 1948, he feared that Harriman was overstating the accompanying program of military aid to the point of doing harm to the treaty itself.[28]

Yet, it was impossible for the defenders of the treaty to distance themselves from a program that was not only required by the future beneficiaries but was vital to the success of the treaty itself. The long-range U.S. military objective, as the Foreign Assistance Correlation Committee (FACC) identified in its policy paper of May 15, 1949, was to "prevent loss or destruction of Western European and Middle East nations and by securing the natural approaches to the enemy sources of power to facilitate the conduct of offensive operations. But for the short-run the United States must "improve to the maximum extent practicable, adapt the earliest date practicable, the capability of Western European nations to provide for their own defense."[29]

While negotiations over treaty's terms were being conducted, the interagency group responsible for military aid was already in motion and prepared to launch a program as soon as the treaty was signed. Over the past year the Brussels Pact powers had created a Western Union Defense Organization (WUDO), at least on paper, complete with a Military Committee, a Chiefs of Staff Committee, and even a Commanders-in-Chief Committee. Their purpose was to demonstrate to the framers of the treaty that the Europeans were doing their part in preparing not only their own defense but also collaborating in the spirit demanded by the United States.[30]

Nothing much was accomplished beyond the display of intentions. A Military Supply Board was supposed to come up with a firm production program within the budgetary limitations of their economies. By April 1949 there was little to justify the plans made by the FACC. The U.S. military advisers attached to each of the committees recognized and were frustrated by the inactivity of their European colleagues. However, they had no choice but to accept what was given them.[31]

If these plans did not materialize, it was not only because of the inadequate preparations of WUDO. More responsible was the widespread concern among pact adherents in the Senate over the linkage of the military assistance program (MAP) with the treaty. Vandenberg in particular did not want to have the importance of the treaty measured by a military yardstick. But the separation of military aid from the purposes of the alliance was even more difficult to finesse than the claims of harmony between the treaty and the charter. Almost all the signatories of the treaty had made known their requests even as the negotiations proceeded. The five Brussels Pact members submitted a single coordinated petition on April 5. It was designed to assure maximum benefit for the Atlantic community, containing as it did assurances that the military programs of the member nations will display self-help, in the spirit of the Marshall Plan, and will not endanger their economic recovery. Although the military assistance program was consciously conceived and developed separately and in advance of the formulation of the pact, there was no doubt in the Truman administration that the Atlantic alliance would benefit from the defensive potential it provides all the members.[32]

Consequently the president prepared to give the secretary of state broad responsibility and authority to administer the military assistance program. As early as December 1948 the machinery to implement President Truman's proposal in his inaugural address to provide "military advice and equipment to free nations" was in place under a Foreign Assistance Steering Committee (FASC), composed of the secretaries of state and defense and the European Cooperation Administration (ECA) administrator. The task of implementing a program was delegated to the

Foreign Assistance Correlation Committee (FACC). Within the State Department an administrator would manage the program and supervise the allocation of funds, with the recognition that the National Military Establishment (NME) would be delegated a large share of the responsibility for actual operation of the program.[33]

The administration even had an estimate of the cost of the program—$1,130 billion for fiscal year 1950. Although not publicly addressed, countries receiving monies from the $1 billion planned would be expected to increase their expenditures for defense by 5 percent over the current fiscal year, and their total expenditures should come to almost one-third of the U.S. $15 billion defense budget. Arms given could not be used outside the North Atlantic area, or used to replace equivalent arms for use outside the area. The FACC intended to ensure as well that bilateral agreements would grant base rights to the United States on a bilateral basis before extending military assistance to the allies.[34]

These arrangements were worked out in advance of the ratification of the treaty and many of them before the signing of the treaty itself on the assumption that they were necessary to give meaning to the commitments made by the treaty. As a CIA report in February 1949 indicated, if the United States failed to provide military assistance, the deterrent effect of the treaty might be lost. Moreover, the allies would also lack the means of containing Soviet aggression.[35]

When Sen. J. William Fulbright (D-AR) took the next step on April 27 of asking if the Brussels Pact organization would be merged with NATO, Acheson was not ready with an answer, except to say that relations would be very close.[36] Acheson's evasions were understandable in light of the negative reaction that greeted the Brussels Pact's package in the Senate after it became obvious that Article 3 would trump Article 5. Concrete military aid now seemed more important to the new allies than the "pledge," and this change of emphasis disturbed the senators. The Western Union submitted its request on the day after the treaty was signed, listing the points its members knew the Americans were looking for—coordination of their efforts in accordance with a common strategic plan and increased arms production consistent with economic objectives. The administration was ready to move ahead immediately even before it received details on the specific needs of the beneficiaries. The State Department sent a similar positive message to Norway, Denmark, and Italy.[37]

While the submission of the allies' requests and the administration's quick response were clear reflections of the treaty's priorities, the Senate's reaction was a mixture of caution and resentment. Many senators suspected that greedy Europeans were more interested in using the treaty to extract military aid from the United States than in guaranteeing security from Communism. Vandenberg's uneasiness about tying military aid to NATO was well known. The senior Republican on the Foreign Relations Committee was not happy with the connection between military aid and the treaty. "When it comes to the supplemental arms program," he observed on April 15, "I really think I would have preferred to leave the Pact stand by itself as an all-out warning sustained by our general pledge but since the State Department has taken this other route (supplementary arms aid) I am not disposed to enter into any *public* argument lest it be misconstrued. On the other hand, I do intend—as far as it lies within my power—to see to it that any such supplementary program is realistic."[38]

Secretary of State Acheson implied that military aid was linked to the treaty even as he tried to avoid a clear answer to Senator Connally's query: "Is there anything in the treaty itself that binds the United States even to adopt the military program? I mean explicitly." Acheson was anything but explicit in his lawyerly response: "There is something in the treaty which required each member of the senate, if you ratify this treaty, when he comes to vote on the military assistance program, to exercise his judgment less freely than he could have exercised it if it had not been for the treaty."[39] In essence, the secretary of state was admitting obliquely that the treaty and military aid were inextricably linked; military aid to the allies would give meaning to the treaty. Without it the defense of the West would be in doubt.

This linkage suggests that the decision of the United States to join Europe in an alliance was insufficient in itself to deter Soviet aggression or suppress Communist subversion. Why this recognition should come as a surprise to American critics is itself surprising. On April 21, the day after the president approved the submission of a military aid request to the Congress, secretaries Acheson and Johnson met in an executive session with the Senate Foreign Relations Committee, explaining in detail the proposed program. The committee then issued a press release announcing the figure of $1,150 billion out of $1,450 billion that would go NATO members. The committee also called for hearings to begin on May 16. While the timetable was revised to have the military assistance bill presented after passage of the treaty, there should have been no doubt about the administration's aspirations.[40]

Former Undersecretary of State Robert Lovett, who had been instrumental in winning Vandenberg's support of the treaty, further added to the senator's misgivings by his unconvincing answers to Donnell's questions at the Foreign Relations Committee's hearings. When asked if the president could send troops without congressional approval in the event Norway were attacked, Lovett assumed that if Congress was not in session, there would be an emergency meeting to deal with the crisis, and that the president could not act until Congress had declared war: "But I am not a lawyer." This lame interpretation of the meaning of Article 5 was no help to Vandenberg or to other friends of the alliance.[41]

The treaty reached the Senate for debate on June 6, fittingly in the old Supreme Court chamber where the Monroe Doctrine was first announced, although unexpectedly since repairs were being made to the regular Senate chamber.[42] There the issue of Article 3 persistently arose despite the administration's decision to postpone a formal presentation until the treaty was approved. Given that so much attention had been paid to Article 3 in the April and May hearings of the Foreign Relations Committee, it was understandable if the senators felt that there was little more to be said on that subject. But Article 5 was a useful target for opponents, since its military character could discomfit supporters of the treaty.

As the time for voting neared, Vandenberg had no doubts about the passage of the treaty, but was troubled by the expectation of pressure from the administration for immediate dispatch of military aid to the European allies. On July 20, he predicted "not more than sixteen votes against the Pact. Then comes the still worse haggle over implementing it. Here I am in sharp *disagreement* with the President and the State Department. They have gone much too fast too soon." George Kennan, as chairman of the Policy Planning Staff, did not share this view. He saw no alternative to acting quickly. The consequence of delay in military aid would mean postponement of all aspects of strategic planning for at least a year.[43]

Sen. Robert A. Taft (R-OH), leader of the small band of isolationists, took up the case of military assistance in his dogged fight in the Senate to defeat the treaty. He assumed with good reason that the subject would strike a nerve among those fearful that the military character of the alliance would undermine the nation's allegiance to the UN Charter. In his last-ditch effort to derail the pact, he formally announced on June 11 that he would link his vote against the treaty to the militarization of the alliance. The arming of the allies, as he piously noted, violated the spirit of the obligations that the United States undertook under the UN Charter.[44]

Although this ploy failed, Taft and his allies could claim some credit for the postponement of the military assistance program. Ultimately, this was a Pyrrhic victory, given the recognition on all sides that arms aid would follow passage of the treaty. Sen. Kenneth Wherry (R-NE), a staunch opponent of military aid, was ready to concede on July 21 that "some sort of arms" would be approved before the Senate adjourned this session. While he felt "morally free to vote against an aid program, he would "do nothing to sabotage" one.[45] Senator Vandenberg also seemed conciliatory when he proposed on the day after ratification that Congress enact a stop-gap arms aid program confined "to the relatively short interim until recommendations can be made to the next Congress." His intention, obviously, was to put off the day when action had to be taken.[46]

As the Truman administration and the U.S. Senate worked to obscure the role of military aid in the ratification process, the Brussels Pact allies did everything in their power to emphasize the aid as a prime benefit of the treaty. Their judgment was that the administration went much too slowly and possibly too late. General de Gaulle observed on the day the pact was signed that to have practical value, it must be combined with binding and precise commitments on American aid. U.S. ambassador to France, Jefferson Caffery, was convinced that a military aid program's fate in the Congress would have a significant bearing on both the passage of the treaty in France and on the increased sense of security so badly needed in that country. Secretary Acheson made the same point in his statement before the Foreign Relations Committee on April 27.[47]

For France the priority of military aid was always in the forefront of their arguments for the treaty. It was no coincidence that Le Monde's headline, as the final debates in the U.S. Senate were concluded, celebrated not the passage of the treaty but rather France as its principal beneficiary of a military assistance program.[48] Opponents of the pact seized on the possibility that neither military aid nor automatic military response would be guaranteed by the United States. René Massigli, France's ambassador to Great Britain, noted the importance of former premier Edouard Daladier's assertion that if military assistance was not included in the Atlantic Pact, the alliance would lose all meaning. In this circumstance he would see no reason to ratify the treaty. President Vincent Auriol also made it clear that Article 5 would be meaningless if Article 3 were not implemented.[49]

The Left and Communists in the National Assembly were not alone in their opposition to the treaty. After the National Assembly had approved the treaty, the Gaullist bloc submitted an amendment to postpone ratification until the United States had acted upon the issue of military aid to France. The amendment failed, 424 to twenty-six. Foreign Minister Robert Schuman did acknowledge the anxieties expressed in the amendment, even though the majority rejected it.[50] France's sensitivity on the matter was manifested in the instructions the Council of the Republic gave to the French ambassador to the United States upon his deposit of France's formal ratification of the treaty: namely, to inform the United States of the need for guarantees of modern arms and equipment to enable French forces to fulfill their obligations under the pact.

Acheson agreed with France's objectives, but feared that such a declaration could be construed as improper pressure and prejudice the Congress against passage of the MAP. France agreed with the recommendations of Foreign Minister Schuman that the treaty would be in the nation's interest without demanding a special codicil.[51]

The priority that the French government placed on military aid was not to be found in the same degree in the assemblies of the other allies as they debated the merits of the treaty. Where Article 3 did come up in the House of Commons, it was as an instrument of the Left to berate the Attlee government and the Conservative opposition who pressed for Parliament's approval. One far Left member of the Labour Party, William Warbey, found a sinister significance in Article 3's obligation to increase each country's expenditure on armaments. The requirement to maintain and develop its individual and collective capacity to resist armed attacks was translated into increasing the cost of living and reducing social services, thus lowering Britain's standard of living to satisfy the demands of the American capitalist economy.[52]

For the most part, Communist and leftist MPs concentrated on the danger of war that membership would entail and on its implied assault against a former ally.

Military aid as a prerequisite for success of the alliance was not a factor in Britain's acceptance of the treaty, although the Brussels Pact powers presented their case as if Article 3 were the equal of Article 5. In retrospect, military aid was a much more sensitive issue in the U.S. Senate than in any of the legislatures of the European partners. Other issues, even in France, competed with military assistance for attention.

The German Question

Arguably, the most divisive obstacle in the way of ratification was the role that Germany would play in the creation of an integrated Western Europe. The question of Germany's place in the new order was particularly problematic for France. The potential resurgence of a militant Germany was an obsession for many in the French establishment, whether or not it was expressed in their communications with the allies. The French were disturbed over German efforts to delay fulfilling obligations to the allies, a prerequisite to the establishment of a provisional constitution of a federal republic. Dismantling of smaller factories without direct connections with war materiel was considered unnecessary, but there were questions about larger plants capable of producing military equipment. If they were not to be dismantled, their production would have to be limited.[53] Expressing this concern was an oblique way of doubting the good faith of the incipient federal republic of Germany.

As the National Assembly considered ratification of the treaty, the president of the Assembly warned that the first step in the regeneration of Germany was the creation of a West German state, but the second would be German membership in NATO. Foreign Minister Schuman hoped that Germans would understand the delicacy of their position, particularly how difficult it was for the French public to accept a treaty that would rebuild a still not denazified Germany. Fear that the Atlantic alliance, under pressure from the United States, would result in German rearmament was widespread in France.[54]

What reconciled the French government to a revived Germany was its failure to win over the allies to France's concerns. Actions to slow the pace of Germany's recovery only antagonized U.S. and British colleagues. Moreover, its efforts to maintain restrictions on German political and economic development facilitated Soviet ability to sow dissension in the alliance. Schuman was well aware that the Soviet Union's goal of a united Germany under its influence posed a greater threat to the security of Europe than the creation of a pro-NATO German state.

In this context the scrapping of the complex agreements crafted by the authorities over the past year was the only reasonable alternative. At least the new Occupation Statute giving extensive powers to the new German government in May did reserve the right of the Allied High Commission to intervene if necessary. In a remarkably short time after the signing of the treaty, France fused its zone with

Anglo-America's bizonia, reached agreements on dismantling and reparations, and, most importantly, endorsed the Basic Law for a new federal German republic.[55]

It was in the spirit of pragmatism that Schuman's calculated solidarity with the British and Americans won over skeptical countrymen to accept a stabilized Germany that would be responsive to its NATO patrons. Had Schuman not prevailed, the May 1949 meeting of the Council of Foreign Ministers might have had different and more dangerous consequences. In unity the allies presented to the Soviets the incorporation of the French zone with the three other zones, to be followed by free election for a federal government, supervised by a four-power High Commission. The Soviets rejected the proposal and, as the French anticipated, wanted nothing less than a demilitarized Germany under Soviet influence.[56]

This pragmatic strain was also present in Ambassador Hervé Alphand's journal in which he recalled that France's reasons for accepting the Basic Law in 1949 establishing the federal republic were based both on the need to oppose the Soviet plan for a single German government and on the assurance that an international commission would oversee the new republic. By following this path Germany would be prevented from playing the East against the West and, at the same time, be freed from the danger of Communist domination.[57]

As for other European allies, fears of a regenerated Germany threatening the continent once again were certainly alive, but not to the degree it was in France. Potential German aggression was subsumed, as a Senate Foreign Relations Committee report observed in June, under the security blanket of the North Atlantic Treaty. When Sen. Walter George (D-Gs) gloomily judged that French antagonism toward Germany would defeat the very purpose of the treaty, Senator Vandenberg quickly took exception. The purpose of the treaty, he asserted, was to allay French fears of a revived Germany. The proof of its success was found in France's "substantial reversal" of its former German policy. The treaty not only removed the possibility of Germans striking a deal with the Soviets, but, as the report indicated, also gave them hope for a brighter future with the West.[58]

Aside from Communist barbs, British parliamentarians would agree with this assessment. In fact, Labour's Herbert Butcher felt that if the allies could accept Italy as a partner, why not Germany? Italy was not only a military liability given its restriction on its rearming but also, like Germany, it was an enemy in World War II. Italy is included without offering the alliance any useful contributions while Germany is excluded and could enjoy certain benefits from its exclusion. "None of the taxation of her people will go to the mutual aid of Western Europe and all the industrial production will be available either for export or for re-equipping of her country. So the allies should take steps now to bring Germany in as a full and proper partner inside the union of Western democracies."[59]

The senior partner surprisingly displayed more emotion on the subject than its European counterparts, as the administration sought to remove Germany from discussion by burying it in closed sessions in the Senate or in secret meetings of the Joint Chiefs of Staff in the Pentagon. Inevitably, there was visceral rejection of the idea of a German membership in the Atlantic community among the public at large. Given that the end of World War II was only four years away and that some 300,000 U.S. troops were killed in that conflict, this reaction was to be expected.

The administration handled the issue by carefully excluding the notion of future German membership from the public debate over the treaty. W. Averell Harriman, U.S. special representative in Europe for the ECA, noted that there was still uncertainty about the solidity of democracy in the new Germany. Only in the future at "such time as there is concrete evidence that there is a real democratic Germany developing" would consideration be given to any kind of military collaboration. Former Undersecretary of State Lovett concurred in this judgment: "We found that its circumstances in the present time make it impossible for it to be considered as a participant. And when Dean Acheson was badgered about the service Germans would provide to the strategic position of the allies, he asserted that although he was no military expert, 'quite clearly at the present time a discussion including western Germany in the pact is not possible.'"[60]

In executive sessions there was more candor on the subject. Unlike most European allies who reluctantly accepted the logic of a German contribution, the idea of a German role in the alliance was attractive to many senators, if only to force Germans to supply their fair share of the common cause of containing Communism. Since Germany, by its geographic position, would have to be defended in the event of a Soviet attack, Senator Watkins blurted that "we certainly are not going to fight all their battles for them if somebody attempts to take their territory." Watkins, a dogged opponent of the pact, used the German question to embarrass the administration. When he pressed Lovett about plans to prepare Germany for "entrance into the pact in the near future," the former undersecretary dodged the question by saying that they were discussed on the exploratory talks.[61]

It is worth noting that Watkins's pressure for an answer did not originate in any hostility to the prospect of German membership in NATO—just the opposite. If there was to be a treaty, it made sense that Germany should be a part of it. He was simply using the administration's reluctance to confront the question as a weapon against the treaty itself.

Watkins and his allies in the Taft bloc failed to break the administration's silence on the issue. As the treaty moved toward ratification, the treaty's managers made no admission that German membership in NATO, let alone rearmament, was necessary to the defense of Western Europe. Although no American lobby was making a case against a German role, the administration was still fearful that an open discussion of the possibility would be as unacceptable to Americans as it would be to the French.

NATO and Spain

The idea of fascist Spain joining the Atlantic community alongside fascist Portugal was outside the realm of possibility as far as the European allies were concerned. Unlike Portugal, which owned valuable bases for potential NATO use and which remained precariously neutral in World War II, Franco Spain was beyond the pale because of its alliance with Nazi Germany and because of the stigma attached to its behavior in the Spanish civil war. Communists and their allies on the Left in France's National Assembly used Spain to strike at Portugal as well, claiming that the admission Portugal linked Spain to the alliance, French opponents of the treaty asserted that Portugal's Iberian pact with Spain was incompatible with its membership in NATO. Communists led the campaign in the National Assembly to identify Spain with an Anglo-American plot to go to war with the Soviet Union. Communist deputy Alfred Biscaret urged his colleagues to "remember Munich" as the party attempted to shelve a vote on the treaty. The vote was 407 to 148 against delay.[62]

The theme of an unholy alliance with Spain through Portugal's membership was aired also in the House of Commons in the course of the final debate in that body. According to H. N. Warbey, a member of the left wing of the Labour Party, if Portugal could be included, it would be impossible to exclude Franco Spain. He included Churchill in a conspiracy to bring Spain into NATO. The former prime minister saw the return of a British ambassador to Spain "as a step in the right direction and sufficient for the time being." Churchill, Warbey insisted, "knows very well that it is a step in the direction of eventual inclusion of Franco Spain. How can it be refused if Portugal is included?" While Churchill disputed this prediction, he believed that the absence of Spain from the Atlantic Pact left a strategic gap in Western defense, and further noted that while he would not want to live under the present Spanish regime, "he cannot see the sense of having relations with Soviet Russia and refusing to have any relations with Spain."[63]

Churchill's was a minority voice in Europe, but even as he equated Franco with Stalin, he was not advocating Spain's admission into the Atlantic alliance. His views were more closely aligned with many in the United States, although often for very different reasons. The Spanish civil war had divided Americans, with a large segment of the population identifying the republicans with destruction of the Catholic Church. Catholics were joined by secular anti-Communists in believing that, much like Churchill, fascism was no worse than Communism and less of a danger in the postwar world. Former ambassador to Spain, Carlton J. H. Hayes, a distinguished historian at Columbia University and a Catholic convert, made an eloquent case for admitting Spain to the UN and for appreciating its opposition to Communism. He emphasized in particular that Spain in World War II was more supportive of the allied war effort than such neutral countries as

Turkey, Sweden, and Switzerland. Among other services, the Spanish government "permitted us to use Spain as the base for invaluable information on Axis activities in France and the Mediterranean."[64]

Rep. Dewey Short (R-MO) took up one of Churchill's themes in asking rhetorically why we do business with Stalin when we refuse to do business with Franco. He felt that the United States lost economically when its European allies had trade agreements with Franco that were denied to American businessmen. From another perspective, Sen. Dennis Chavez (D-NM) saw the United States playing into the hands of the Soviet Union by demonizing Franco and weakening Western European defenses.[65]

The anti-Communist mood of America, combined with perceived economic and strategic advantages in resuming ties with Spain, prevailed over the opposition. Lacking the psychological scars of Europeans, the United States could bring Franco into its orbit more easily than its NATO allies. Bilateral arrangements with the Spanish dictator brought economic aid to Spain in exchange for air and naval bases on Spanish territory. Not until Franco died a generation later would a democratic Spain take its place with a democratic Portugal in the Atlantic community. But in 1949, Spain, as a fascist ally of Hitler, was too great a burden for the NATO allies to resume normal diplomatic relations with, let alone consider admitting to NATO.

Ratification Completed

While the signing of the treaty set in motion heated debates in the United States, France, and Italy that required four months to resolve, other signatories had few problems with the treaty. Canada was the first to complete the process. Ratification was one of the last acts of the Canadian Parliament before its dissolution on April 30. The vote was unanimous in favor of the treaty, and the instrument of ratification was deposited with the U.S. State Department on May 3.[66]

Britain, too, had no difficulty in ratifying the treaty on May 12, with Conservative Winston Churchill praising Labour Foreign Secretary Bevin for his motion to approve the treaty, noting that "The House will not be surprised if I begin by saying that I find myself in very general agreement with the somber speech which the Foreign Secretary has just made." The vote was 333 to six, two of whom were Communists. When Sir Oliver Franks, British ambassador to the United States, officially deposited the instrument of ratification with the State Department on June 7, it was a ceremonial occasion. The document was bound in blue leather with the coat-of-arms of the United Kingdom stamped on it in gold. Franks had justification for asserting that Parliament's overwhelming majority in favor of the treaty expressed the convictions of the British people.[67]

In the Low Countries Luxembourg's Chamber of Deputies ratified the treaty on May 31 with only five Communist deputies in opposition. Belgian premier and foreign minister, Paul-Henri Spaak, claimed that the U.S. Senate's ratification on July 21 "was greeted with joy by Belgian public opinion." Communist members of Belgium's Chamber of Deputies and Senate were the only dissenters, one by abstention in the lower house and thirteen in the Senate, when the treaty was ratified on May 4 and 12, respectively. Similarly, the negative votes of sixty-five to seven on July 19 in the lower house of the Netherlands' States Assembly and twenty-nine to two in the upper house on August 3 were from the Communist Party.[69] Portugal's National Assembly ratified the treaty on July 27 by a vote of eighty to three; the three negative votes were in protest over Spain's exclusion from the pact, a sentiment expressed also by Premier Antonio de Oliveira Salazar.[70]

The Scandinavian members ratified the pact with little opposition, given that most of their reservations had been settled in the February and March negotiations over terms of membership. Norway deposited its instrument of ratification on July 8 and Iceland on July 22, a day after the U.S. Senate acted. Denmark, the most ambivalent of the northern allies, would have preferred an independent Scandinavian alliance. Still, it voted in the lower house in favor of the pact on March 24 by a vote of 119 to twenty-three, and in the upper house the next day by a vote of sixty-four to eight. Proponents of the pact had to beat back not just Communist amendments demanding refusal of bases to a foreign power, but also the Radical Party's demand for a referendum on membership in the alliance. Ultimately, Denmark joined the other core members in depositing its notice of ratification with the U.S. State Department on August 24.[71]

The passage of the treaty in France and Italy raised tempers and tensions to a far greater degree than in the other European signatories. The French National Assembly would not begin the final debate until the United States had completed its ratification on July 21. Communists were ready to paralyze proceedings with their uncompromising opposition to the treaty, while Gaullists intended to add amendments assuring U.S. arms before supporting the treaty. In introducing the bill on July 22, René Mayer, reporting for the Foreign Affairs Committee, justified the treaty by citing the dangers the Soviet Union posed to the security of the West. The German problem was never far from their minds. Foreign Minister Schuman wanted to make it clear on July 25 that there was no question about the admission or the rearmament of Germany.[72]

The treaty passed the National Assembly on July 27 by a vote of 398 to 187; all but fifteen of the negative votes were from the Communist deputies. The Gaullist effort to couple ratification with a U.S. guarantee of French membership on a NATO defense committee was defeated as well by 348 votes to sixty-six. The session did not end before fists flew in the Assembly. During a recess that day, Communist deputies struck the former minister of the armies in the face and a Conservative deputy suffered a gashed lip in the melee that followed. Nevertheless, two days later, the Council of the Republic ratified the treaty by 284 votes to twenty.[73]

In Italy as well as France, Communists led the opposition to the treaty, and accompanied it with violence in the legislatures and in the streets. They were abetted by the Soviets whose notes to Italy and France as debates over ratification began charged that Italian membership in the alliance would violate the Italian peace treaty. The Communists had no more success with this charge than they did in the UN General Assembly in April. On July 21, the same day that the U.S. Senate ratified the treaty, Italy's Chamber of Deputies voted 323 to 160 for its passage. Communists had done as much mischief as they could after the vote was taken by demanding its nullification on the grounds that more votes had been cast than there were deputies at the session.[74] Their efforts to derail the treaty failed.

As noted, the United States Senate generated considerable discussion over compatibility with the United Nations, over the treaty's ties to military assistance, and—to a lesser extent—over the roles of Germany and Spain in the future Atlantic community. By the time of the final vote, the arguments against the treaty had been exhaustively vented. Opponents from the old isolationist bloc had become dispirited, assuming that passage of the treaty was inevitable. But the surprise intervention of Sen. Walter F. George (D-GA), a supporter of the treaty who was dissatisfied with the Foreign Relations Committee's report, forced a postponement of any action until the second week of June. George wanted assurance that the president would not send troops to the rescue of any member nation without the approval of Congress.[75]

Once this hurdle had been passed, a challenge from the Left appeared on the last day of debate in the person of Sen. Glenn Taylor (D-ID), vice presidential candidate of the Progressive Party in 1948, who joined with its leader, Henry A. Wallace, in an attack on the treaty for the secretive and devious behavior of its proponents. They professed to find Churchill abandoning a Western alliance in favor of a "new understanding" with the Soviet Union.[76] Presumably, this information would inspire rethinking of the North Atlantic Treaty. Wallace had to pass out his statement from the press gallery, but Taylor would cast his vote against the treaty on the following day.

The final act in the Senate did not take place until it had rejected three amendments in succession, first from Kenneth Wherry (R-NE) ,Taft, and Watkins, asserting that Article 5 would not commit the United States to any moral or legal obligations to supply military aid to an ally. This was defeated by a vote of seventy-four to twenty-one. The other two reservations were from Senator Watkins, denying the use of force in defense of an ally without congressional approval, and denying the president the power to declare war without explicit congressional approval if a signatory state were attacked. The former was defeated eighty-four to eleven, the latter eighty-seven to eight.[77] In the end Taft could muster only twelve other senators to vote against the treaty—thirteen nays, eighty-two yeas. An awareness of America's new weight in the world combined with the weakness of Western Europe and the menace of Soviet Communism to win over the Senate and the nation.

Yet it was obvious that America's history of non-entanglement was not forgotten. The Truman administration felt the need to qualify the promises in Article 5. Unlike the clear commitments of the Brussels Pact's Article IV, the U.S. framers of the Atlantic alliance had to display a deference to unilateralism, even if the deference was more apparent than real. Taft's rearguard assault against the treaty recognized that the prevailing arguments of 1919 would fail in 1949. So did the European partners, who understood that the inhibitions against U.S. military action in Article 5 were undercut by the president's powers as commander-in-chief. Taft doubted if Congress's constitutional authority to declare war could cope with the president's ability to deploy armed forces in a war zone. "I am inclined to think such action is not necessary," he noted ruefully, "if the President chooses to use our armed forces when an ally is attacked."[78] Although the opponents of the treaty repeatedly invoked the tradition of non-entanglement that was so feared by the administration, the eighty-two to thirteen votes on July 21 reflected a different consensus on U.S. foreign policy in the Senate and in the nation.

3

Mutual Defense Assistance Program

July 1949–January 1950

Anticipating the Bill

The contentious congressional debate over the ratification of the treaty derailed the concerted effort on the part of the European allies to win an immediate U.S. response to their urgent requests for military aid. In fact, once the treaty had been signed, Article 3 superseded Article 5 as the priority for members of the Brussels Pact. Although the meeting of the UN General Assembly dominated headlines on April 5, the Western Union submitted its package of requests of that day. The administration shunted it aside until more detailed information was available. At least this was its rationalization. For many friends of the treaty, the mingling of aid to the allies' military establishments with the guarantees of the treaty would be a gratuitous obstacle to its ratification.

Yet it was understood by advocates and adversaries alike that the military assistance program, formulated before the treaty was signed, would be the administration's first order of business after ratification. As early as March 1948, in reaction to the Communist coup in Prague, State and Defense officials produced a Title VI to the proposed economic assistance bill. If it failed to be included in the future Marshall Plan, it was not because of the absence of Western Europe's need for military aid; rather, the House Foreign Affairs Committee worried about the implications of an open-ended program for the health of the U.S. economy.[1]

The machinery for implementing such a program, after all, was in place by the winter of 1949. Two weeks before the treaty was signed the JCS had even come up with a recommended figure of $995,647,000 for Western Union nations, a figure that the Foreign Assistance Correlation Committee (FACC) lowered to $830,850,000 on April 5, and the Bureau of Budget furthered lowered to $817,630,000 on April 15. On April 20, 1949, the president approved $830,600,000 for the Brussels Pact members.[2]

While the administration was responsive to the requests presented by the Brussels Pact allies immediately after the signing of the treaty, it was even more responsive, as noted in Chapter 2, to the delays demanded by Congress. The con-

tents of the hearings and debates over ratification of the treaty gave the administration ample warning of the trials ahead. Opponents of military aid had forced
the administration to accept the treaty as a bar to aggression completely apart
from any military aid. Supplies sent abroad would be only those not needed by the
U.S. military, and none of the aid would interfere in any way with the economic
recovery program. Despite these concessions, the enemies of the treaty were convinced that a secret understanding had been made between the administration
and the European allies. The inability or the unwillingness of the defenders of the
treaty to give details of a military aid program nurtured these suspicions.

As the ratification process came to an end, the administration found itself in
a dilemma. It recognized that a failure to follow up the implications of the treaty
with an aid bill could seriously affect Europe's ability—and will—to resist Soviet
aggression and, at the same time, understood that a major assistance program
could harm the allies' economic recovery efforts. Not least of its concerns was the
political damage that exposure of the inextricable connections between the treaty
and a military assistance program would do to the administration's relations with
a restive Congress. Such was the situation in Washington when the MAP bill was
introduced in the House and referred to the Committee on Foreign Affairs on the
same day—July 25—that the president signed the instrument of ratification.[3]

To calm the storm of criticism that the administration knew would follow
the formal request for military aid, bipartisan advocates of the Atlantic alliance
joined State Department spokesmen to mount a campaign on behalf of military
aid in advance of its introduction in the Congress. Demonstration of widespread
support for military aid was all the more important given division within the
administration itself. Edwin G. Nourse, chairman of the President's Council of
Economic Advisers, exacerbated those divisions when he suggested that the costs
of arming Western Europe be squeezed from the military budget.[4]

ECA officials, for their part, were understandably concerned that any military
aid program would impact the effectiveness of economic recovery no matter how
vigorous the denials from other agencies. And from within the State Department
itself, George Kennan, director of its policy planning staff, repeatedly deplored
the emphasis on the military aspect of military aid even as he acknowledged the
importance of defending Europe.[5]

Gov. Thomas E. Dewey, titular leader of the Republican Party, opened a pre-
emptive defense of a military aid program in a commencement address at Wil-
liams College on June 19. He strongly supported arms and money for Western
Europe: Europe by itself "cannot successfully meet . . . the external threat of a
colossus which stretches from the Elbe to the Pacific Ocean for the first time since
Genghis Khan." A united Western Europe with access to the resources of Africa
could cope with Soviet power, but in the immediate future only with U.S. help.[6]

The State Department took the initiative in emphasizing the relationship between the MAP and U.S. strategic interests. As a policy paper approved by the FACC stressed on July 1, "In most instances the basic consideration is the military factor with the assistance designed to strengthen the military posture of free nations to resist aggression and thus strengthen U.S. security. In other instances, however, political considerations are paramount, leading to the provision of military aid to withstand Communist-inspired internal disorders and to enhance political stability. In all cases, the psychological factor is of major importance in that military assistance will increase the determination to resist." Moreover, the resulting benefits to their economies will help diminish their dependence on the United States.[7]

The State Department's voice was heard, too, at Colgate University's annual conference on American foreign policy, where Francis H. Russell, director of the State Department's Office of Public Affairs, was keynote speaker before an assembly of two hundred government and academic groups active in foreign affairs. On July 22, the day of the final vote on the treaty, he outlined the executive branch's plan to implement the Atlantic Pact, observing that the program was to hold off an aggressor until the United States was ready to respond. This transfer of arms, he pointed out, "is not solely to the advantage of the European nations that received them. It is to the advantage of the United States as well." He explained that the program did not envision "large and costly armies" necessary to cope with an all-out attack but rather a well-trained force able "to prevent surprise attacks and piecemeal conquest." Francis O. Wilcox, chief of staff of the Senate Foreign Relations Committee, complemented Russell's approach by citing, somewhat wistfully perhaps, the successful executive-legislative teamwork that produced the North Atlantic Treaty. The "rich dividends" produced from this cooperation made it wise for the administration to build on this success in other areas, such as military.[8]

Just how nervous the treaty's sponsors were about anticipated Republican attacks over military aid was clearly evident in Senator Connally's unusual step of issuing a formal statement a week before the ratification asking for "prompt action on this program. It is my hope and expectation that the Foreign Relations committee will take it up as soon as the North Atlantic treaty is disposed of." He was speaking for the State Department, which was pressing for early approval of the administration's $1,130,000 program of military aid to Europe as a companion piece to the treaty. And he was speaking as well to skeptics in his own party in the Senate, where the majority leader, Scott Lucas, appeared to worry about the economic implications of the military assistance program.[9]

Connally had reason to ask for immediate action before the final vote for ratification in light of the rising opposition of the Republican leadership. As noted in Chapter 2, Senator Taft was prepared to use the linkage between arms aid and the treaty to help defeat the treaty itself. He asked rhetorically on July 8 "whether it was possible for a Senator to vote for the treaty and then take the position that we are not obligated to provide arms?" He knew that it was not possible, and condemned the proponents of the treaty for their efforts to deceive their colleagues.[10]

The administration played into the opposition's hands by suggesting that the MAP be taken up in the House before the Senate had completed the ratification process. For the administration, this would have the advantage of winning a simple House majority before taking it to the Senate, where a two-thirds majority was necessary. When Acheson proposed this arrangement on June 23 at a closed meeting of the House Foreign Affairs Committee, Chairman James P. Richards (D-SC) rejected it. Southern conservative Democrats joined with the Taft Republicans to stop this procedure. The administration's program was not helped by *Le Monde*'s boast on July 24 that France would be the principal beneficiary of the military assistance program. While this would be the outcome, if only because of the pressing need to rebuild a French army that had not recovered from World War II, it could raise suspicion of U.S. collusion with France at the expense of their allies as well as of the American taxpayer.[11]

The administration's case rested on the credibility of Vandenberg's argument that the pending military assistance program "would be necessary even if there were not treaty just as the treaty would be necessary if the military assistance program had not been formulated. . . . The military assistance program is separate from the treaty, except that the treaty and the MAP both serve the national interest and security of the United States and in this way supplement each other."[12] Vandenberg was quoting from the State Department's statement, which he hoped was sincere.

There was never a question about the senator's own position. He complained in a letter to the influential columnist, Walter Lippmann, about Sen. Wayne Morse's insistence (R-OR) that we have a legal and moral basis to furnish arms to the new allies. Vandenberg had interrupted Morse on the Senate floor to say that "Our obligation is not to furnish arms. Our obligation is to our responsibility as an honorably participating member of the North Atlantic Community in quest of objectives to which the Treaty is addressed." He went on to tell Lippmann that he would make a last effort to clarify the matter before the final debate on the treaty. He planned to say that "this Pact establishes no right anywhere to demand arms. It establishes a right to present a request under Article Nine and to have it considered by us in the light of our mutual responsibility to the Pact and our own estimate of the need and of our capacity to respond." Vandenberg displayed frustration as if he were not convinced about his Senate colleagues' understanding that the negotiation over a MAP "*preceded* the negotiation of the Pact (even though its publication was more or less simultaneous) and that there are no negotiations under Article Three of the Pact until *after* the Defense Committee of the Advisory [North Atlantic] Council has made a recommendation under Article Nine of the Pact."[13]

Lippmann agreed that Vandenberg's speech was "entirely sound. But I can't get away from the fact that there is a real basis for Taft's argument, arising not out of the text of the treaty nor out of the interpretive declarations." Rather, the circumstances in Europe itself—the knowledge that Norway and Denmark's adherence to the pact as well as France's persistent demand for aid—conflated the treaty and the

MAP. Denmark professed to have only thirty-six anti-aircraft guns in the whole country, virtually no radar equipment, and seventy military planes. As the gateway to the Baltic, Danes believed that their country would be one of the first targets of a Soviet attack. France put its case more generally but more starkly. In conversations with the French ambassador, Lippmann knew that the French general staff and the majority of the French General Assembly felt that if there was no military aid program, the pact itself would be valueless. He asserted that "these are political realities that cannot be disposed of by statements from the floor of the Senate or from the Department of State." While he was convinced that the treaty should be ratified without reservations, "the whole matter should be clarified beyond the possibility of misunderstanding in the text of the arms bill itself."[14]

Although the treaty was ratified without dangerous reservations, Lippmann's—and Vandenberg's—need for a clear statement on military aid necessary to get rid of "the open objections of the very real segment of American opinion which Taft represents" was never addressed. It was unlikely that any statement separating the treaty from the MAP would appease opponents of the treaty. Nor would any disclaimer really satisfy Vandenberg himself. Acheson anticipated trouble "in view of the Vandenberg-Dulles attitude, which is that we should not take definitive action until the machinery under the Atlantic Pact has been set up and has had a chance to function."[15]

The Joint Chiefs of Staff's Role

The critics were right. There could be no genuine separation between the treaty and the MAP. The treaty's success would rest on its passage. In other words, Article 3 was inseparable from Article 5. Presumably, it was important for the cogent arguments of Secretary Acheson and the steadfast position of President Truman to enjoy the valuable backing of the Joint Chiefs of Staff. The united stance of the American military leaders in favor of military aid to Europe should have overwhelmed the sniping of Taft and the grandstanding of Vandenberg. Sen. Millard Tydings (D-MD), chairman of the Armed Services Committee, spoke of the deference the senators would pay to the words of the nation's military leaders: "It is up to the Chiefs of Staff to explain in terms of guns, tanks and planes the need for the full $1,450,000,000. I think the Congress will give them what they say is necessary to carry out the defense plans."[16] Tydings was too optimistic about the influence of the Joint Chiefs, and not knowledgeable enough to recognize their difficulties in defending the administration's program, although these obstacles were not initially visible.

The JCS certainly waged a vigorous and very public campaign for the military assistance to Europe. Their very appearance in uniform aroused admiration from members of the House Foreign Affairs Committee on July 29, when Gen. Omar

S. Bradley, army chief of staff, accompanied by navy Adm. Louis E. Denfeld and air force Gen. Hoyt S. Vandenberg (Senator Vandenberg's nephew), appealed to Congress for approval of the administration's $1,450 billion to NATO members as well as to other non-Communist nations. No military figure, aside from Eisenhower, had the respect of Congress that Bradley enjoyed. The soft-spoken, unassuming Missourian was perfectly cast as the spokesman of the National Military Establishment (predecessor of the Department of Defense) in general, and the Joint Chiefs of Staff in particular. Eisenhower was serving as temporary presiding officer of the Joint Chiefs, but Bradley was the logical candidate for the new position of chairman, to which he was appointed in August.[17]

The army chief told the committee that he was anxious for "every American" to know the status of defensive plans for NATO. The Joint Chiefs, he claimed, had "given the most serious consideration to every detail" of the military aid plan, and had found it to be a means of acquiring "at a minimum expense, additional measures for our own security." Western Europe marked the defensive frontiers of the United States. To the Senate Foreign Relations Committee Bradley reported that "the Western European countries which are the principal ones involved and to which a majority of this equipment goes, already have an organization which has been functioning for about a year and we do think they have arrived at a point in their plans and their organization, where as far as they are concerned, the conditions you have been talking about have been met." Secretary of Defense Johnson was even more explicit in his endorsement of the Western Union as "a working reality and not a mere paper organization. It has been studied by the Joint Chiefs of Staff who considered it to be basically sound and in consonance with their strategic thinking." In short, the military leaders seemed to have thought through the outcomes of military aid and found them indispensable to American security.[18]

Adding to the drama of their presentations was the departure of the Joint Chiefs for Europe immediately after the House hearings, where they would meet their counterparts in Frankfurt, London, and Paris. Only limitations of time would prevent the chiefs from visiting the capitals of all the members of the alliance, although the military leaders of the other allied nations were expected to meet with them in the course of their itinerary. Inevitably, there was speculation about the military aid program being on the agenda despite the efforts of the Joint Chiefs to avoid discussion about assistance until Congress had acted on the president's recommendations. The credibility of this disclaimer was open to question in light of the JCS's intention to inspect the progress of the Western Union's defense program.[19] The U.S. military was clearly committed to building up the defense establishments of the allies.

They returned to Washington a week later with appreciation for the work done by the Western Union Defense Organization (WUDO). Adm. Louis E. Denfeld, speaking for his colleagues from Paris, made a point of saying that WUDO had done "some very successful planning." Back in Washington on August 10, Bradley pleaded the cause of the MAP, telling the combined Senate Foreign Relations and Armed Services committees that prompt military aid to Western Europe would be "a supreme test of leadership" in an area where Communist advances were being checked. Bradley had Connally by his side in urging the committees to enact the bill quickly without cuts. It was not a crisis, he made clear, or fear of impending war that demanded action now. Rather, the alliance should take advantage of "a moment of possible success for which we are well prepared." The military assistance program was just the instrument to serve the West at a critical moment.[20]

The assumption that underlay their findings was the satisfactory progress they perceived in the activities of the WUDO, the Western Union's military arm. The Joint Chiefs wished to leave an impression in Congress that Western Europe's military organization was not only a going concern but that it only awaited the delivery of weapons, supplies, and funds from the MAP to become fully effective against potential Soviet invasion.

Such a conclusion would have been mistaken. Since its creation in 1948, Western Union had a clear vision of the function of its military plans, which was to convince Americans that Western Europe was doing its part to justify immediate and extensive military assistance. They had no expectations that their combined defense efforts in 1948 or later would be sufficient to cope with Soviet power. If they could not manage their own defense, they at least could demonstrate to Americans that Europeans were doing on the military level what they had promised to do on the economic level: namely, to help themselves in rebuilding their military, and to collaborate with allies to break down barriers blocking integration of their forces. They would then be worthy of the kind of support that the Marshall Plan was in the process of giving their economies.[21]

It was not that the Joint Chiefs were predisposed to believe WUDO's claims. They had been suspicious of European designs on the limited military budget imposed by the administration from the outset of negotiations for an Atlantic security pact in 1948. WUDO would be competing for the same resources that the JCS believed were vital to U.S. security. Years later Gen. Lyman L. Lemnitzer, as former director of the Office of Military Assistance, recalled Gen. J. Lawton. Collins, army deputy chief of staff in 1948, only half-jokingly greeted him with the comment, "Lem, I understand you are up there doling out all the equipment that you're going to take away from the army and give it [to] European allies."[22] Yet the chiefs ultimately recognized that they had few choices. Military aid was inextricably linked to a future Atlantic alliance, and the Western Union, the product of the Brussels Pact, would be the primary vehicle for transmitting the aid. As historian Steven Rearden observed, "by the end of 1948, despite the Joint Chiefs' cautions, the United States had moved extremely close to a *de facto* alliance with the Western Union."[23]

These cautions gradually dissipated in the course of that year. When the Vandenberg Resolution opened the way for exploratory talks in the summer of 1948, it also opened the way for military talks in London with European leaders. Although the JCS dispatched Maj. Gen. Lemnitzer to London in June "on a non-member basis" to head a group of U.S. officers assigned to the WU Military Committee, the committee pressed the general to participate in their activities. Lemnitzer responded with enthusiasm as he recommended the early establishment of a Military Supply Board, and advised the Military Committee to pool all weapons.[24] While Lemnitzer may have taken an excessively proprietary interest in the workings of the Military Committee, his reasons served U.S. national interests. As he observed in the course of his visit, "If [the] US is to participate in the activities of Western Union Military Committee as envisaged in JCS 1868/11 it will necessary for [a] US representative in London to have access to all committee information and documents."[25]

In making this recommendation he attested to potential American influence in all their councils. The pattern set by the first U.S. representative became the template that his successors followed over the next two years. The price the American military had to pay for its deep connections with the numerous committees the WUDO established was involvement in deception. The U.S. delegates knew how illusory were the accomplishments touted by the European allies and participated, though often unwillingly, in WU's campaign to convince the American ally of their good faith. If the Western Union managed to keep any credibility in 1949, it was only as a result of the administration propping it up before a reluctant Congress as an example of European progress in self-help and integration of their forces.

The failure of Bradley and his colleagues to recognize the full extent of the disarray at the time of the August trip to Europe was due in large part to the reluctance of the U.S. delegates in Europe to explain that WUDO's activities were a charade. The American officers attached to WUDO committees in 1948 were too close to their European colleagues for objective reporting of their problems. Maj. Gen. A. Franklin Kibler, U.S. delegate to WUDO's Military Committee, was present in all its deliberations and was party to its failings as well as to its slim list of successes. On the basic question of U.S. military assistance, he was well aware of the deficiencies in the first estimate of equipment to be sought from the United States. Even though he knew how important it was for the WU to present to the Pentagon and Congress a well-researched long-term plan, he also knew that there was no time to wait for this result. No matter how inadequate the proposals of the Military Committee were, he reported that they "would afford the basis of a reasonable approach to the U.S. government." As for their possible effect on Congress, he was prepared to guarantee that the Western Union "was making the best use of the means at present available."[26]

The American generals in London were more than passive observers at WU committee meetings and more than conduits of information from London to

Washington. They were actors in the relationship, both influencing their European allies and being influenced by them. They were not consciously deceiving the JCS. They may not have been aware in many instances of a distinction between the impression they made on their colleagues around the table in London and the impression they made on their superiors in the Pentagon. The differences were often more in tone than in substance. Lengthy exchanges in committee meetings were not always clearly encapsulated in cables.

In short, there was no conspiracy between U.S. representatives and their European colleagues to deceive the Joint Chiefs. The exigencies of the time encouraged empathy with the plight of the European military. Consequently, the generals reacted in the same spirit that animated the State Department's Hickerson and Achilles when they drank a toast to the end of the isolationist tradition, knowing that they could not share this understanding yet with Congress or with the public. A dangerously weak Europe had to be rescued, and to do this required convincing congressmen that principles of the Marshall Plan were being applied to the military sphere. The Europeans knew, as did their American advisers, that even their best efforts would not achieve a credible integrated defense system. Change would come only through a major U.S. commitment of resources, and to secure this was a transatlantic goal in 1949.

It is questionable if the Joint Chiefs, in their vigorous advocacy for the military aid program, were ever convinced by the assurances of the Western Union leaders or by the positive reports of their delegates to WU committees. Seeing firsthand how limited were the advances made in the year after WUDO was established must have been dismaying even if too little sense of disillusion was reflected in the report the Joint Chiefs delivered to Congress. British Field Marshal Bernard Law Montgomery, chairman of WU's Commanders-in-Chief Committee, loudly and regularly displayed his disgust over WUDO's status. Despite a contentious personality that ruffled sensibilities wherever he went, Monty's judgment was respected in Washington. His assertion, in 1950, that Europe's defense efforts amounted to an "opera bouffe" would have made little difference in 1949.[27] The Joint Chiefs were too firmly committed to the administration's agenda to express dissent.

HR 5748: Mutual Defense Assistance Program Bill

Notwithstanding Senator Tydings's assurance that Congress would give the military everything it asked, the Senate forced the administration to make extensive revisions to the bill in the midst of their testimony. The Joint Chiefs' European trip and the report they delivered turned out to be irrelevant to the congressional debate despite Bradley's claim on August 10 that the United States stood at "a fleeting moment" of opportunity to "exploit the advantage" it had gained in advancing the security of the West. Military aid was at the heart of this opportunity.[28]

Immediately following the ratification of the treaty, the president had sent a special message to Congress on July 25 on the need for a military assistance program. The linkage could not have been more evident. The essence of his message was embodied in three kinds of aid: (1) a limited amount of dollars to increase production of military equipment without hampering economic recovery; (2) direct transfer of essential military items from U.S. stocks; and (3) assistance in the use of military equipment and in the training of personnel. He made a point of noting that the assistance proposed "will be limited to that which is necessary to help them create mobile defensive forces . . . in the shortest possible time."[29]

HR 5748, the Mutual Defense Assistance bill of 1949, had been introduced in the House on July 25, and two days later in the Senate, where it was referred jointly to Committees on Foreign Relations and Armed Services. The administration spokesmen—Acheson, Johnson, Bradley, and Harriman—thought they had anticipated all objections in their presentations before the House Committee on Foreign Affairs on July 28 and 29. Its very name—Mutual Defense Assistance— was designed to soothe critics. They skillfully repeated points already accepted by the majority of Congress, and Acheson noted there were no initial defections on the Democratic side. The administration tried to hold fast as Republican critics asked to have the initial figure voluntarily cut. Acheson appealed to Congress to withhold their judgment until all the facts were presented.[30]

Yet it was obvious that the administration was unprepared to cope with new questions resulting from the bill. Historian Steven Rearden observed that Secretary Johnson's testimony in support of the bill was perfunctory, leaving the size and goals of the program to the State Department and the military issues to the Joint Chiefs or to Lemnitzer as director of the Office of Military Assistance. The reasons may have been his unfamiliarity with its details or unwillingness to be too closely identified with a program in which he did not participate.[31]

Advocates of the treaty immediately joined with the irreconcilables in condemning the bill. Vandenberg, as leader of this unlikely collaboration, was always lukewarm about his acceptance of a limited aid, but appeared willing to accept it until he saw the terms. Rebuking a Michigan newspaper editor on August 1 for his full support of the bill, he believed "it would be a supreme tragedy if this session of Congress should adjourn without passing some kind of preliminary 'arms bill.'" But he asserted that "not even the most devoted friends of the Pact can swallow the pending arms proposal. If they cannot do so it becomes a cinch for the isolationists to beat this bill." He saw it as his mission to work with newly appointed Sen. John Foster Dulles in "cutting this arms bill down to size."[32]

The Michigan senator appeared to relish this prospect from the moment the bill was proposed. As he told his wife, "I served blunt notice today that I simply would not support the present bill."[33] It revived his long-standing discomfort with the militarization of the treaty when he asserted that "its statement of policy put too much emphasis on arms. Since some sort of action is necessary before adjournment, I think study should be given to an interim measure while major plans await reports to the next Congress under Article 9 of the pact." Vandenberg's reference to Article 9 underscored his conviction, expanded on by Senator Dulles, that the program be rewritten until a plan had been worked out under that article of the treaty, which sets up a council of the associates of the pact to make aid recommendations. As Vandenberg vented to the Jackson editor, "the pending bill totally *ignores* these [sic] treaty articles and proposes to set up the implementation of the Pact entirely *outside* the Pact. This is intolerable. The thing we should do now is to provide a very brief *interim* bill to demonstrate our good faith pending the development of an integrated arms program as directed by the Pact itself." Acheson attributed Vandenberg's attitude to "a misapprehension of the degree of consultation which has already taken place with the Atlantic powers." And he told Dulles, who shared Vandenberg's views, that as "an interim program," it was exactly the sort of program the newly appointed Senator Dulles had advocated.[34] Acheson was too optimistic about his ability to clarify the situation.

Vandenberg's most passionate response to the proposed legislation concerned the president's putative use of the arms bill "as an *excuse* to seek more general peace-time power than was ever concentrated in the White House in the history of the United States." It distressed the senator that Truman could "upon the request of any nation to furnish assistance on such terms as *he* deems appropriate." By the time he finished his tirade, he was ready to believe that the president "would become the top warlord of the earth. Can you imagine that the American people would for an instant surrender such supreme and exclusive authority to the Chief Executive?" He had exhibited similar indignation and used similar language in his letter to his wife on the day the new bill was delivered: "I served blunt notice today that I simply could not support the president's bill" that would make him "the number one war lord of the earth." He felt comforted by a bipartisan consensus in the Foreign Relations Committee, which agreed with his objections.[35]

The old isolationists, senators Kenneth W. Wherry (R-NE) and Taft, quickly associated themselves with Vandenberg, adding their own angles to the argument. Wherry charged that the administration had hatched a conspiracy through secret commitments to the Western Union signatories of the treaty, and saw evidence of it in the fact that the substance of the bill had been completed before the treaty itself had been ratified. Taft played on Vandenberg's sensitivity about excessive powers in the hands of the president. He claimed that Truman had exceeded Roosevelt's arbitrary exercise of power in the Lend Lease Act of 1941.[36]

In the face of the Republican onslaught, Democrats were remained relatively silent. Some key Democrats, such as Walter George (D-GA) and Richard Russell (D-GA), may not have shared Vandenberg's fears about overreaching executive power or Wherry's paranoid obsessions with conspiracy, but wanted delay out of concern for the economic impact of the military aid program. Connally led the administration's defense, with a special interest in outperforming Vandenberg. Despite his and Acheson's heroic efforts to prevent the postponement of the bill, they had no choice but to present a new version.[37]

The administration's retreat was no surprise. The president felt he had no special stake in the executive powers the initial bill conferred on him. The opponents had an easy victory on August 2, but it did not inhibit Vandenberg from crowing over the outcome in his customary hyperbolic fashion: "We had our telltale show-down on the arms program in the joint meeting this morning of the Foreign Relations and Armed Services Committee. I bluntly laid the 'facts of life' before Secretary of State Acheson and Secretary of Defense Johnson. I gave 'em an ultimatum—write a new and reasonable bill or you will get no bill and it will be your fault."[38] It is obvious that Vandenberg's earlier agreement with the need for some aid immediately lost urgency; it was subsumed under his many grievances against the terms of HR 5748.

The Michigan senator had an influential figure on his side in the person of Walter Lippmann, who saw Vandenberg's arguments against the military aid bill in the light of a constitutional challenge to American tradition. He raised the issue after the administration had limited the authority that the original bill had bestowed. Lippmann found the bill to be a "shocking example of utter disrespect for our constitutional traditions and for the very processes of law." He recommended that the senator deliver "a stern lecture" "without jeopardizing the support of the avowed purposes of the bill, which we all want to see go through."[39] The pundit appealed to his vanity, which may have been in conflict with his sense of the national interest. Did Vandenberg regard the deficiencies in the bill as a challenge to his reputation?

Ego aside, Vandenberg remained true to his long-standing conviction that the military aspect of the Atlantic alliance was a diversion from the goals of the treaty. The very creation of the alliance was the inherent deterrent to Soviet expansion, a point he emphasized in a letter on August 23 to the former banker and constructive critic of U.S. foreign policy, James P. Warburg, in which he said that he "would have infinitely preferred to rely upon the potentials in the North Atlantic Pact as a discouragement to Soviet aggression." He was convinced that relying on military buildup of allied forces, in which military assistance played a vital role, was unnecessary. The MDAP could be "an inadequate down-payment on a stupendous future account." His preference was to maintain a small nuclear force "around which the potentials of tomorrow if necessary can be swiftly organized."[40] Vandenberg's acceptance of military assistance was always accompanied by these caveats.

HR 5895: Mutual Defense Assistance Program Bill

On August 5 the administration came up with a new bill—HR 5895. Vandenberg hailed the changes, but only grudgingly. While pleased that the State Department "totally surrendered on eighty per cent of my criticisms," he still felt it was too expensive and failed to "adequately subordinate itself to the machinery provided in the Atlantic Pact for its own implementation."[41]

The administration had no problem with restrictions on executive power, but it worried about the effect wrangling over the program would have on fragile European morale. As Acheson had pointed out to the House Foreign Affairs Committee, on July 28, "the failure to provide military assistance to those joined with us in that effort would . . . inevitably weaken the confidence of the other free peoples in the determination of the United States to carry out the task we have jointly undertaken."[42]

This was not Vandenberg's primary concern. The reservations he expressed were not addressed. He and other friends of the alliance confronted Acheson with the dangers of uncoordinated expansion of national armies rather than a coordinated program envisioned under Article 9 of the treaty. They urged cutting back the amount of aid until the North Atlantic Council's voice could be heard. The administration's case was not helped by Secretary Johnson's admission that the proposed military supplies would require two years before they could be available. This led to demands that only those funds that could be spent in the current fiscal year would be authorized. Nor was Congress favorably impressed with Johnson's explanation that a large sum of money granted now would permit him to make a good impression the next time he approached Congress for less money.[43]

Once again the administration retreated. Just as congressional pressure had imposed limits upon the president's authority to grant aid at his discretion, so now it forced a reassessment of the amount of aid to be given. At the hearings of the Senate Foreign Relations Committee on August 8 and 9, revisionists asked for a 50 percent cut for NATO countries in fiscal year 1950 since much of the aid would not arrive in that year. Instead, they suggested that the excised funds be placed under contract authority, chargeable to the fiscal year 1951.[44]

The administration received this congressional advice with good grace; the substitution of contract authorization indicated a change in form rather than substance. The FACC that originated the program recognized that the MDAP was in an early phase, and that its short-range objectives could be no more than a modest improvement in the recipients' ability to withstand a Soviet assault. Its impact should stem from the psychological comfort that the prospect of U.S. aid would demonstrate the seriousness of American involvement in Europe's defense.[45]

But Congress did not stop with the foregoing revisions. While the House Foreign Affairs Committee approved $1,160 billion in aid for NATO countries of

Western Europe on August 15, this figure was still too much for an important segment of Congress. Three days later the House cut this sum in half before passing the bill by 238 to 122, with amendments sponsored by Rep. James P. Richards (D-SC) that eliminated the contract authorization previously approved by the Foreign Affairs Committee and authorized only $819 million for NATO members. This was a considerable reduction from the $1,450 billion asked for by the administration.[46]

The difficulty in mid-August was less with Vandenberg's objections than with members of the president's party who were skeptical of Europe's reliability and even more worried about the size of the program. Still, Sen. John Foster Dulles (R-NY) further slowed the administration's progress when he and Vandenberg proposed to eliminate funds that would encourage arms production in Europe. But these Republicans opponents of the MDAP posed a lesser challenge. On the other hand, senators Walter George and Richard Russell of Georgia, speaking for a small but important band of southern Democratic senators, raised persistent questions about the cost of the program that were heard until the very end of the debate.[47]

It was often difficult to distinguish between senators who wanted revisions and those who opposed both the treaty and the MDAP. In mid-September eleven senators from both parties proposed support for an Atlantic police force, recruited in Europe from the smaller members of NATO, along with West Germany. No mention was made of the Western Union when Ralph E. Flanders (R-VT) spoke of an international military force that "will serve as a nuclear international police force whenever we decide, as we should, to extend the Atlantic pact into a world pact under proper world authority." Ostensibly, the nation would not have to "spend our millions on building up the weak and dispersed armed forces of the smaller nations." To further this goal, Sen. John J. Sparkman (D-AL) introduced an amendment of the MDAP bill that would earmark for such a force 10 to 25 percent of the $1 billionallocation proposed for NATO countries. Connally questioned the seriousness of the proposal, as it was made primarily by former isolationist Republicans, such as Harry P. Cain (R-WA) and Homer Capehart (R-IN), and conservative cost-conscious Democrats, such as John C. Stennis (D-MS) and Edwin C. Johnson (D-CO). Connally described the amendment as putting "barnacles into the military aid bill."[48] The amendment failed.

It was obvious that the old isolationists were fighting a rearguard battle against both the treaty and the MAP. Some of the opponents labeled the MDAP a British plot against the U.S. Treasury or a scheme for the enrichment of the Rockefellers. The arguments of others were more generalized. According to Taft, "this program is completely illogical, completely vain in respect to what it proposes to accomplish; not only does it seem to me that it is contrary to every principle we have formerly pursued in connection with the United Nations; but I also believe it to be a policy which is dangerous to the peace of the United States and the peace of the world." The Ohio senator's reference to the UN may have been an attempt to tap a sensitive nerve that would arouse Vandenberg once again. It was Rep. William Lemke (R-ND) who was most candid about the hopes of the former isolationists. He intended "to vote for all crippling amendments and then vote against the cripple.⁴⁹

The Truman administration had not expected the progress of the Mutual Defense Assistance bill to require almost two months before passage. Its outlines had been known before it was launched as a necessary accompaniment to the North Atlantic Treaty. The European allies had confidently anticipated it, as their submission of the Western Union's list of priorities had indicated. Nevertheless, the extended time required for final congressional approval could not have been a total surprise. The isolationist bloc's opposition was expected and the misgivings of the Vandenberg circle were also well known. The suspicion of Europeans taking advantage of American largess, after all, was not confined to irreconcilables.

In addition to these factors holding up action on behalf of the European allies, the question of aid to China's faltering struggle against the Communists and the need for continuing support for the still precarious success of Greece's suppression of Communist aggression could not be ignored. These areas held priority over Europe's needs in the eyes of many congressmen, and to fulfill their requirements meant reducing those of the NATO allies. Such was the rationalization for categorizing aid under titles. Title I—Western Europe—ultimately was the primary beneficiary, but Title II (with $211 million for Greece and Turkey) and Title III (providing $28 million for Iran, Korea, and the Philippines) represented more than a token awareness of their needs. Nationalist China would receive $75 million that Congress imposed on the administration.⁵⁰

These diversions helped to account for the protracted process of passing HR 5895. The Senate's verdict proved to be more generous than the House's perhaps, as Steven Rearden suggested, because it had a stake in complementing the treaty that it recently approved.⁵¹ By the third week of September, the logjam was broken, largely in favor of the Senate's version. On September 22 the House passed the bill authorizing a total of $1,340 billion to the recipients under the three titles. The authorization for Title I amounted to $1 billion, with $100 million immediately available in cash after NATO had fashioned a strategic plan for the integrated defense of the West. Five hundred million dollars would be available in contract authority when the strategic plan was approved. While the law would provide "equipment, materials, and services" to strengthen the allies' capabilities for individual and collective defense, it forbade the transfer of manufacturing equipment abroad. MDAP's opponents succeeded in withholding nine-tenths of the $1 billion authorized for the NATO allies.⁵²

The restrictions were modest in light of the criticism expressed over the summer months and, for the most part, reasonable. Vandenberg endorsed the Senate's version as "a bargain insurance policy for peace," the cheapest in "blood and treasure," and as the best way to prevent a third world war.⁵³ It is tempting to credit the completion of the process to the president's announcement on September 23 that the Soviet Union had detonated an atomic device, even though critics such as Senator George felt that it "confirms my contention that you can't contain Russia by land arms built up around her." Soviet possession of an atomic bomb seemed irrelevant to the Georgia senator. Rep. John Kee (D-WV), leader of the House negotiators on the House–Senate conference committee, told reporters that the House restoration on September 26 of the aid earlier denied was not connected with the Soviet detonation of an atomic device.[54]

If the Soviets' atomic capability was not persuasive enough to push the bill through, Connally's warning on September 19 that Russia has five million men in arms should have alarmed other senators. The "Soviet army," he warned, "is not organized for the purpose of playing polo." Connally went on to observe that "we cannot permit our friends to remain so weak that they will invite aggression and be picked off one by one like pigeons in a shooting gallery." Although George, among others, continued to be skeptical about the judgment of the "highest military opinion" invoked by the chairman of the Senate Foreign Relations Committee, the movement toward passage was irresistible by the third week of September. The House had capitulated to the Senate version of the MDAP because, as Representative Kee admitted, with Senator Connally smiling at his elbow, "the matter is so transcendentally important."[55]

Nightmare scenarios of Soviet armies on the march and its atomic power deployed were probably unnecessary at this point. Both houses had made up their minds. At the House–Senate conference on September 26 the Senate voted for the full $1,314 billion, but required NATO to formulate workable plans before the monies would be released. To satisfy House colleagues, the Senate abandoned the $869 million figure it had agreed to in August. The Senate vote of fifty-five to twenty-four on September 22 signaled that it had won more bipartisan support than the bill's managers had expected. The final bill passed by a vote of 223 to 109 in the House and by voice vote in the Senate. The president signed the act on October 6, 1949.[56]

It was an impressive victory for President Truman, Secretary of State Acheson, and chairman of the Senate Foreign Relations Committee Tom Connally. The administration spoke of the effect on European morale the $1 billion aid program would have, with more to follow. Given the long and intense debates over military assistance, it is understandable that the implications of military aid were not fully explored. An exhausted Senator Connally, sitting on a bench outside the Senate chamber after the conference adjourned, told reporters that he judged the controversy to have been the most difficult since the passage of the Lend Lease Act of 1941. The Times (London) added a postscript to this observation when it noted on November 11 that with the defeat of Senator Dulles in the New York election and the illness of Senator Vandenberg, there were no longer prominent Republicans to carry the banner of bipartisanship.[57]

This observation was not strictly accurate. Although both senators repeatedly had claimed at the time the military aid bill was presented that the administration had turned its back on a bipartisan foreign policy, Vandenberg and Dulles supported the final version as vital to the success of NATO. To underscore his sense of sacrifice in endorsing the final version, Dulles noted that he interrupted his campaign to retain his Senate seat in a special election for the unexpired term of Robert F. Wagner to return to Washington and vote. He did so despite the president's pledging his full support for his opponent, former New York Governor Herbert H. Lehman: "We may differ among ourselves—indeed, we do differ—as regards domestic policies. . . . But in the face of external danger we unite to help our friends and to bring confusion to our enemies."[58]

Bilateral Agreements: The Survey Teams

The voice of the Joint Chiefs of Staff was heard frequently and usually respectfully in the congressional debates over military assistance, but with limited impact. As late as September 19, Senator George testily asked, "Is the military opinion to be taken without question? Gen. Omar Bradley is not a member of the Senate, with responsibility for a policy." Senator Tydings's response that "he is the poor fellow who will have to do the job if trouble comes" quieted the Georgia senator, but this exchange showed the limits of the Joint Chiefs' influence on Congress.[59] Neither the Joint Chiefs nor Secretary of Defense Johnson controlled the course of the debate over military assistance even though the chiefs would be responsible for carrying out the commitments made under the new Mutual Defense Assistance Act.

The momentum behind the program was propelled by the State Department and its allies in the Senate. The reason lay partly in the authority Secretary Acheson projected in his first year in office, as compared with his counterpart in the Defense Department (despite the new powers he acquired under the revision of the National Security act of 1947).[60] Johnson often seemed to be lost in the complexities of the program. But the reasons for the State Department's predominance in a program dependent on the military services for its implementation went beyond the personal qualities of the respective secretaries. The threat of financing the MAP from current military appropriations had come from the Bureau of the Budget and, more pointedly, from Edwin Nourse, chairman of the President's Council of Economic Advisers. It had been turned aside with the help of the State Department.[61]

The three agencies—State, Defense, and the Economic Cooperation Administration—that had been instrumental in drafting the aid bill continued their oversight of the administration of the MDAP. The Foreign Military Assistance Coordinating Committee (FMACC), under which the diplomatic, military, and economic officers served, reflected the dominance of the State Department. On October 17,

1949, James Bruce, U.S. ambassador to Argentina, was appointed as director of Foreign Military Assistance and chairman of the FMACC, as well as special assistant to the secretary of state. Within Defense, General Lemnitzer, an early advocate of the MDAP, was named director of the Office of Military Assistance, helping the Joint Chiefs develop policies for the program. Secretary Johnson made it clear to Lemnitzer on November 9 that "all dealings with other Departments in this Program will be to and through my office." He then gave the JCS responsibility not only for directing all overseas military operations but also for recommending broad criteria for military assistance.[62]

The implication in these directives was that the leadership in the administration of military assistance would be in the office of the secretary of defense. This was not to be the case. The European Coordinating Committee (ECC), the agency maintaining the MDAP in Europe, would be under the direction of the U.S. ambassador in Britain, Lewis Douglas.[63] The other members of the ECC— Gen. Thomas T. Handy, commander in chief of the European command, and W. Averell Harriman, special representative in Europe for the ECA—had impressive credentials, equal if not superior to those of Ambassador Douglas. Nevertheless, it was Douglas, not Handy or Harriman, who was the dominant figure in Europe. Given the immediate storm in NATO that the Mutual Defense Assistance Act created, it was fitting that a diplomat be the key person in calming tensions.

The most emotional problem emanating from the implementation of the MDAP derived from the requirement that the distribution of aid be monitored by U.S. officials on a bilateral basis in each member nation.[64] Here the military played a significant role through the country-level Military Assistance Advisory Groups (MAAGs) But important as military expertise was in this process, the chief of the diplomatic mission in the host country chaired the country teams. The JCS was also involved in assisting the MAAGs, but played a subordinate role in the development of programs.

The European beneficiaries of aid had two major objections to the way the United States perceived the relationship between donor and recipient. While the United States insisted at every opportunity on Europeans breaking down national barriers and moving toward integrated defense, the Mutual Defense Assistance Act required the completion of detailed bilateral agreements with each recipient nation as prerequisites to the release of funds. These involved thorough examination of just how the monies would be used, and this in turn meant that each country would serve as host to American political, military, and economic inspectors.

The bilateral emphasis distressed Europeans at a time when multilateral goals were the professed objectives of the Atlantic alliance. They could claim that the Americans were creating a double standard: demanding the integration that the Western Union was in the process of developing and that the North Atlantic Council would promote, and then securing for themselves bilateral advantages denied to the allies. The requirement of reciprocal aid in the form of military bases was an example of this discrimination. Granting the United States base rights could be seen as a species of nineteenth-century extraterritoriality, a humiliating deference to power of the senior NATO partner. France reluctantly accepted the conditions as long as the agreement took into account the nation's sensibilities.[65]

From a U.S. perspective, such complaints had no basis in fact; the precedent of Marshall Plan aid should have been understood by Europeans.[66] The charge of American imperialism or neocolonialism was unfair given that the transfer of a European installation to American use should be considered a reasonable quid for the quo of military aid. Unlike the Marshall Plan, directed solely toward European recovery, military aid was in the service of an integrated program that embraced Americans as well as Europeans.

The more specific complaints from the European allies dealt with the implementation of the aid program, and here they were vulnerable to U.S. criticism. However responsive the Joint Chiefs were to the administration's acceptance of Western Union's claims of progress in building up their own individual defenses and in advancing integration of forces, they knew the inadequacy of those efforts and the lack of coordination in determining requests for specific aid. Not much had been accomplished between WU's submission of its lists in April and the passage of the Mutual Defense Assistance Act in October. Too many of the items on the allies' individual lists conflicted both with the congressional requirement of efficient utilization of the aid and the NATO requirement of conformity with an overall strategic plan.

France, at head of the line, had admitted that each of the French military branches had presented budget needs without consulting the plans of the others. The French navy, for example, wanted to construct several large aircraft carriers that the country could not afford and that NATO did not need.[67] France was not alone in looking upon the MDAP as an opportunity to fulfill the military's wish lists at the expense of outstanding gaps in the nation's capability for self-defense. Few countries could resist the temptation to use U.S. arms in place of those they could have financed themselves had there been no MDAP. The Netherlands proposed to abandon its program to build six destroyers needed for sea patrols because an equal number was expected from the United States under MDAP.[68]

What the Americans asked of the NATO allies was not only proof that military aid would advance an integrated European defense, but also that they demonstrate a spirit of reciprocity by means of bilateral agreements between each beneficiary and the United States. This prerequisite was written into the Mutual Defense Assistance Act guaranteeing that the president would safeguard the defense needs of the United States, much as the ECA had done on behalf of the U.S. economy. Bilateral agreements would assure Congress that the administration would have control over the use of aid. Equally important was the recipient's "furnishing equipment and materials, services, or other assistance . . . to the United States . . . to further the policies and purposes of the Act."[69] Section 402 did not specify military bases or special installations under "assistance," but this was its primary purpose and the source of considerable European discontent.

The Western Union tried to cope with U.S. pressure by a show of unity. At the ninetieth meeting of its Permanent Commission the WU asked that negotiations on bilateral agreements be "undertaken on the basis of complete agreement between the five." The delegates recognized that they would have to conduct negotiations from their own capitals rather than collectively in Washington, but hoped that the bilateral treaties would be signed only after full consultation in advance by the members of the Brussels Pact. In the meantime, they protested that too many of the draft agreements depended on the will of Congress, which, as the Belgian delegate pointed out, could be changed unilaterally by subsequent congressional legislation.[70]

The beneficiaries of MDAP understood they lacked the power to reject bilateral negotiations. This meant that they had to put aside their resentments and host special investigating teams that would survey their current capabilities and verifiable needs. Not surprisingly, State Department representatives headed the survey teams, although the Defense Department was an important partner. Time was a factor in advancing negotiations. The inspection process had to be finished before the new NATO Defense Committee met on December 1. Acheson emphasized to the missions in Europe that the full $1 billion for military assistance would be available only after the bilateral agreements had been signed.[71]

Inevitably, there was grumbling over the teams' recommendations, and not just from the European partners. Secretary Johnson had reservations about allowing the retransfer of lend-lease goods. A redistribution of surplus materials in Europe from one ally to another would provide a striking example of mutual aid principles in action. But even before the MDAP came into being, he had objected to the idea; the secretary of defense felt that any proceeds from the retransfer of Lend-Lease items should not be at the expense of the U.S. taxpayer. It required considerable explanation on the part of the State Department to budge him from this position.[72]

Dissatisfaction with various aspects of the retransfer idea was expressed by Europeans who could not come to a consensus about the transfer of excess goods. Ideally, the allies would prefer to place all military stocks in Western Europe into a pool with an international clearing system to arrange for exchanges among the NATO members. Realistically, they had to deal with internal conflicts in Europe over the burden of costs. For example, should Britain, with its considerable stocks of U.S. origin, supply the needs of the continental allies without compensation from those countries or from the United States? And even if this problem were solved, a potential beneficiary, such as Italy, was reluctant to accept British planes and engines because it preferred U.S. equivalents and feared Britain's supply might run out.[73] Britain, in turn, protested vigorously against the provision in Article I of the bilateral agreement that could prohibit exchange of arms with Commonwealth nations without U.S. approval. France also objected to this article if only because it gave credence to the Communist charge that the MDAP placed France in bondage to America.[74]

To each of these complaints the United States gave sympathetic attention to Europeans' concerns. Acheson assured Ambassador Franks that the transfer of military materials to other countries would apply just to the actual items supplied under the bilateral agreement. The British also noted the requirement in the MAP bill that 50 percent of equipment transferred to other nations be carried on U.S. ships was "unrealistic and uneconomic." Theodore Achilles was sympathetic and n substantial agreement with the British complaint, but "doubted that anything could be done."[75] Congress had spoken.

Still, U.S. negotiators sought not only to avoid the stigma of dictating the provisions of the bilateral agreements but also to impress upon the recipients that a "mutuality of interest" was the basis of each article. A change in—or omission of—wording sometimes silenced complaints. It was a point of honor for France to have the adjective "advisory" removed from the text of the agreement. The Quai d'Orsay further asserted that the bilateral agreement must be approved by its legislature and will not be legally binding before this is done. The British continued to resist granting full diplomatic immunity to the MAAG. The United States then conceded that military personnel at least would not be in uniform. And rather than monitor "utilization" of aid, the U.S. military advisory groups would observe its "progress."[76]

As for British resentment over having to seek permission to export their own manufacture made with U.S. materials, the offensive provision was removed. On page 4 of *The Times* (London) on December 22 there were three articles with reports of U.S. compliance with the British viewpoint. Assistant Secretary of State George W. Perkins made a point of noting that the "unwillingness of the U.K. to sign a bilateral would, we believe, have very serious repercussions both in Europe and the U.S. which would be very far-reaching. We fear it would raise doubts in the minds of Europeans as to the ultimate intentions of the U.K. in the European defense. We are certain it would precipitate a storm of public opinion in the United States which would threaten the continuance of military assistance."[77]

Unfortunately, much of the goodwill engendered by U.S. efforts to respect the sensitivities of the recipients was dissolved in the application of Article VI of the bilateral agreements. No matter how much care the U.S. supervisors took to avoid conflict with the European allies, they could not avoid the appearance of infringing upon their national sovereignty and offending their national pride. The very act of setting up an American headquarters in a foreign capital itself was humiliating. It was hardly surprising that Europeans preferred NATO to determine employment of weapons and equipment, even though the United States was the dominant partner in the organization. Bilateralism was in variance with procedures whereby NATO would act as a multilateral entity at the same time that the United States demanded bilateral arrangements.

For the most part, the arguments the host countries raised against the imposition of U.S. advisory teams had considerable justification. Denmark, remembering the Nazi occupation, feared that comparisons were unavoidable. Norway, with equally vivid memories, wondered why the United States intended to send a military mission larger than the entire Norwegian foreign office staff.[78] All Europeans worried about the impact on NATO's adversaries—Communists, nationalists, neutralists— of the spectacle of Americans officials occupying lavish quarters in their capitals where housing was scarce, dining at the best restaurants in cities where food was rationed, and unwittingly giving the appearance of superiority over their allies. The Italians, though, seemed less disturbed by the trappings of American imperialism than by the potential cost for the upkeep of a large American delegation.[79]

There was a perimeter beyond which the United States could not bend to the wishes of the recipient countries. Under the leadership of the former ambassador to Argentina, Walter Surrey, special consultant to the director of the MDAP, the negotiations required U.S. control over the transfer of MDAP items from one country to another, as well as arranging for securing base and other specific military operating rights from the NATO allies. It took time to iron out the many differences between grantor and grantee. Acheson was too optimistic when he announced on November 30, 1949 that "negotiations on agreements with eight Atlantic Pact countries are in the final stages."[80] Not until January 27, 1950 were the bilateral agreements signed with eight NATO members.

Bilateral Agreements: Export Controls

Although the European beneficiaries of military aid had won some compromises, they had to accept the teams that the FMACC dispatched and the duties they were to perform. They were less compliant about a provision in the bilateral agreements restraining trade in strategic materials with Eastern European countries. Control of trade with the Soviet bloc was a major issue with the United States. The administration and Congress identified denial of vital materials to the Soviet adversary as an integral part of the Cold War. Defense officials were not alone in pressing this issue. Ambassador Harriman, the ECA's representative in Europe, stressed that the allies should recognize the importance that the United States attached to export controls as a factor in mutual aid. In agreement with the Defense Department, he recommended that primary responsibility for directing control procedures be transferred from the ECA to the State Department. Harriman was convinced that this would be the best way of applying pressure on the allies.[81]

Understandably, the reshipment of U.S. goods to Communist countries would be a major preoccupation of the Truman administration. The Defense Department wanted even more stringent measures than the ECA or the State Department to stop trade with the Soviet bloc. The Department of Commerce, which was responsible for export licenses, extended license controls in November 1949 on the eve of bilateral negotiations with NATO allies. Ultimately, the Defense Department watered down its demands, but the message was clear: Europe should follow America's lead in denying economic advantages to the Communist nations.[82]

The Europeans did not share the U.S. sense of urgency with respect to East–West trade. Unlike the Americans, they thought less about the hardship the Soviets would suffer if vital materials were cut off than of the economic consequences to themselves if trade were interrupted. Such a policy, they feared, would undo the benefits of the Marshall Plan and undercut a sound rearmament plan. Even if a reduction of trade in strategic materials weakened Communist power, their economic ties with the East were too important to their national economies to allow a sudden disruption. Moreover, they argued that Communists in the NATO countries might use U.S. pressure for export controls as unwarranted interference in their domestic affairs. Alternatively, such action might provoke the Soviets into dangerous retaliatory acts. The perceptive French commentator, Jean-Jacques Servan-Schreiber, identified transatlantic differences over the perception of the Soviet challenge as the source of the problem. He urged Americans and Europeans to recognize that the principle of Atlantic uniformity does not necessarily apply to all issues, and that these differences should be understood as the allies made their decisions.[83]

Considering the depth of U.S. official feelings on the matter of export controls, it is noteworthy that the bilateral agreements, signed on January 27, 1950 by eight NATO recipient countries, made no mention of this provision. Unlike the inspections on the use of military aid by U.S. military and civilian personnel in each allied country, the FMACC, despite its misgivings, felt that its absence from the final agreements did not jeopardize U.S. national security. If necessary, the question of export controls could be revived at a later date. The MAAGs, on the other hand, could not be sacrificed; they had to be set up before shipments were made if the MDAP was to fulfill its mission and retain public confidence in the United States.

The patience of the U.S. negotiators and their NATO partners was rewarded by the overwhelming approval of the bilateral pacts by those countries requiring legislative action. The American embassy in London was particularly pleased that the British announcement would link the bilateral agreement to MDAP, so it put a positive spin on the connections between military assistance and NATO. It was expected that the French also would make a positive statement identifying the signing of a bilateral agreement as a step forward for NATO.[84]

MAP 1949: In Retrospect

NATO could not have come into being without the military assistance program. From a U.S. perspective, the program was a momentous step in America's relations with Europe. Committing the nation to abandoning a cherished tradition of non-entanglement with the Old World was unquestionably more traumatic, but implementing it turned out to be politically more contentious. It was not just that the shriveled but articulate remnants of the old isolationist bloc spoke out against the program. For them it was an invitation for Europe to plunder America's resources, as well as to lure the United States into conflicts that the nation had avoided since its founding. Rather, the problems lay with the supporters of a binding commitment to European defense.

Senator Vandenberg represented a large community of believers in internationalism even as they opposed the expansion of Communism. But if they recognized the inadequacy of the United Nations as the primary instrument to maintain world order, they feared the consequences of excessive militarization of the Atlantic alliance. Military aid conceivably could distort the purpose of the treaty. By itself the very creation of an alliance should have deterred Soviet aggression and also assure Europeans of America's long-term dedication to their economic recovery and security. Such military aid that would be sent should be minimal, limited to internal protection, and organized with coordinated efforts in self-defense.

These reservations were at the heart of the objections raised by advocates of the alliance. They were supplemented by the initial alarm that the military aid program would exaggerate presidential authority at the expense of the legislature. The substitution of a new bill just a week after the initial bill was presented was a measure of the concerns of arguably a majority of both houses of Congress. Another bloc, many of them Democrats, continued to fret over the cost of the program and the negative impact it might have on both the American and the European economies.

The European beneficiaries of aid prolonged the progress of the legislative process by their exaggerated sense of entitlement. France, in particular, made a point of identifying itself as the first to receive arms and the most important participant in the program. While the Truman administration essentially agreed with France's role in MDAP, the manner in which it trumpeted its superiority was offensive. Not that it was out of character. Its provocative positions were familiar to the framers of the treaty. It was particularly galling, though, when France, as the leading member of the Western Union, assumed that the Brussels Pact five would continue to be elevated above the other European members of the alliance. The unseemly competition for supremacy between British Field Marshal Bernard Law Montgomery and French Gen. Jean-Marie de Lattre de Tassigny illuminated the dysfunctional relations among the European allies in their attempts to convince the American partner of their success in creating an integrated force. The Pentagon's pretense at accepting WUDO's accomplishments at face value was barely credible, but there was no choice. If the remaining $900 million was to be released, the United States had to accept them, no matter how reluctantly.

The Truman administration, in turn, alienated the European allies by the requirements of the Mutual Defense Assistance Act and the associated bilateral agreements. It seemed hypocritical for Americans to impose bilateral arrangements with the allies when multilateral integration was the premise on which the North Atlantic Treaty was built. American use of European bases was an appropriate exchange for aid, but the way it was obtained was an affront to their national pride. The Western Union had to recognize as well that it was not to be the exclusive partner of the United States.

That the European partners were able to hold their own in negotiations despite their grievances over the behavior of the senior partner was a tribute to the vigor with which they argued their positions, both separately and as members of the Brussels Pact. It was also a reflection of American concern to put the pieces of the alliance into place as quickly as possible as well as appreciation for the validity of their arguments. Deliberate as the debates in Congress were, they had to take into account that the administration's failure to conclude agreements would risk the loss of funds authorized by Congress and, more significantly, constitute a setback in the struggle with the Communist world.

Ultimately, there were few opportunities for substantive accomplishments from the $900 million military assistance in a program whose life span was more than half completed before the military items would be in European hands. Almost all the equipment promised for Europe required a year or more to manufacture, and what was ostensibly available immediately in the form of excess stocks often required extensive reconditioning. The fiscal year 1950 would end on June 30, 1950, and the first planes and ships would not arrive until the spring of that year. Given this situation, the success of the MDAP could not be measured by the amount of aid delivered abroad, or by any quantifiable increase in NATO's strength in Europe, or by the accuracy of the U.S. survey teams' determination of the military deficiencies of the recipient nations. Instead, initial achievements had to be measured by the extent to which diplomats—both military and civilian—had worked out a system of cooperation within the alliance, by the increase in a sense of security in Europe, and by the soundness of the structure erected to administer the MDAP.

Still, there were other more important issues than the mechanics of delivery aid, which were not resolved as MDAP was set in motion. Historian Chester Pach observed that while the legislators debated the extent and application of military aid, they did not turn their attention to the evaluation of the effectiveness of an armaments program: "At a time when military assistance was still a secondary and even somewhat novel instrument of national policy, Congress demanded from the Truman administration only a superficial justification of its preference for large-scale arms aid to accomplish its foreign goals."[85] Arguably, its very novelty precluded anticipating its end results.

The more immediate problems of the day absorbed the attention of all the allies. The role of the Western Union remained unsettled. Integration beyond the five to include the Scandinavian and Italian recipients was in the background in NATO's first year. When the position of the WU did surface, American negotiators expressed annoyance with its persistent claims to serve as the exclusive unit for distributing military aid to Europe. Secretary Johnson told the Senate Foreign Relations Committee in August that U.S. equipment could not be transferred directly to the Western Union because "it is not a sovereign entity which has the means of receiving and employing such equipment."[86]

What lessened tensions and permitted questions to go answered in the fall of 1949 was the parallel establishment of NATO machinery that could take the sting off the American-imposed bilateralism. The organization that the allies were creating was, by definition, multilateral, and the concessions on such issues as bases on the part of the Europeans or yielding on exports controls on the part of the Americans could be rationalized as confidence in the new agencies the North Atlantic Council was establishing at the very time the MDAP was being set in motion.

4

The North Atlantic Council at Work

September 1949–January 1950

While transatlantic attention in the late summer and fall of 1949 centered on Capitol Hill in Washington, where Congress was fashioning a military assistance program, NATO's twelve foreign ministers met at the Interdepartmental Auditorium on Independence Avenue to constitute the North Atlantic Council (NAC). In a single day, September 17, 1949—in fact, in a single hour—NAC established an array of subsidiary bodies under Article 9.[1] As noted in the introduction to the texts of final communiqués, "It is from Article 9 that the whole North Atlantic Treaty Organization, both civil and military, derive[s]."[2]

It is Article 9, too, that permits a comparison to be made between the treaty and the U.S. Constitution. Both seminal documents are succinct in their clauses and open to expanded interpretations. Article I of the Constitution, vesting in Congress all legislative powers, evokes resemblance to the treaty. Section 3 (18), which allows Congress to "make all other laws which shall be necessary and proper for carrying out" legislation already passed, brings to mind the following quotations from NATO's Article 9. That article establishes a "Council . . . to consider matters concerning the implementation of the Treaty. . . . The Council shall set up such subsidiary bodies as may be necessary." All the subsequent NATO committees, groups, and agencies owed their legitimacy to Article 9.

The linkages between the Constitution and the treaty, of course, are limited. The essential military character of the alliance, as opposed to the American union, was made clear in the functions given to the Council in Article 9. The "subsidiary bodies" it was charged with establishing were not vaguely to be created "as may be necessary." Rather, NAC was specifically required to "establish a defence committee which shall recommend measures for the implementation of Articles 3 and 5." Here was the conjunction of military aid and a defense structure with the promise of security for each of its members. The specificity of this mandate differentiates Article 9 from the more general charges of the Constitution's Article I, Section 3.

The temporal linkage of the Mutual Defense Assistance Program (MDAP) with the creation of a NATO infrastructure was not coincidental. The legislative process resulting in the Mutual Defense Assistance Act extended from July 25, 1949, when the first version of the military aid bill was introduced, to October 6, when it was enacted as PL329. A Working Group prepared the first NAC ministerial meeting on September 17, during which a series of committees was created— the most important being the Defense Committee under which a Military Committee and its Standing Group, along with five Regional Planning Groups, would function. Two more NAC meetings to set NATO in motion met in Washington in the fall of 1949 and the winter of 1950 with Dean Acheson as chairman.

The first was on November 18, when the council established a Defense Financial and Economic Committee and a Military Production and Supply Board. The second was on January 6, when NAC approved recommendations for a strategic concept for an integrated defense of the North Atlantic area, which had been drawn up by the Defense Committee in Paris on December 1. The strategic concept could not be completed until the U.S. Congress released funds for military aid to the allies under the terms of the Mutual Defense Assistance Act.

North Atlantic Council: Ministerial Meeting, September 17, 1949

The working group preparing the agenda for the first NAC meeting seemed to have fulfilled its assignment in every respect. In the lengthy communiqué that followed the sessions, NAC asserted that "all Parties are united in their resolve to integrate their efforts for the promotion of lasting peace, the preservation of their common heritage and the strengthening of their common defence."[3] In light of the progress of congressional negotiations for military assistance, "defense" loomed larger than "lasting peace" and "common heritage" in the communiqué. While it appropriately lists relevant information about the council itself—its composition of foreign ministers or their designated representatives, annual meetings of ordinary sessions, rotating chairmanship, and the equality of English and French as official languages—its primary charge was the establishment of a Defense Committee that would develop the organization's means of resisting armed attack: "the Defense Committee should therefore immediately take the requisite steps to have drawn up unified defence plans for the North Atlantic area." Accordingly, Secretary of Defense Louis Johnson, as chairman, was to call the first meeting of the committee on October 8, just three weeks after NAC adjourned.[4]

Detailed but not complete functions of the Defense Committee and its subordinate agencies followed from this instruction. This committee would be tasked with recommending measures to implement articles 3 and 5 under council guidance.

Many more specific responsibilities were given to the Military Committee, composed of chiefs of staff or their representatives. Unlike the North Atlantic Council and the Defense Committee, the Military Committee would meet periodically in Washington and would be dependent for most actions on a subcommittee, the Standing Group, which would be housed in the Pentagon and would meet continuously. This important body consisted of one representative from France, Britain, and the United States.[5]

The Standing Group's special responsibility would be to monitor defense plans of the five Regional Planning Groups, which would immediately come into being. They included a Northern Regional Planning Group composed of Denmark, Norway, and Britain, with the United States and Canada participating as "appropriate"; a Western European Regional Planning Group with the Low Countries and Britain as members, the United States and Canada again participating as "appropriate"; a Western European–Mediterranean Regional Planning Group with France, Italy, and Britain, and once again with participation by the United States as "appropriate." A Canada–United States Regional Planning Group would include European participation as "appropriate." Every member of the groups, with the exceptions of Italy and Luxembourg, would be charged with some aspects of the defense of North Atlantic regional planning. Even Iceland, without an armed force, would be included here, and would be part of subgroups responsible for specific functions.[6] On the basis of the amount of space given to the Regional Planning Groups and their relationships with the Standing Group, they were obviously intended to be the motor driving NATO's efforts. Supported by U.S. military aid funds, they were to provide in as short a time as possible a credible defense program for the alliance.

Don Cook, the veteran European correspondent for the *New York Herald Tribune* and observer of most NATO ministerial meetings since the birth of the alliance, was not impressed with the results of the first NAC meeting. He observed that it lasted only one day and produced only "a loose collection of uncoordinated committees." He noted that there was no mention of a headquarters, a secretariat, or an international budget. In fact, it was not clear who would be in charge of foreign relations in the alliance.[7]

Cook overstated the shortcomings of the meeting. The Working Group had done its job well in putting together a variety of tasks for the many subordinate committees that NAC would immediately set to work. Cook granted that the Standing Group was organized for continuous activity under the leadership of the military chiefs of the United States, Britain, and France, but qualified his appreciation by noting how wary the United States was of becoming too involved in the Regional Planning Groups that the Standing Group was intended to monitor.[8] Dean Acheson, always alert to absurd situations, found in NATO's pre-integration organization just the program General de Gaulle would have approved: "general plans for uncoordinated and separate action in the hope that in the event of trouble a plan and the forces to meet it would exist and would be adopted by a sort of spontaneous combustion."[9] This, too, was an overstatement of NAC's defects. The results of the NAC meeting may have been as much as the council could produce at the time.

European Reactions to the First NAC

Given the relatively short time the NATO Working Group had to cobble together the elaborate program unveiled at NAC's first meeting, it should have come as no surprise to the American framers that the partners had reservations about the arrangements and were not reluctant to express them. These ranged from the membership of the Standing Group to the composition of the Regional Planning Groups. No ally could complain about the leadership role taken by the United States. This was welcomed. Among the common complaints of Europeans was that the United States was not sufficiently central to the planning process in Europe, and would participate only as it determined "appropriate." The chairmanship of NAC would be rotated at future sessions, but the first three ministerial meetings met in Washington and were chaired by Secretary of State Acheson.

Turkey's Grievances

Nations on the periphery of NATO that were anxious to play a part in the organization felt all the more excluded as they observed the array of committees and groups that emerged from the Washington meeting on September 17. Greece and Turkey had been offended when they were denied the privilege in 1948 of even applying for membership in the alliance. Having been the beneficiaries of the Truman Doctrine the year before, they had a sense of entitlement as the earliest warriors against Communism. They felt that the Western allies had not sufficiently recognized their contributions. While they obviously were not "Atlantic" powers, they could point out that Italy did not meet that criterion either. If Italy, a former enemy in World War II and a minor presence in the alliance, could be brought into NATO, then the vital strategic position of Turkey, along with its considerable military potential, should have been a valuable addition to NATO.

Turkey, along with Greece, was to benefit from Title II of the Mutual Defense Assistance Act, potentially receiving up to $211 million to carry out defense measures first appropriated in 1947. This evidence of support was not enough to satisfy Turkey. When NAC set up the Southern European–Western Mediterranean Regional Planning Group in September, the counselor of the Turkish embassy spoke with Assistant Secretary of State George C. McGhee about plans for the Eastern Mediterranean.[10] This inquiry was part of Turkey's continuing campaign to acquire some role in the North Atlantic Treaty, if not direct membership in the alliance.

Response to the first inquiry was easy enough for McGhee to manage; it was too early for a newly created planning group to consider planning outside its area. The larger question was not as easily resolved, particularly when framed as a query about the status of the United States in the event that Britain and France were brought into war as a result of an attack against Turkey. The Turkish diplomat was referring to the 1939 Treaty of Mutual Assistance, which was recently reaffirmed by all three countries. Turkey's solution was to join NATO, and the counselor of the embassy wondered if the announcement of the USSR's atomic explosion might change the status of Turkey's relationship with NATO.[11] McGhee temporized, saying "that we could only move forward a little at a time, and that when we felt that the conditions were favorable for an extension of the treaty to Turkey, we would discuss the matter further with him."[12] While Turkey understood the U.S. reasoning, it was obvious that its government would not abandon the subject.

The Swedish Connection

There was uneasiness as well on the northern periphery of NATO. The Norwegian and Danish allies entered the circle of charter members late in the negotiations over the terms of the North Atlantic Treaty. Denmark, if not Norway, would have preferred the path of Swedish neutrality in place of a military pact with the West. All three Scandinavian countries, despite some Norwegian reservations, would have been happy to have a neutral Nordic bloc with its security backed by the United States.[13] While Norway and Denmark were tempted by Sweden's invitation, their acceptance hung on the U.S. response. The answer: only if there was anything left after the allies' needs had been served.[14]

Sweden did not join NATO, unlike Norway and Denmark. Still, lingering doubts remained in Denmark and Norway about the wisdom of replacing a Nordic alliance with an Atlantic alliance. Even as the Regional Planning Groups were being established in the fall of 1949, they were still hoping for eventual Swedish membership in NATO. The independent Norwegian newspaper, *Verdens Gang*, felt that Scandinavian defense would need an alliance with Sweden. Although they recognized that a separate Scandinavian union would not materialize, the editors saw indications that Britain might join Norway and Denmark in approaching Sweden on behalf of NATO.[15]

U.S. diplomats in Oslo were no more sympathetic in the fall of 1949 to discussions with high-ranking Norwegian officials about the desirability of having Sweden join the Atlantic Pact than they had been in 1948. H. Freeman Matthews, U.S. ambassador to Sweden, threw cold water on the idea. Noting that no matter how many advantages Norway might perceive in Sweden joining the alliance, he felt that "there is no possibility of such a move in spite of public and especially Swedish military discussions on the subject in the foreseeable future." Matthews asserted that Sweden's key ministers made it "abundantly clear that Sweden has no intention to depart from its neutrality policy. Traditional neutrality that succeeded in two world wars remains popular in that country."[16]

It was Denmark more than Norway that displayed persistent discomfort with NATO's defense policy. Sentiment for neutrality never disappeared, and the Communist press took advantage of Danish ambivalence toward the alliance, particularly after the U.S. representative of the MDAP arrived in Copenhagen. The U.S. chargé d'affaires in Copenhagen attributed Danish hesitancy about NATO to the fact that the change in the Danish mentality from neutrality to participation in a major power grouping had been of very recent origin and dictated more by the pressure of events than by enthusiastic acceptance of the idea of bringing Denmark into a new international organization. He found Denmark's behavior roughly analogous to that of the United States with respect to foreign entanglements.[17]

Italy's Problems

The results of the seminal first NAC meeting evoked an emotional response in Italy that was arguably more serious than that aroused in Scandinavia. It stemmed initially from the ambiguous position Italy always held in the Atlantic alliance. First, as a defeated party in World War II, it had to confront the hostility of the Soviet Union, which at every opportunity denied the legitimacy of Italian participation in any Western defense organization. No matter how vigorously the Americans or the British asserted that by joining NATO Italy was not violating the terms of the peace treaty of 1947, the Soviets would accuse Italy of repudiating its pledge "to abstain from undertaking any actions directed against the states with which the treaty was signed."[18] On each occasion the allies would reject the Soviet charge, and yet the issue remained troublesome. The State Department was concerned that Italian compliance with the military clauses of the peace treaty might create difficulties with respect to Italian production of military equipment for the Military Production and Supply Board.[19]

Italy's membership in NATO generated problems beyond those raised by the Soviet Union. NATO's role in Italian politics was a more contentious issue in that country than in any of the other allies. A united front of Communists and left-wing Socialists ignited riots in the streets and in the legislature with a vehemence that might have deterred its pro-Western leaders from requesting membership in the alliance. Italy's Communist Party had a tradition of intellectual leadership and mass following that was not matched by any other Communist party, including France's.[20] The survey team negotiating a bilateral agreement between the United States and Italy was a particular target for agitators. A case in point was the arrival of a special representative overseeing the MDAP in Italy as an occasion to label him a second U.S. ambassador with the mission of subjugating the nation to U.S.

domination.[21] The conjunction of military aid with a pro-consular figure fired the emotions of enemies of America and NATO.

Italy did not help its cause by seeming ambivalent about joining the pact. Its touchiness over a perceived inferior role in NATO was always in evidence. It occasionally took the form of excessive demands that the able Foreign Minister Carlo Sforza knew would be unacceptable, such as making the retention of return of Italy's African colonies as the price for joining the alliance. This was an absurd ploy from which Sforza quickly backed off. He agreed not to complicate the negotiating process by raising extraneous as well as explosive issues.[22]

Italy's sensitivities over what it considered unfair slights on its sovereignty and on its potential contributions to the alliance continued to be exhibited in the NAC meeting in September. Rather than feel comforted by its acceptance in NATO, uneasy as it was, Italy seemed to forget its former pariah status when it asked for membership in the new Standing Group. That the matter of representation would be a delicate one for members not included in the group was very much on the mind of the State Department. On August 3, when the Canadian ambassador heard informally that a Steering Group was being formed that might include Canada, he informed State Department officials that Canada would accept if invited, but would not voluntarily apply for admission. The Portuguese foreign minister, talking with Acheson on September 16, suggested adding two other members to the Standing Group chosen annually in alphabetical order, but, like the Canadian ambassador, he did not intend to raise objections to the existing arrangements.[23]

These comments must have relieved the Americans, who responded that while no decision had been made, the Joint Chiefs leaned toward a small executive group made up of just three members. On the assumption that there would be opposition from some of the allies, U.S. planners speculated that it would not be advisable to propose a Standing Group at the outset but wait until there was a demonstrated need for its existence. This advice was not followed when the Standing Group was singled out at the first NAC meeting as the most significant instrument in military planning. The three members named did not include Italy.[24]

Within a week the United States had to explain just why Italy was not considered for membership in the group. Acheson himself spelled out to the Italian chargé d'affaires that the Standing Group would not be effective if enlarged. The secretary of state urged the chargé to impress upon Sforza the possible intrusion of the Italian peace treaty again if he pushed for Italy's membership. Italian pressure would "only serve [to] confuse and delay progress." British Foreign Minister Bevin subsequently made it clear that Italy should not be allowed to join the Standing Group. Instead, Acheson would have Italians recognize that their interests would be represented in the Regional Planning Groups as well as in the Military Committee, which would oversee the Steering Group.[25]

On September 15, two days before the first NAC met in Washington, Sforza withdrew Italy's candidacy. Although it still rankled Sforza that France would be part of a triumvirate with Britain and the United States, Italy accepted this decision reluctantly. But the solution to this problem did not extend to Italian concerns about membership in Regional Planning Groups. Italy, France, and Britain comprised the Southern European–Western Mediterranean Regional Planning Group, but the Italians were unhappy about their exclusion from the Western European Planning Group; that group seemed to be an exclusive club of the Brussels Pact members. Italy argued for membership in the Western European Planning Group on the grounds that planning encompassed a line from Trieste to the North Sea via the Rhine.[26]

Sforza was not alone in complaining about the arbitrary composition of Regional Planning Groups. Among the many objections General de Gaulle had against NATO was the absurdity of metropolitan France being part of one regional group and Mediterranean France of another, with the two linked only via Washington.[27] But this was not the only French perspective on the Western Mediterranean Regional Planning Group. The French had reason to approve its composition. The nomination of Gen. Alphonse Juin, commander of French troops in North Africa, as France's representative in that regional group could be seen as NATO's granting its imprimatur to the integration of French North Africa into that regional group. It seemed to confirm the legitimacy of the inclusion of Algerian departments of France into the Atlantic alliance under Article 6 of the treaty.[28]

Although Acheson emphasized that membership in the Western European group was a matter of discussion between Italians and Western Europeans, he promised to help work out a compromise. Joint meetings of two or more planning groups to discuss common problems could be the solution. When Sforza reacted unfavorably to this idea, the secretary of state once again warned Italy of the consequences of rejecting the best available formula. If the allies' failure to settle this matter should block the establishment of the treaty's machinery, the blame would fall on Italy.[29]

On the eve of the NAC meeting, the Italians accepted the compromise. And they also had to accept London as the headquarters of the Southern European–Western Mediterranean Regional Planning Group despite their preference for Rome. The United States refrained from an outright rejection of Italy's bid, noting that this was a matter for the European governments to resolve. But Acheson leaned heavily on the Italians when he asserted that Northern and Western regional groups could not meet anywhere but in London. The "highest caliber US personnel in this field" were all concentrated in London and Washington: "If [the] Southern group located elsewhere it will have second string US representation." Professing understanding of prestige attached to this issue as well as the need to satisfy Italian public opinion, and he still maintained that "real collaboration" could be achieved only if groups were located in the same place. There could be no satisfactory collaboration if the Southern group were located in Paris or Rome.[30] This was another blow to Italian pride, although it was unlikely that Acheson realized how patronizing his remarks were.

Anglo-French Tensions

The unveiling of NATO's organization in the first NAC meeting should have relieved most of France's anxieties about its future. Its place in the Standing Group, the most significant of the many committees established in September, should have given its leaders confidence about France's security in the postwar world. As an equal partner of the United States and the United Kingdom, it could stand up to the internal Communist threat and marginalize the Gaullist dissenters. With Britain by its side, fears of a revived Germany dominating Europe, even in a truncated form of West Germany, should have been put to rest. They were not. France's relations with its two major allies were no less fractious than they had been before the formation of the alliance. Discord centered on two aspects of British foreign policy: first, the depth of Britain's commitment to the continent as a counter to Germany; and second, the tightness of the Anglo-American bonds at the expense of France's interests.

The two issues were not necessarily discrete; one often overlapped the other. The roles of France and Britain in the newly created Council of Europe were a case in point. The council had its ideological origins in the passionate efforts of partisans of European unity that grew out of World War II.[31] Britain was well represented at The Hague meeting in May 1948, which advocated a European assembly and a European parliament to promote European unity. Despite the visibility of Winston Churchill as leader of the British delegation, French, not British, initiative propelled the efforts to create a Council of Europe. The U.S. State Department appeared to give its blessing to the drive for European unification. But rather than endorse the movement, Bevin made it clear that a European parliament could damage Britain's relations with the Commonwealth and—less openly—with the special relationship he was nurturing with the United States.[32]

British doubts notwithstanding, the Council of Europe was founded in London on May 5, 1949, just a month after NATO, in a treaty signed by ten European states. All were members of NATO except Ireland and Sweden. Its major instruments were the Council of Ministers (the foreign ministers of each member state), a parliamentary assembly in Strasbourg, composed of representatives of each member nation, and a secretary-general heading a secretariat.[33]

Britain felt pressure from both the United States and France to make its adherence credible to its European colleagues. The idea of a complete immersion of parliamentary powers into a European assembly was unacceptable to even the most ardent Europhiles in Britain. When Foreign Secretary Bevin spoke warmly of the Council of Europe, he was referring to the Council of Ministers, not to the

Assembly, which implied an integration the British were not prepared to accept. "I am sure that the bringing together of this Committee of Ministers, will prove vital to the unity of Europe," Bevin told the Commons on November 17. "They represent their Governments. . . . In making this statement I do not wish to be derogatory to the Assembly, which have [sic] a different mission to perform."[34]

This clear distinction between the Council of Ministers and the Assembly stoked French fears that Britain was not fully engaged. A test case was the admission of Germany into the Council of Europe. France would prefer to postpone that day as long as possible, even as it gave lip service to integrate Germany into the council as quickly as possible. The sticking point was a demand that the Saar be admitted simultaneously, or France would not give its consent. Foreign Minister Robert Schuman did concede that in the comfortably distant future, reconsideration of the Saar as an independent entity could be made.[35] Britain recommended an associate membership for both Germany and the Saar since Germany did not yet control its foreign policy. A week later the Standing Committee of the Council of Europe's assembly approved the inclusion of both Western Germany and the Saar as associate members of the council.[36]

Although in this instance the British Cabinet passed the test, France's doubts about Britain's commitment to the Council of Europe persisted, and for good reason. Too often British officials failed to conceal their satisfaction in their special relationship with the senior partner. Its reluctance to grant genuine parliamentary powers to the assembly was always transparent. British hesitations could disrupt NATO's defense plans by reinforcing French suspicions of its ally's seriousness in identifying itself as a "European" nation. Britain's stance was all the more important when the issue arose of German military integration into Europe's defense. In referring to Bradley's and Montgomery's positive assessment of Germany's military potential, Le Monde editorialized that "it is not so much a new German army that is envisaged but a European army that will include Germans. But this could not materialize until Germans can be considered as allies by their partners."[37]

How far Britain would commit itself to the unification of the continent remained unclear. Its membership in the Council of Europe was always hedged by its commitments to areas beyond Europe, notably its Commonwealth obligations. Bevin quoted the chancellor of the Exchequer on November 17 to clarify this point: "Our position . . . is such that we could not integrate our economy into that of Europe in any manner that would prejudice the full discharge of these other responsibilities. . . . Yet, at the same time we regard ourselves as bound up in Western Europe, not only in the economic terms and in political and strategic interests, but in our culture and, indeed, in our participation in the heritage of Christian civilization."[38] Given the double message in this declaration, it is understandable that the French were skeptical of Britain's commitment to the continental allies. Speaking in the National Assembly a week later, Deputy Louis Terrenoire of the

Liberal Catholic party (Mouvement républicain populaire [MRP]) concluded that Britain judged France and Germany to be two impossible nations, the first in time of peace, the second in time of war. The role of Britain, then, would be that of referee, not participant.[39]

Britain's future course in Europe could depend on how far the United States wished Britain to go into Europeanization. The special relationship between the two countries was a factor on the American as well as the British side. U.S. embassy officials in London were sympathetic to feelings in the British Cabinet that it was "being pushed too hard and too fast" on European integration. There were, after all, skeptics in the United States who did not want Britain to become a fully European nation. Yet, Britain's unwillingness to state in advance how many troops it would dispatch to the Rhine in light of its Near East commitments sent a negative message to France. British reservations were reinforced by U.S. unwillingness to become full members of European Regional Planning Groups.[40]

Despite American concerns about excessive pressure on Britain, there was unanimity among the diplomats at the conference of U.S. ambassadors in Paris in October 1949 that without the active involvement of Britain, Western European integration will have little, if any, value. The key problem as always was the German question, not just as France conceived it but as it was perceived by other NATO allies. Pressure was rising in Germany for West German integration into Western Europe, while the USSR was in the process of establishing a Soviet-controlled government in East Germany. The ambassadors were convinced that France would not take any leadership in advancing European integration without British participation.[41]

Charles E. Bohlen, Soviet specialist and adviser to the Secretary of State, was particularly emphatic about the need for a British presence on the continent to offset Germany's future power. George Kennan, however, questioned the wisdom of pressing too hard for Britain's absorption in Western Europe. It might be counterproductive in the long run if the British or American presence in Europe inhibited the unification of Germany. In essence, the Council of Europe could be the instrument to effect a unified Europe that enfolded Germany. His conception of a unified Europe would have minimized NATO's as well as Britain's role in Europe. As he noted in observations to Acheson in July, "what we should aim for was a continental union, sufficiently detached from Britain to have some chance of absorbing Germans into something larger than themselves . . . quite separate from the Atlantic Pact, and thus eligible to provide a framework into which the smaller Central and Eastern European countries eventually could be fitted."[42]

Kennan should have been reassured by Bevin's continuing reluctance to have Britain drawn deeply into continental affairs. Britain's abstention would permit France to take charge not just of the Council of Europe but the unity of Europe that the council was promoting. With Britain effectively removed from the scene, France should have felt itself free to proclaim itself the prime mover of European integration.

This was not the case. Instead, Kennan perceived a paranoia in that country, fueled by an unreasonable fear of a revived Germany and by an obsession with an Anglo-Saxon conspiracy to repudiate its commitments to the security of Europe: "I don't see that there is anything we can do for the French. If any one can entertain the proposition that the efforts made in this Government to put through and implement the Marshall Plan, the Atlantic Pact, and the Military Arms Program were some sort of cynical joke and that all these things were done only with a view of sudden abandonment of the continent in precisely September 1949, I am afraid, then, there is no place here for rational arguments." As for the German question, if a partitioned, disarmed Germany poses a threat today to a France linked by treaty with the United States, "Can we really expect that the French will show greater capacity for leadership and initiative in Europe at some future date, when Germany has emerged from many of the present controls and handicaps?"[43]

The behavior of French diplomats confirmed Kennan's pessimism. Henri Bonnet, France's ambassador to the United States and defender of French interests on every occasion, displayed his sense of the Anglo-Saxon disengagement from Europe when he asserted in September that "a historical policy decision" had been made whereby the economies of the United States, Britain, Canada, and the Commonwealth countries would be removed from the U.S. involvement with Europe. He charged that this decision would not only fracture relations with the Organisation for European Economic Co-operation and with the WU and Council of Europe as well, but, more importantly, would leave France alone on the continent with the Germans. Foreign Minister Schuman, according to Acheson, wondered how Bonnet could have gotten such an idea.[44]

Acheson had an answer. He felt that leading U.S. pundits, Joseph Alsop and Stewart Alsop, unwittingly left this impression with the French ambassador when they conflated the "decision" with the familiar Kennan proposals for two strategic groupings within NATO—the United States, Great Britain, and Canada versus Western Europe under France's leadership. What particularly disturbed Bonnet was the implication that there was no practical possibility of an effective union between Great Britain and the continent. Walter Lippmann took up the issue a few weeks later when he expressed his worry that the idea of two groupings "would create the dangerous impression that Britain, Canada, and the United States are now an exclusive club within the Atlantic community. If that impression becomes a general conviction, the fine promises and hopes of the Marshall Plan, the Brussels Pact, the Atlantic Pact and of the European movement will go down in cynicism and suspicion."[45]

Neither Acheson's nor Foreign Minister Schuman's firm denial of such a historic decision could allay these suspicions. It was obvious that France's insecurity was not going to be resolved by membership in the Standing Group triumvirate, let alone by U.S. assurances of its long-term support. Nor was Britain's gesture in the Council of Europe to back France's position on the Saar sufficient to convince France of Britain's permanent presence on the continent or what the limitations in the special relations between the Anglo-Saxon countries might do. No matter how often American diplomats tried to convince the French that World War II's Combined Chiefs of Staff no longer existed, some commentary always seemed to arise to thwart understanding. In the aforementioned inflammatory column, the Alsops prolonged doubts by assuming that the combined Anglo-American political staffs would "parallel the existing Combined Chiefs of Staff." It is unlikely that the French press or public were relieved by the British minister of defence's response in Parliament that "the Supreme Chiefs of Staff Committee in Washington has been disbanded." Gen. Pierre Billotte, France's representative on the Military Committee, felt that the Combined Chiefs of Staff, whether it existed formally or informally, was a natural Anglo-American combination that inevitably made Britain America's premier ally.[46]

Given the record of grumbling, laments, and protests arising from the first meeting of the North Atlantic Council, NATO's evolution might have been stopped in its tracks. NATO's foreign ministers took the projections of the Working Group seriously and presented ambitious and remarkably detailed actions for the alliance to take immediately. That it evoked a cascade of dissents from the European partners was to be expected. Even as they jousted over which member would have the advantage over the other in regional groups, or in the Standing Group, they could coalesce in their resentment at the senior partner's refusal to become a member of any regional group outside the Atlantic Ocean and the North American region.[47] "Participation as appropriate" was too Delphic to be satisfactory to the allies.

Yet no member of the organization elected to reject the decisions made at the NAC meeting in September. European insecurity in the face of Soviet power and a reviving Germany, and dependence on increased American support, required acceptance of the course the alliance was following no matter how unhappy an individual ally may have been about one or more of the decisions.

North Atlantic Council: Ministerial Meeting, November 18, 1949

The second NAC meeting lacked the excitement that the act of creation brought to the first, two months before. The promise of a new order, which despite the frictions it generated among the allies, suggested that America's presence in Europe would bring security to all and accelerate the movement toward European unification. The next meeting of the alliance's leaders would require implementation of the plans the first NAC had promised. And this would create new problems for NATO, resulting in deeper frictions within the organization.

The Defense Financial and Economic Committee and the
Military Production and Supply Board

Following the recommendations of the Working Group, the ministers established
two committees: the Defense Financial and Economic Committee (DFEC) and
the Military Production and Supply Board (MPSB). The DFEC, composed of representatives at the ministerial level from each signatory country, would report
"directly" to the NAC and consult "as appropriate" with the Defense Committee. It would provide "information on those requirements of defense programs
relevant to the consideration of economic and financial questions and then offer
guidance on such financial and economic arrangements needed to fulfill their
requirements of the defense program." These would involve examination of the
member nations' individual financial and economic resources, and then facilitate
interchange among NATO members of military equipment and surplus stocks.
The DFEC would appraise the financial and economic impact on member states
of individual defense projects formulated by the MPSB or Standing Committee.
The committee would have a working staff located in London.[48]

The relationship of the DFEC with the MPSB was a primary feature of the DFEC's
mission. Its success was dependent on the information provided by the MPSB and
the organs of the Defense Committee. Its powers and indeed its role were limited
and vague compared with the more specific functions of the MPSB. The linkage
of the MPSB with the Defense Committee implied an authority the DFEC lacked.
Its responsibility for advising the NAC on the financial and economic aspects of
defense measures was not on the same plane as the connection between the MPSB
and the Defense Committee, even though its U.S. representative was the veteran
diplomatist W. Averell Harriman, who would "look primarily to the Sec State for
guidance."[49]

Although the MPSB was placed after the DFEC in the communiqué, its members
to be drawn from the subministerial level of each NATO country were instructed to
report to the Defense Committee rather than to the NAC. It had a more central role
from the outset than the DFEC. This was implicit in the reference to the MPSB, as
noted above. The board was to "work in close coordination with the military bodies . . . to provide them with technical advice on the production and development
of new or improved weapons." A liaison group would be set up in Washington to
work with the Standing Group. Unlike the DFEC, the MPSB held its first meeting
in Washington, on November 1, 1949 with N. E. Halaby, of the Office of Secretary of
Defense, the chair before either body was officially established.[50]

The dominance of the military through its functions on the Defense Committee was a potential problem for the DFEC. An official of the staff of the assistant
secretary of state for economic affairs worried about its "appropriate independent status." Equally important was the assurance it needed that its members were

"not military men but are representatives of the responsible economic or financial ministries of the countries concerned." Its mission "to maintain in particular close working relations with the Military and Production Supply Board and provide it with guidance on all relevant economic and financial factors" was not an assurance of equality. The apparent imbalance of power weighed on the minds of U.S. civilian officials.[51]

Historian Steven Rearden noted that Secretary of Defense Johnson had been quick to assert as much control as he could over NATO and MDAP matters through his deputy, Maj. Gen. James H. Burns, appointed in November as liaison between NATO and the Defense Department. Johnson's appointment of General Bradley, the chairman of the JCS, as U.S. representative on both the Military Committee and Standing Group, was a further indication of a heavy military hand in NATO councils. The U.S. representative on the MPSB was Johnson's choice. The secretary made his preference clear in a letter to the president on April 16 that since the National Military Establishment "will be carrying such a heavy proportion of administrative responsibility . . . policy direction from the State Department concerning the military assistance program should come from a high-level administrator "to and through my office."[52] Although the institutional arrangements in the fall of 1949 did not convert NATO into a military arm of the U.S. Defense Department, they represented a challenge to the authority of the State Department and the alliance's foreign ministers.

Arguably, the most critical part of the MPSB mission was to recommend to the Defense Committee ways of increasing available supplies where they fall short of requirements. While the board was to take into account limitations of physical capabilities of individual countries to produce military material, the thrust of the paragraph was emphasis on "the importance of maximum efficiency and integration of production." Toward this end, the MPSB was to promote more efficient methods of producing military equipment, "including advice to appropriate military bodies on the production problems involved in proposed new weapons or modifications in existing weapons." The board could delegate to any regional supply board any of its functions that could be better performed by regional boards. In carrying its assignments, the MPSB's liaison group in Washington would work closely with the Standing Group, thereby assuming more importance than its permanent working staff in London.[53]

Unlike the array of committees set up at the first NAC meeting in September, the MPSB intruded into the affairs of individual member states to a degree that had unanticipated repercussions. No longer could allies sit back and expect America to take over the responsibilities for such actions as NATO would take, even as they deplored the occasions when the United States abstained from assuming leadership in a particular committee or conference. With the MPSB in place, it was up to the allies to show just how they would contribute to the needed military buildup.

The obligations identified on November 15, two days before the NAC formally established the board, were extensive. The board presented an outline of proposed studies that included the physical capacities of the NATO partners for producing military end items; a review of currently planned programs for military production in the next phase of integration; and plans for standardization of production and production methods. The DFEC then would determine the costs of the production recommendations.[54] This was not only an ambitious agenda for the allies to execute but forced them, particularly the Western European Planning Group, to bear the main burden of response. This Regional Planning Group was comprised of the members of the Brussels Pact who presumably had been addressing those very questions for a year and a half.

The planning group was both a valuable resource for all NATO planners and a source of frustration for the senior partner. In light of the activities of the Western Union Defense (WUDO) over the past year, this group should have been in a position to incorporate its plans without delay into an integrated defense of Western Europe. After all, WU had its own committees seeking to fuse financing with military production. But there was little to show for the time spent in talking about the defense of Europe. The reality was that members of Western Union were waiting for the United States to give meaning to their deliberations. And the Joint Chiefs knew this, having served as witnesses and advisers to WUDO from its inception.[55] It was one of the reasons why the Defense Department turned down repeated requests that the United States be a member of the Regional Planning Groups. The Joint Chiefs knew how little had been accomplished and wanted to limit their responsibility for the situation.

The alliance witnessed a self-defeating cycle. The Europeans looked upon American military entanglement in the defense structure of Europe as the only way they could continue their economic recovery and develop defense capabilities. The Americans, by contrast, were determined to minimize their exposure to Europe's efforts to disengage from responsibility for their own security. The substance of American hesitancy with respect to participating in European planning groups was largely the result of JCS fears of losing control of the ultimate strategic concept. The U.S. position was complicated by another familiar issue: the active involvement of altruistic pressure groups in the establishment of an Atlantic union. Its origins went back to journalist Clarence Streit's concept of Atlantic democracies in 1940 establishing a union modeled on the American experience in 1787. It had attracted such luminaries as Supreme Court Justice Owen Roberts and Sen. J. William Fulbright.[56]

In December 1949, just as the United States was pressing its partners for more contributions, Congress passed a resolution asking the president to invite the NATO democracies to a convention that would promote a federal union to which the United States would belong. Kennan's State Department's Policy Planning Staff urged a vague endorsement, but warned against raising unrealistic and dangerous expectations from the NATO community. Convocation of a federal convention could undermine the movement toward European integration by increasing dependence on the senior partner.[57]

The AMP Program

Intrusion of the Atlantic union issue was a distraction the American partner did not welcome. In the weeks leading up to the second NAC meeting, a particular feature of the MPSB took center stage for the organization and absorbed much of its time. The issue preceded NAC's formal announcement of the establishment of the board. At the first meeting on November 1, the MPSB recognized its obligation to "recommend ways and means of increasing available military supplies where they fall short of requirements, either from production, surplus equipment or equipment economically capable of rehabilitation."[58]

Lip service, at least, was given to the goal of accomplishing its objectives without jeopardizing essential economic rehabilitation. The United States was anxious to gather more details on military equipment and services, particularly on net requirements that could not be met from local production or from imports from other NATO countries. The FMACC expected the survey teams to gather appropriate information on the proposed Additional Military Production (AMP) program, which became central to MPSB as the year drew to a close. Recognizing the shortage of experienced U.S. personnel on these matters, the coordinating committee asked embassies to discuss financial and military production capabilities with the survey team in London.[59]

Although no commitments were expected to be made at that time, a sense of urgency pervaded the atmosphere when the survey teams met with the representatives of each member state in the following week. The U.S. secretary of defense and the director of MDAP, as well as ECA officials, needed to know as soon as possible the estimated overall costs of projects for increased military production in Western Europe. When the director of MDAP approved basic programs, they would be a firm guide for allocation funds for specific purposes. Careful monitoring of supply actions was to follow, with special attention to earmarking equipment from U.S stocks and placing orders for new equipment. The State Department, in overall charge, was expected a devise a way to measure actual progress in implementing the program. None of the agencies was satisfied with the long lapse in receiving reports.[60]

Acheson understood how sensitive the U.S.'s prodding of allies for more financial effort would be for the European allies, but felt that "although painful [it] will not significantly retard [a] recovery program" or risk internal financial instability. In this context there was appreciation for France's plan to increase French expenditure on the AMP program by shifting credits between military services. America's appreciation was reflected in $85 million for assistance it made available to France. This would be in addition to $12 million for France's AMP in 1950, amounting to 27 percent of the entire French program.[61] How meaningful this show of confidence was had to be measured against France's complaint that there was nobody in NATO able to make quick decisions. Waiting for final clearance under the current pact mechanism might cost the country a year's delay, according to France's Minister of Defense René Pleven.[62]

This moment of relative harmony between the senior partner and a key ally was not typical of the relationship. The AMP program inevitably stirred emotions as each member saw a conflict between military expenditures and economic recovery. Moreover, it exposed the delicacy of the patron–client relationship between America and Europe. Even the Pleven proposal evoked U.S. criticism on the grounds that an individual country was seeking the largest possible share of AMP dollars without regard for its impact on the integrated defense of Europe. U.S. concerns included assurance that proposed AMP projects would represent a net increase in the production of equipment.[63]

NATO vs. WU

The formal launching of the DFEC and the MPSB revived the dormant but potentially inflammatory relationship between NATO and the WU. The latter's most visible imposition on NATO had taken place immediately after the signing of the treaty when the Brussels Pact powers presented their package of requests for military aid. Since then American connections with the Western Union had been with individual members of the alliance, which was the relationship the United States preferred. In fact, a major theme in transatlantic correspondence among U.S. officials had been the need to ensure that the non-WU powers in NATO were not neglected. This was not easy to manage when the most important Regional Planning Group—the Western European—consisted solely of members of the Brussels Pact.

The State Department's advice to Harriman as U.S. representative on the DFEC was that the "secretariat should be separate and distinct from the WU Financial and Economic Committee." When transfer arrangements of military equipment were under consideration, the State Department was anxious to avoid distinctions between WU and non-WU countries. This question arose from concern that Britain might insist on preferential treatment in transfers with other WU countries.[64]

The potential for conflict over the relationship between NATO and the Western Union was evident in the agenda for the meeting of the Brussels Treaty's Consultative Council on November 5. The council recognized that the correlation between the Atlantic Pact machinery and the Western European Regional Group required "immediate study." It assumed that many of the same people would serve in both organizations, "but the question of responsibility and line of command will have to be worked out separately." What gave urgency to this study were the differences in the guarantees of assistance in the event of attack. Under Article IV of the Brussels Treaty, military aid would be automatic. Under Article 5 of the North Atlantic Treaty, the response would not be as clear.[65]

While the differences between Article IV and Article V involved hypothetical challenges, the functioning of the machinery of the MPSB had to be addressed as quickly as possible. At the first meeting of the MPSB on November 1 the WU representative initiated controversy by noting that the Western Union Supply Board had proposed that the secretariat of the WU take over the secretariat of NATO's MPSB. This arrangement was unacceptable to the U.S. member. A mutually acceptable compromise involved the creation of a separate NATO secretariat with a deputy to work out arrangements for joint utilization of the facilities and resources of the Western Union secretariat.[66]

Other differences were not as easily resolved. WU's representative, British Gen. Sir Harold Parker, objected to NATO's permanent working staff reviewing the MPSB's program for additional military production that the WU defense ministers had already approved. Parker professed to be worried about unnecessary delays resulting from NATO's review. Resolution of this issue devolved on an understanding that the United States could not justify its MDAP without satisfactory oversight of its implementation. A similar American veto was cast on the possibility of regional MPSBs, including non-WU members, supplementing the work of NATO's MPSB. The diplomatic language stated that for the present, "it was not proper to delegate any functions to the Western Union MPSB (admitted to be a *de facto* regional MPSB), but rather to wait and let the problems be worked on . . . until we could have a clear picture of the role which the Western Union could properly play as a regional board with NATO."[67] With some reluctance on the part of those delegates waiting to seek their government's reaction, the allies accepted this verdict.

Despite irritation over the claims for special privilege by the WU, the United States inevitably favored its Regional Planning Group over the other regional groups. Britain and France were the primary allies and through the Western Union, their financial and production plans received priority over those of other less sophisticated planning groups As the European Coordinating Committee (ECC), chaired by the U.S. ambassador to Britain, pointed out in October, many projects within the WU program were "clearly in line with military priorities" and these projects should proceed "at earliest possible moment." Moreover, the FACC admitted in November that "due to the advanced stages of WU additional production planning, the delays in MDAP legislation and the prospect for slow development of over-all NAT requirements and organizations, interim procedures will be necessary for most of the fiscal 1950 additional military production program." This bias in favor of the WU was always evident, even though its production program had never been screened. No matter how unsatisfactory its production schedules were, they could not be scrapped.[68]

The executive director of the ECC, Charles H. Bonesteel, noted after the meeting of the Defense Committee on December 1 that approval was expected for WU projects that are unlikely to be produced in quantity in other NATO countries. Aircraft, minesweepers, land mines, and anti-tank weapons were among the high-priority items cited.[69] The push for projects that would demonstrate the success of NATO's integrated defense efforts to impatient congressmen often trumped objections to the hollowness of the allies' claims. The NATO committees, boards, and groups were under constant pressure from the Standing Group to provide enough details to fulfill the organization's planning needs.

Nevertheless, the senior partner's impatience over the insistence of the Western Union to make its voice heard at all times was met by a mix of resistance and compliance. At the NATO Defense Ministers meeting in Paris on December 1, the WU assumed that if a NATO directive "appear[ed] to conflict with responsibilities assumed under the Brussels Treaty, the Western Union Defense Ministers should be able to appeal it to the North Atlantic Defense Ministers." The report on which this request was made obliquely indicated both dissatisfaction with American dominance and willingness to accept it under terms that respected their dignity.[70]

A response to the underlying frictions between NATO and the WU could be to fuse the two organizations. After all, the primary purpose of the WU and its military arm, WUDO, was the entanglement of the United States in Europe. NATO, in essence, had fulfilled this purpose, despite periodic jitters over the permanence of the U.S. commitment. In November *Le Monde* speculated about the possible fusion of the WU with NATO. In the same month, *Figaro* saw that the first problem facing NATO was integrating the WU organization into the Atlantic Pact. Still, there was no signal in 1949 that WU would be enfolded into NATO.[71] There were too many advantages for the WU allies vis-à-vis the non-WU nations in NATO to relinquish their own special relationship.

The year ended without NATO confronting, let alone resolving, the relationship between the two organizations. On the agenda for the NAC meeting on January 6, 1950 were allocation of costs of the Standing Group and relations between NATO and the Brussels Treaty, but the only item of significance in that meeting was the strategic concept for defense of the North Atlantic area. The State Department's foreign relations volume merely lumped the WU among five other items on the agenda of the forthcoming NAC meeting. The WU was not even mentioned in the NAC communiqué detailing the highlights of that meeting.[72]

Ambivalence over German Rearmament

The year also ended with continuing debate over the relations between NATO and the Federal Republic. The nub of the issue was always the need to harness German resources into an integrated European defense structure. How to do this in the face of unrelenting French suspicion shared, if not to the same degree, by most of the allies? The United States and Britain, however, were convinced that there was no alternative to German involvement in the alliance, but when and how were unanswered questions.

By December 1949 the rarely spoken word—rearmament—was in the open. In diplomatic exchanges and in the press, the subject of rearmament, if not of immediate German membership, was in the air. American leaders did their best to understand the concerns of the European partners, and demonstrated their understanding by removing the question of German contributions to NATO from the negotiating table until all the allies were satisfied that a reformed democratic Germany was ready for partnership. Sincere as their efforts may have been to calm European fears, they could not prevent outbursts about the German role from congressional committees or private speculations in the Policy Planning Staff or in extensive deliberations by the JCS. Sen. Francis Case (R-SD) expressed a widespread sentiment in Congress when he wrote in August to Acheson that "Even if for strategic reasons no outward evidence of including West Germany is deemed advisable at this time, surely, I hope, that our strategic planning does not contemplate turning over [its] resources and man-power to the Russians."[73]

Acheson recognized just how touchy the subject of dismantling German industry was. He had no objection per se to dismantling if he could be sure it would be done right. This was unlikely. He foresaw that dismantling would have an effect on other things. As he observed on September 15, "the Germans are going to be difficult no matter what happens. No one likes to be occupied. . . . They will never have loyalty to the Occupation Statute. All we can do is to try to create a German self-interest in it."[74]

Given its uneasy relations with the Anglo-American powers, France would have been suspicious even if the United States had spoken with one voice on the subject. But the combination of the exigencies of the Cold War and the ambitions of the new German state for equality raised the level of suspicion. It was apparent to France that a resurgent Germany was already in motion in the fall of 1949.[75] Under the Occupation Statute following the establishment of the Federal Republic, there should have been enough curbs to delay any changes. The statute reserved to the allies supervision over disarmament and demilitarization, foreign affairs, control over foreign trade and exchange, and "respect for the Basic Law and the *Land* constitutions." Any amendment to the Basic Law would require the express approval of the occupation authorities before becoming effective. The signatures of the three military governors were appended to this document.[76]

France's military governor, Gen. Pierre Koenig, had doubts from the outset about how meaningful the decentralization of power in the new Federal Republic would be. As the laws were being framed in the spring of 1949, Koenig charged that the Basic Law was a sham—"hypocritically federal but actually centralist." President Auriol shared Koenig's skepticism about the future of the Federal Republic, but was unhappy later in the year with Koenig's premature advocacy of a conference on Franco-German rapprochement. Auriol envisioned the shallow German democracy surrendering to traditional nationalism, employing its industrial capacity once again to wage war.[77]

Certainly, the role of the chancellor, as played by Konrad Adenauer, offered no comfort to French sensibilities. A Rhinelander prominent in the Catholic Center Party in the Weimar republic, he was sidelined and briefly imprisoned under the Nazis. As mayor of Cologne under British auspices, he proved to be an able if autocratic figure, ready to challenge both Communists and Social Democrats. Adenauer immediately assumed a status of equality with his Western peers. The replacement of military governors with high commissioners in September 1949 enhanced the status of the Federal Republic and its leader. The ceremony accompanying the change gave Adenauer an opportunity to appear as an equal of the commissioners when, as *The Times* observed, "a guard of honour was mounted by the military police of the three Powers, and when Dr, Adenauer, the Chancellor, arrived, with a number of Ministers, he was ceremonially received with a salute." The symbols were more important than the substance of the speech he addressed to André François-Poncet, John McCloy, and Sir Brian Robertson, the high commissioners of France, the United States, and Britain, respectively.[78]

The Cold War in the fall of 1949 had occupied an important place in encouraging Adenauer to challenge many of the restrictions that had limited German authority since the establishment of the republic. The Soviets appeared to lay down a gauntlet when Gen. Vassily I. Chuikov, commander in chief in East Germany, announced that the Kremlin would transfer to the new People's Chamber administrative functions handled in the past by the Soviet military administration. While the action could be seen as a counterpart to the NATO allies' transfer of power to the new Adenauer government, it was accompanied by the creation of a militia, presumably a defensive action against potential West German aggression. It set off alarm bells in the Federal Republic. An aggressive East Germany, prodded by its Soviet master, revived the ongoing question about the extent of dismantling of heavy industry and a newer question about rearming West Germans, a subject that the United States had formally avoided since the formation of the North Atlantic Treaty.[79]

A meeting in Bonn in mid-November was to begin negotiations on ending dismantling of industry and on bringing West Germany's economy into closer integration with its neighbors in the West. It sparked a controversy over the reliability of German democracy and affirmed the skepticism of General Koenig over the centralizing tendencies in the Federal Republic. It even divided Bevin and Churchill, who had been allies for the most part on the direction of British foreign policy. When Bevin wanted to continue dismantling, Churchill lashed out in Parliament asserting how dangerous it was to continue dismantling while allowing Germans to "stimulate every force hostile to the Western democracies to give full vent to their passions."[80]

Increased French uneasiness over the dismantlement issue emerged from a meeting of the three allied foreign ministers in Paris in mid-November despite the insertion of significant reservations. McCloy unwittingly roiled the waters after he reportedly told a representative of a news agency that dismantling was no longer justified when it affected serious unemployment in Germany. The immediate reaction was jubilation in Germany and criticism in France and Britain. McCloy quickly amended his comments, telling the press that "the matter of dismantling is now not in the hands of the commissioners. It is entirely a Governmental matter. . . . My personal view does not favor a cessation of dismantling until guarantees as to security and reparations can be given by Germany sufficiently to justify it."[81]

But the persistent linkage of the dismantling issue with German rearmament nullified the soothing words of the high commissioner. In the debate in the French National Assembly on a European political authority, Foreign Minister Schuman was pressed to say that at no time and under no circumstance was there a question of rearming West Germany. He was able to win a qualified vote of confidence from the assembly on November 25—325 to 249—but only after the assembly asked the government to be vigilant about separating Germany's industrial restoration from any links to military power. Additionally, it continued to oppose restitution of Ruhr industries to its former owners and reiterated that the internationalization of the Ruhr was an indispensable prerequisite to the creation of a united Europe. Schuman's mention of German rearmament before the National Assembly, even as he dismissed the prospect, caused Ambassador Bonnet to complain to Acheson that the issue of rearmament was still on the table.[82]

Schuman's promise was undercut in an interview with General Bradley in *Le Monde* on the same day when the chairman of the U.S. Joint Chiefs of Staff suggested that once a democratic Germany had achieved economic stability, the allies should consider the nature of a German contribution to Western defense. Bradley's cautious voice on behalf of ultimate German rearmament was in contrast to the frequent congressional outbursts of impatience over the unreasonable delays on the part of the allies. Sen. Elbert Thomas (D-OK) was chided in the French press for his remarks at a press conference in London on seeing Germany as necessary to the defense of Western Europe. He recommended raising several divisions of German troops, armed by the United States, without Germany being permitted to manufacture arms.[83]

Given the mixed messages from American and British leaders, it was understandable that as the Standing Group met on November 28 to begin the first formal move toward giving military and economic substance to the Western Europe regional planning, French nervousness about the future increased. The issue was less NATO's swallowing the Brussels Pact organization, although this was a concern, than the role the Federal Republic would play as plans materialized. The denials of Secretary of Defense Johnson and JCS Chairman Bradley that Germany was involved in their planning were not convincing. The use of German resources "for the present"—translated into French as "for the moment"—was hardly reassuring in light of so many hints about the need for German manpower in building the defense of the West.[84]

Just a few days earlier, the British high commissioner gave an ambiguous commentary on dismantling by saying that it "should not be regarded as a stepping stone for further demands" and then suggesting that the present arrangements would be reviewed next autumn. Adenauer underscored the uncertainty by noting that there would be no immediate demands on the allies, but that there were still issues to be settled in Germany's favor. In an interview with the *Cleveland Plain Dealer,* Adenauer's ambiguities were apparent in almost every line. First, he noted that he had to resort to interviews with American newspapers to explain German views on foreign affairs since under the Basic Law, the Federal Republic was not allowed to have a foreign ministry or a foreign policy on its own. While he protested about unfounded rumors of German rearmament, and asserted he would refuse to establish German armed forces even if the allies demanded this contribution, he would consider a German contingent in the military framework of a European federation.[85]

That French opponents of German rearmament under any circumstance would not be appeased by Adenauer's argument was obvious. Gen. de Lattre de Tassigny, of WUDO's Commanders-in-Chief Committee, informed a receptive President Auriol about his deep differences with Montgomery and with the British in general. Not only did he witness Montgomery's hostility to French interests but speculated that the British had not lost the habit of disembarking in a potential replay of Dunkirk. De Lattre envisioned West German rearmament under British patronage.[86]

Like the future of the Western Union, the future role of Germany in the defense of the West was not to be settled in 1949. It had the capability of upsetting transatlantic relations in the next year and beyond. A plaintive memorandum from a special assistant to the State Department's director of German affairs illustrated the uncertainties as NATO prepared to issue an authoritative strategic concept for the alliance. He observed that "we have a sufficient array of words and names and alphabetical agencies to permit any official spokesman to write or speak in such manner as to make it appear that the people of the other nations can safely hover beneath the benevolent wings of a gentle but powerful American Eagle." But he then went on to ask why should Europeans be comforted about American military support when Secretary of Defense Johnson had announced sizable reductions of the military establishment? Why should they give up sovereign rights for "political integration" when the United States made no commitments as to which armed forces would be stationed in Europe, at the same time that it seemed to encourage the formation of a German army? "Why argue that

France is our greatest problem in Europe when the French, living with the realities of history, have only words as defense and the evidence of an ever stronger
Germany as a growing offense?"[87]

It was just as well that this note to his superior remained personal. His message
was both a warning against a revival of German militarism and a plea for a more
rational American policy toward Europe. If the success of European integration
hung on arming Germany, he felt that the United States was playing a dangerous
game. Even if Chancellor Adenauer pledged to free Germany from its destructive
past (and he did not doubt Adenauer's good faith), he asked "Who then protects
a new sovereignty? Not we, who have no military! Not the MAP because we can't
assure the other nations of the extent of our participation. The MAP is still in
chaos. Must we arm our former enemies and gamble their choice of allies?[88] These
were disquieting questions, even if steeped in hyperbole, but they were raised in
the course of setting the organization in motion. They could not be answered in
NATO's first year.

North Atlantic Council: Ministerial Meeting, January 6, 1950

The third meeting of NAC, like the first, was held in Washington, but unlike the
NAC session of September 17, it was understandably anticlimactic. The communiqué after the meeting consisted of just two paragraphs. The work had been done
over the period from September to December. All that was needed was for the
foreign ministers to approve the recommendations that the Defense Committee
had made in Paris on December 1, emphasizing the strategic concept for the defense of the North Atlantic area.[89]

The record of activities of the Defense Committee and its subordinate bodies
was substantial, given the enormous pressure NAC and its senior partner exerted.
NATO's incentive to complete their missions was irresistible: the $900 million
in MAP appropriations would not be available until the council had approved
the strategic concept. This document, developed by the Military Committee and
its Standing Group, identified the immediate objective of the organization under
Article 3 as the "achievement of arrangement for collective defense among the
Atlantic Treaty nations." In furthering this goal, "each nation should undertake
the task, or tasks, for which it is best suited. Certain nations, because of the geographic location or because of their capabilities, will be prepared to undertake
appropriate specific missions."[90]

There was nothing cryptic about this language even if the foregoing paragraph
did not spell out assignments. Subsequent paragraphs did precisely that. To carry
out strategic bombing promptly "is primarily a U.S. responsibility." The securing and
control of sea and air lines of communications would fall primarily to the United

States and Britain. The neutralization "as soon as practicable" of enemy air operations against NATO powers would be the responsibility of the European members. But the arresting and countering of enemy offensives in Europe was the principal assignment of the continental allies: "Initially, the hard core of ground forces will come from the European nations. Other nations will give aid with the least possible delay and in accordance with over-all plans." Cooperation was the key word in other measures under the strategic concept relating to standardization, combined training exercises, and military operating arrangements in peacetime.[91]

The most specific elements of the strategic concept were evident in the assignments given to individual members. They reflected the weight the United States carried in the alliance, but they were also rational reflections of the abilities of the different members. It made sense that American air power perform strategic functions; no other ally had the kind of capability the United States Strategic Air Command possessed. It was also reasonable for Britain to join with the United States in dealing with ocean lines of communication. Britain was the premier naval power in Europe, with a naval tradition unmatched by any other, with the exception of the Netherlands in the seventeenth century. Although the continental members were not ready to assume the burdens the NAC imposed, the military aid sent from the United States was designed to advance their readiness to supply the needed ground forces in the event of an attack.[92]

The major features of the strategic concept were appealing to the senior partner. The United States would provide its major assets—military aid and air power—without having to dispatch troops on the ground. The document omitted the troublesome matter of a German role and exuded an optimism about allied cooperation in collective defense planning. It is not surprising then that publication of the concept did not draw the usual congressional criticisms of excessive American contributions and inadequate European action.

European reaction was muted, at least initially. The Italian and Portuguese delegations had reservations in the form of relatively minor proposals. The Italian delegate proposed calling combined regional meetings when requested by two or more members and establishing a permanent liaison between the European regional groups. The Portuguese delegate wanted the formation of a planning subgroup within the North Atlantic Ocean Regional Planning Group. The Defense Committee rejected the Italian proposal on the grounds that the issue of a formal liaison "is a matter for Regional Planning Groups themselves to resolve, and we consider it would be undesirable for rigid directions to be issued by the Military Committee to put this into effect." The Portuguese initiative was more successful. NAC agreed to the Portuguese amendment in its meeting in London in May 1950.[93]

A more serious challenge came from the Danish representative on the Military Committee two days before the meeting of the Defense Committee ministers. He objected to the sentence in Section 7-a of the document that insured "the ability to carry out strategic bombing including the prompt delivery of the atomic bomb." His point was that Danes feared that the Soviets would use this language to justify dropping an atomic bomb on Copenhagen upon the outbreak of war. But when Secretary Johnson devised a formula to eliminate the offending phrase yet retain its implications, other allies complained that its elimination would remove an important element in the deterrent against Soviet aggression. Ultimately, the Defense Committee accepted Johnson's language in more general terms that could cover other forms of warfare. Atomic weapons were removed from the text, but not from potential use. This was a distinction without a difference. Danes, however, had no choice but to accept the consensus of their colleagues. Acheson still had to be assured that the overriding authority of the president as commander-in-chief was not compromised by Johnson's formula before he could recommend U.S. approval of the Defense Committee's report to NAC.[94]

Although NAC accepted the terms of the strategic concept, fissures opened as the allies recognized the extent of U.S. control of the process. A thoughtful reaction appeared within a week in two articles in a prominent Dutch newspaper, *Algemeen Handelsblad,* which began with a recognition that some form of West German contribution to the defense program should be made even if full German military power was not to be revived, at least until a Western European federation came into being. A more serious flaw in the concept from a Dutch perspective was the British refusal to delay building a large army until hostilities commenced. The history of World War II was very much in the minds of the editors. It was left to the continental nations to hold the fort until the external powers were ready to intervene. But American and British air forces would not be sufficient "to save Europe from being trampled underfoot during the first attack." A precondition for a successful strategic concept then would be the presence of strong Anglo-American ground forces on the continent.[95]

The matter was posed delicately, but the nub of the newspaper's argument was that the Europeans were expected to be the expendable cannon fodder while the Americans and British safely in the air would not be vulnerable to massive acts of aggression and would not intervene until they were ready. This was a prescription for disaster and accounted for a rising French interest, according to the Dutch paper, in having Western Union leave NATO and develop instead the idea of linking Germany with a European federal army.[96]

As fanciful as this scenario may have been, European suspicions that Western Europe was indefensible in the short run were for the most part reasonable. So were their suspicions of the Joint Chiefs' intentions. In October 1949 the JCS advocated abandoning the heart of Europe in favor of outposts in the Iberian Peninsula and Britain until plans were completed to defend Europe As the strategic concept was in progress, the United States emphasized that the key to successful defense lay in the threat of making an attack too costly to undertake. Under the umbrella of this deterrent, NATO would prepare to coordinate plans to defend the continent. If this approach failed, then the present state of military readiness could sustain only evacuation of U.S. forces to a line that might be drawn in the Pyrenees. Even the possibility of a bridgehead in Spain might be sacrificed to budget cuts mandated by the president in the summer of 1949. This was the Short-Term Defense Plan (STDP).[97]

This plan was so unsatisfactory to the European allies that it had to be replaced by a Medium-Term Defense Plan (MTDP), to be completed in phases by 1954. Whether or not the projection was realistic, it projected ninety ready and reserve divisions and a tactical air force of approximately six thousand planes.[98] Though the medium-term defense plan may have been a charade, it was a boost to the morale of Western Europeans and was favorably received by the U.S. Congress. An integrated allied effort was the prerequisite it had demanded before release of the $900 million earmarked for NATO.

There were no surprises in the final presentation of the strategic concept on January 6, 1950. The basic strategy had been outlined in July. The period between July and January allowed ample time for doubts and grievances on both sides to be aired. All parties realized the limitations of the alliance even as they rationalized the pretensions of most of the pronouncements made in its name. Nevertheless, the alliance sparked a momentum for the development of an infrastructure of Western European defense. As Acheson observed on January 3, 1950 in his recommendation to the president to approve the strategic concept, "I believe that this document represents the first major achievement under the North Atlantic Treaty. That these twelve nations could agree on a common basis for defense would have scarcely seemed possible a relatively short time ago."[99] For all its shortcomings, the military development of Europe, first under the Western Union and then under NATO, was more substantial than the progress made in the political and economic movement toward integration of Western Europe.

5

Winter Uncertainties

January–March 1950

Acheson's optimism over the completion of a NATO committee structure in a remarkable short time was surely understandable. Some of the new committees, such as the Defense Financial and Economic Committee and the Military Production and Supply Board, were borrowed, with only slight change of titles, directly from the Western Union Defense Organization. The most important— the Standing Group and the Regional Planning Groups—were specific to NATO, yet disillusion quickly set in. Much of the frenetic activity displayed in the NAC meetings was designed primarily to satisfy congressional requirements that defense plans be in place before aid would be dispatched.

Although the "strategic concept" appeased Senate critics, it was a promise, not a reality, in 1950. Still more assurance was needed. As Acheson recognized, aid would not be available until bilateral agreements had been concluded.[1] Four more weeks would pass before these were completed.

Britain vs. Europe

It was not the French who caused the delay, although their resistance might have been expected; they consistently had been a thorn in the side of the senior partner from the very beginning of negotiations for the treaty. Rather, it was the British ally, the special partner of the United States, who took on this role. Anglo-American tensions had been brewing from the inception of the bilateral requirements under the Mutual Defense Assistance Act. The British expressed unhappiness over transfer of materiel that would affect their ties with the Commonwealth nations. They shared with the continental allies irritation over the privileges accorded the Military Assistance Advisory Group (MAAG) officials in London. Particularly galling was the full diplomatic status initially given to its members.[2]

British emotions were encapsulated in what Acheson felt was Ambassador Franks's "long, confusing document" of December 15, 1949. It expressed resentment at loss of British exports resulting from the additional military production program (AMP).[3] Given the close personal relations between the personable Oxford don and the acerbic American secretary of state, Acheson's was an unusual complaint against the diplomat who, in his biographer's words, "guided and persuaded. Almost as a matter of habit, he clarified."[4]

Most of the problems were quickly redressed, but not before some agonizing in Washington. Immediately after NAC accepted the strategic concept, the State Department admitted that obstacles in the management of bilateral agreements were responsible for delaying the release of the remaining $900 million, but felt that the difficulties were being resolved. In fact, the administration left the impression that arms shipments would start about February 1, 1950. It was important, Assistant Secretary of State George W. Perkins noted, to minimize the time gap between the conclusion of the bilateral negotiations and the president's announcement of the release of funds, now set for January 16. It actually took until January 27, 1950 before the action was completed.[5]

But the difficulties with the special ally were deeper than mutual frustration over the terms of the bilateral agreements. They centered on the question of whether Britain was truly a European nation. This was not a question that the United States wanted raised. It was British ambivalence over its relations with the "continent" that animated the issue. The trauma from the devaluation of the British pound from its wartime level at $4.20 to $2.80 in September 1949—which forced Britain to go to Washington, hat in hand, for assistance—had accentuated the decline from its status as a world power. Consequently, its position as head of the Commonwealth nations was all the more important to its self-esteem. British diplomatists would invoke the Commonwealth as an excuse for dragging their feet on closer ties with the continent. The global Commonwealth's economic as well as political associations with the former mother country provided reasons to be wary of submerging itself in the Western Union or in any purely European organization.

For France in particular, British behavior, whether in the form of its seemingly exclusive partnership with the United States or in its wish to minimize its ties to Europe, continued to jeopardize France's acceptance of a German contribution to the alliance. Without Britain's unreserved commitment to Europe, Western Europe's sense of security, the integration of Germany into the West, and the MDAP itself would be at risk. Should France continue to feel itself alone with Germany, NATO itself might not survive. American diplomatists recognized the necessity of Britain's leadership and expressed their feelings at every opportunity as NATO's defense system was put into place in the fall of 1949. Despite the sporadic attempts of Foreign Secretary Bevin to reassure the French ally, along with the more wholehearted efforts of Foreign Minister Schuman to reassure his countrymen, the fulfillment of congressional requirements for military aid did not solve the problem. Britain's ambivalence seemed to be at its heart.[6]

Belgian Foreign Minister Paul-Henri Spaak, president of the Consultative Assembly of the Council of Europe, ripped the scab off of Britain's European credentials on January 14, 1950 in a speech at the Founders' Day celebration at the University of Pennsylvania. An admirer of Churchill and Britain, particularly in World War II, Spaak was distressed by Britain's continuing reluctance "to step boldly on the way that leads to European order." Britain's traditional posture of disengagement from the continent was no longer tenable. "There is today no really great Power in Europe," he asserted. "A balance-of-power policy has become impossible. Great Britain can no longer be the beam of a balance, the scales of which no longer exist." The consequence of British failure would be a Europe under excessive German control.[7]

This was not an impromptu address. Later that week Spaak spoke with Acheson, noting that "the great aversion to playing any close role in Europe was deeply ingrained in the British by history." While appreciating this legacy, he went on to claim that it would be disastrous if this tradition persisted. Without British involvement, the German problem would worsen, arguably in the form of a revival of Germany as "an arbiter in Europe which could ask for bids from the East and West and attempt to play off one against the other."[8]

At a meeting the next day, this time with Ambassador Robert Silvercruys present, Spaak asked for U.S. pressure to help Britain overcome its unwillingness to enter into binding continental arrangements, even though he could not specify just what concrete steps should be taken. While agreeing with the thrust of Spaak's argument, Acheson urged the Belgian foreign minister not to press too hard for European integration when he met with members of the Senate Foreign Relations Committee. He would risk a Senate demand for specific requirements from Europeans that might prove embarrassing. Spaak "said he would be more cautious than he had intended to be."[9]

The secretary had to cope as well with angry British reactions to Spaak's speech. Ambassador Franks made two visits to the State Department to ask Acheson to press Spaak to withdraw his candidacy for head of the Organisation for European Economic Co-operation (OEEC) Acheson temporized, noting that Paul Hoffman, the ECA administrator, had informed Franks that he did not consider it appropriate to raise this question with Spaak. Acheson concurred. Hoffman made it clear that he "considered it an unfortunate turn of events for the British to oppose an individual simply because he had made some critical statements about the UK and its policies with respect to Europe." From Acheson's perspective, it was important to have a strong political figure as leader of the OEEC, but both "the exact nature of the position as well as the personality were matters for the European countries to determine." Ultimately, it was Britain that determined Spaak's fate at the OEEC. It decided against him on January 30. Dutch Foreign Minister Dirk Stikker subsequently was elected "political conciliator of the OEEC."[10]

Acheson's caution was mirrored six months later in Ambassador Lewis Douglas's comments about continental Europe's anxiety in forming a real political federation. No British government would join at this moment, even if the Labour government exaggerated the Commonwealth's opposition. If there were a choice between the European federation and the Commonwealth, the latter would prevail. Douglas thought that "the national interests of the US . . . would be better served by the preservation of the Commonwealth association with a strong UK than by the disintegration of the Commonwealth which would necessarily be the result of the UK's becoming part of a European federated state." Remembering Spaak's address in Philadelphia in January, he quoted the foreign minister's recognition that if Britain had to choose, its choice would be the Commonwealth. With all his annoyance about Britain's behavior, Spaak would not want to put Britain in that position, nor would any American official in this period.[11]

U.S. Obstacles

Like so many issues in NATO's first year, Britain's relations with the continent would remain unsettled, but it was contained. The uneasiness of Europeans over Germany's ascending power and slow movement of the MDAP were also evident on the alliance's radar in the winter and spring of 1950 and more difficult to push aside. The progress—or rather the lack of progress—in the implementation of military aid was the more quantifiable of those two irritations. Arguably, it was also the more frustrating.

The negotiating process between the Truman administration and Congress, and between the United States and each of its allies, absorbed more than half of the fiscal year 1950. Many of the military items promised for Europe required a year or more to manufacture, and what was supposedly immediately available in the form of excess stocks often required extensive reconditioning. The products of the additional military production (AMP) programs inevitably would require even more time to complete. Maj. Gen. Lyman L. Lemnitzer, as the Defense member of FMACC, made a point on February 10 of expressing concern about the lack of progress despite delivery of project statements from France and Norway. As of July 28, 1950, the Netherlands received only 10.8 percent of the programmed amount of aid; Italy 10.2 percent; Belgium 4 percent; and France 5.1 percent. Historian Steven Rearden noted that "obviously an effort of this sort could not be launched overnight. The AMP had a budget of $85 million in the fiscal year 1950, while the Department of Defense received 190 separate projects by 30 June 1950."[12]

This situation was no surprise to the Bureau of the Budget. Since so little aid would reach its markets by the end of the fiscal year, it recommended as early as December 1, 1949 that the president's budget message on military assistance allow no new obligational authority for NATO countries, and that the unexpended funds be reappropriated for fiscal year 1951. The reasoning behind this recommendation centered on the seeming differences between State and Defense over the objectives of military assistance, which prevented any decision about continuing the program at this time. Moreover, planning within NATO would be so slow that no new program could be ready in time for submission to the next Congress.[13]

Assistant Secretary of State James W. Webb vigorously contested this prognosis. He was particularly upset by the mindset the bureau reflected. It was dangerously short-sighted, given that the West, for the first time, was about to go on the offensive against Communist advances in Europe. NATO and the MDAP, along with the ECA, were indispensable to the success of the efforts: "Failure to provide aid, and substantial aid, in support of the North Atlantic Pact would have a profound and disastrous psychological effect and would for all and intents and purposes knock the props from under the treaty." As long as the dollar figure was considered only an estimate, the bureau backed down, and was willing to recommend extending the $1 billion aid for fiscal year 1951.[14]

The Bureau of the Budget's position was only one of the reasons for prolonging implementation of the MDAP. Its director, James Bruce, on January 3, 1950, raised an obvious objection that provision for military assistance to such countries as Korea, Austria, and Yugoslavia not covered under the Mutual Defense Assistance Act would be at the expense of programs intended for NATO allies. They would also further deplete U.S. military stocks in order to meet the MDAP schedule. Bruce urged the National Security Council to defer any new proposals for military assistance until they had been cleared by the FACC.[15]

An unexpected delay grew out of the question of whether those nations requiring legislative approval of the bilateral agreements could still be eligible for shipments. A loss of a few weeks in the start of shipments could have negative consequences. From the administration's vantage point, just signing bilateral agreements should supply a sufficiently binding contract between the United States and other governments.[16] While this unilateral understanding would meet the requirements of Section 402 of the Mutual Defense Assistance (MDA) Act, it might run counter to the interpretations of senators Vandenberg and Connally, who felt that ratification by that country's constitution would be necessary before assistance was delivered. When General Lemnitzer observed that the proposed initial shipments needed extensive preparations, he asked if it was necessary to wait for a parliamentary ratification before deliveries could be made. The State Department lawyers judged that parliamentary approval was necessary.[17]

The French National Assembly voted 416 to eight, and the Council of the Republic registered 296 against two in favor of ratification on March 19, 1950. Belgian ratification was more complicated. In light of disarray in its parliament over the future of the monarchy, embassy officers wondered if some modus vivendi could be worked out, putting the bilateral agreement into effect provisionally pending ratification. After all, this was an executive agreement not subject to ratification by the U.S. Senate. Still, Acheson was uncomfortable with the "provisional" label; it would not meet the terms of the MDAP. Fortunately, the Belgian parliament acted two days later. Prime Minister Van Zeeland noted that formal approval only awaited the Prince Regent's signature.[18]

A solution was found for other recipients by having the United States retain title to shipments pending completion of the ratification process. This may not have been the ideal solution, but if deliveries were to begin in March, there was not much choice. Other interim measures in the absence of functioning MAAGs had to be made. Ports with suitable shore facilities in each recipient country had to be designated. Given that some of the NATO allies failed to make financial arrangements for off-loading initial shipments, General Lemnitzer proposed that the United States assume such charges to avoid further delays. That this proposal was ultimately offered, even if it was not implemented, was a measure of the administration's concern for the future of the program.[19]

Some of the hitches pushing back the schedule were self-inflicted. After the signing of the bilaterals on January 27, three days later the Dutch and British military asked what was in the approved programs. The answer was embarrassing. The FMACC had to admit that it had not yet approved the 1950 programs, even though approval had to be given before the MAAGs arrived at their assigned embassies. General Lemnitzer's response at a subsequent FMACC meeting was to have Defense work up as quickly as possible one or two simple projects to put AMP machinery in motion.[20]

But the problem of just what the AMP was supposed to produce was not easily solved. Shipments of surplus equipment, by contrast, encountered few obstacles. Trouble arose out of the inability of the DFEC to evaluate the costs of the MPSB projects. The most that the DFEC could come up with was devising financial arrangements to facilitate the transfer of military equipment in Europe to those countries most in need. Small wonder that Ambassador Harriman was motivated to use his influence to break the logjam created by the two agencies.[21]

Harriman's intervention could not make much difference considering that there was no possibility, according to the ECC, of getting satisfactory information from the European governments to justify Congress's continuation of the AMP program.[22] Responsibility for this situation, however, rested with the United States for failing to define clearly the AMP program for Europe. If Congress was to be won over, an argument should be made that new projects would increase European industrial capacity, thereby relieving dependence on the United States for such items as spare parts and ammunition.[23]

This approach was too hypothetical for Secretary of Defense Johnson. In light of the successive delays in slowing the MDAP operations, he felt it imperative to extend the period for obligating funds in fiscal year 1950. Too much of the $1 billion remained unallocated, and it was unlikely that much more would be allocated before the end of the fiscal year. To avoid conflict with Congress over the proposed MDAP bill for fiscal year 1951, he insisted on an interdepartmental approval to extend the contract authority from June to December 30, 1950. The State Department seemed agreeable, but wondered if December 1950 was the appropriate date.[24] Both State and Defense were understandably depressed by the obstacles in the way of advancing the delivery of military assistance, and in the late winter of 1950 feared that the entire MDAP would not survive congressional scrutiny.

The administration's response to the setbacks in the timetable was to put the best face possible on the deliveries of the initial military aid to the European allies. Both the State Department and Defense Department spokesmen were willing to overlook the shortcomings in the program in the interest of moving MDAP materiel to Europe as quickly as possible. The ECC agreed to postpone NATO's encouragement of standardization and integrated production since these "will be evolutionary over a period of years." In the meantime, rapid processing of many AMP projects would be manageable if aid was limited to filling high-priority deficiencies.[25]

MDAP Deliveries: Mission Accomplished?

While the first shipments of MDAP equipment were en route to European ports, Congress was debating the overall foreign assistance appropriations for fiscal year 1951. NATO was not its focus, but inevitably dissent in the Senate over the bill had implications for the MDAP. Senator Connally threatened to end all dollar aid to Britain until it withdrew its order curbing imports of U.S. oil. Its action would have been excusable six months earlier in the wake of the sterling crisis, but nondiscrimination was a principle underlying Marshall Plan aid. American oil companies, he asserted, had lost markets for refined products in Britain, Scandinavia, Argentina, and Egypt. Senator Walter George (D-GA), chairman of the Senate Finance Committee, charged that military aid to Western Europe at this time was "simply a waste of money." Such arms as the United States was supplying would fall into Soviet hands in the event of war since none of the beneficiaries could resist a Soviet assault at this time.[26]

The administration survived these displays of temper. The omnibus foreign aid bill passed, and the ships went on to their assigned destinations. Intra-service negotiations would be completed. These did not require a change in program, but involved placing ships under navy rather than army control. Interdepartmental issues also had to be resolved, such as the Commerce Department's reluctance to grant export licenses on materiel where title had been transferred to a foreign government. Moreover, care had to be taken with respect to sending P-51 aircraft to Italy to ensure that the treaty limitations on the size of the Italian air force would be respected.[27]

The first of forty-eight navy fighters and bombers set out from Norfolk, Virginia, on March 8 on the French aircraft carrier, *Dixmude,* bound for the French port of Toulon. France's acting ambassador to the United States, Jean Deridan, along with representatives from the State and Defense departments and ECA, was present at the modest ceremony marking the occasion. He was pleased to note that the French insignia was already painted on the planes. As for possible Communist resistance to unloading this shipment at this or any other French port, he declared defiantly, "If the communists want a showdown they will get it."[28]

State Department officials, responsible for the successful delivery of military assistance, were not as confident as Deridan seemed to be in meeting the Communist challenges. They had good reason to be wary of the reception the ships would receive when they reached Europe's ports. NATO's adversaries had ample time to mount their opposition. As early as January 25, 1950, The U.S. ambassador in Moscow noted increasing Soviet press attention to Communist plans to obstruct the unloading of MDAP supplies in European ports.[29]

The Communist presses in each of the eight recipient countries did their best to rouse dockworkers. The Italian Communist Party issued a call for national resistance to MDAP arms shipments and particularly for support to longshoremen and railroad workers on the front lines against the distribution of military equipment. The party organ, *Unita,* reported that the Italian National Committee of Peace Partisans met in Rome to mobilize the nation against the "threatened arrival of foreign arms." The British *Daily Worker* claimed that European workers understood that American arms "are a badge of Europe's servitude and are a proof that western European foreign policy is being made in Washington." The paper urged British workers to support the militants of Europe who were refusing to unload American arms.[30]

Anticipating trouble, the American embassy in The Hague recommended that vessels carrying the initial shipment of MDAP materiel arrive at all European ports at the same time. If this was not possible, synchronize arrival times for shipments to Belgium, the Netherlands, and particularly to France, where the first ships would dock. Such plans would help to eliminate the possibility of Belgian and Dutch port workers staging sympathy strikes if their counterparts in France refuse to unload equipment. To further block opposition, the embassies should leak information that the ships would arrive twenty-four to forty-eight hours later than the estimated time of arrival.[31]

State Department officials were conflicted about responding to the troubles that public knowledge of the arrival of the first MDAP shipments would arouse. On the one hand, they were sensitive to the embarrassment the recipient governments would experience if the ships encountered violence at the ports, and they responded with low-key announcements of the first deliveries. At the same time, Secretary Acheson noted that U.S. public interest had increased over the past weeks and any friendly response to U.S. contribution to Europe's defense would be as beneficial to the program at home as it would be abroad. Moreover, Communist organizations planning demonstrations would be well aware of the loading of the MDAP equipment in U.S. ports before ships sailed. Even if no publicity were given to them, Acheson judged that the "wiser course is to refrain from issuing formal press release on materiel arriving at US ports and on its departure for Europe, but to answer legitimate news queries stating where materiel [is] loading for and when it is expected to be shipped."[32]

So while there would be no excessive celebration of the occasion in the United States, the three constituent parties of the MDAP—State, Defense, and ECA—agreed to have all crated MDAP materials stenciled in black paint with the words "Mutual Defense—supplied by USA," the words translated appropriately into the language of the recipient countries. The spectacular failure of Italian Communists to stop the unloading on April 12 of the first shipment of U.S. arms in Naples underscored the wisdom of the U.S. decision. Granted that precautions were taken; the port was heavily guarded as forty-eight teams of anti-Communist workers completed the unloading at high speed under large floodlights from 5:30 in the afternoon to the early morning of April 13. The Communist-inspired strike was unsuccessful because anti-Communist workers refused to walk away from their jobs. The scene in Naples and other Italian ports made U.S. officials optimistic about a peaceful unloading of a U.S. freighter with MDAP arms in Cherbourg on the same day. U.S. confidence was bolstered by the knowledge that the CIO and AFL had given the full weight of U.S. labor support publicly to the MDAP.[33]

There was a sense of relief in NATO circles when the supplies arrived in Europe without serious incident, but it was hard to gloss over the impact of the extended delays in dispatching the shipments in the first place. Such equipment that did reach European ports in the spring of 1950 were barely more than tokens. The French in particular had been uncomfortable about the inevitable gap between the initial shipment of MDAP materiel and the beginning of main deliveries. Some French army circles would have preferred to reduce the interval as much as possible even if it meant delaying the arrival of the first shipments. They worried that a long delay would play into the hands of the Communists. Defense Minister René Pleven disagreed, although he knew that the Communists were preparing an "all-out effort to sabotage [the] MDAP program and the arrival of [the] first shipment will be their D-Day." Pleven was convinced that the Communist effort can be smashed and, like Daridan in Washington, he wanted as many shipments as possible in the first wave to provoke a "real showdown" with the Communists.[34] Both these views placed an exaggerated value on the military equipment and so missed the point the United States wanted to make, namely: the symbol was more important than the substance at this juncture.

Ambassador Bruce's response from Paris was to emphasize to Europeans that "NATO and MDAP are essential components [of] US foreign policy," and so every opportunity must be taken to "hammer home to European opinion this concept . . . rather than to dwell on military strategic and tactical factors which invite invidious comparisons [of the] relative strength [of the] armed forces [of the] Soviet Union with those [of] west European countries." His key point was that "the strength of MDAP lies not in what it provides in terms [of] military statistics but what it means as [a] contribution to [the] common task [to] prevent aggression [from] ever occurring.[35]

The Wave of Neutralism

These were brave words, but whether they reassured the European allies was another matter. Jean Chauvel, France's representative to the United Nations, did not seem convinced about the symbolic value of the first shipments. He gave President Auriol the impression that the United States and the West were not working hard enough to seek accommodation with the Soviet Union. Since the French public, according to Auriol, did not believe that sufficient strength could be built up in the next several years to cope with a Soviet invasion, "the door should not be slammed on negotiations with the USSR in the intervening period." Secretary of State Acheson's extemporaneous remarks at a press conference on February 8 confirmed Chauvel's misgivings. Acheson asserted that "If we could reach our goal by agreement, of course, that would be highly desirable and the simplest and easiest way to do it. But I think years of experience have brought us the realization that that is not possible." Chauvel's response dwelled on the need for the United States to make greater effort to reach agreements with the Soviet Union in light of the West's military weakness in Europe. He rejected Acheson's primary message that only firm resolve on the part of the West would maintain peace.[36]

A pessimistic cable from the ECC in mid-February over "flagging enthusiasm or renewed doubts" about both the defensibility of Europe and the extent of American commitment evoked mixed reactions in Washington. The ECC saw signs of a resurgence of the neutrality complex in Western Europe that could threaten the viability of NATO and U.S. foreign policy toward Europe. Too many unsettling events—such as Soviet successes in Asia, Churchill's proposal of talks with Stalin, and the announcement of the H-bomb—had led to the decline in public enthusiasm for the alliance.

Even if no NATO government wavered in its support of the alliance, the ECC feared that a "significant decline [of] public enthusiasm would remove stimulus to governments to take specific measures in furthering NAT [North Atlantic Treaty] objectives." To remedy the situation, the ECC called for more publicity about the positive actions that the alliance, particularly the NAC, had taken over the past year.[37]

Ambassador Harriman agreed that the West had been too lax in educating the European public about the stakes involved. He noted that there had been no information from the organization since the signing of the treaty, or at least since the vigorous debate over ratification in the French National Assembly. The result was Communist propaganda filling the gap. If the sour mood was not counteracted, he felt that the wave of neutralism would continue to rise.[38]

Reactions to the ECC cable from the embassies in Brussels and Paris were more circumspect. Both felt that there should be concrete new developments rather than empty publicity measures. The Communists could consider a publicity campaign as a sign of NATO's weakness. While the United States could not do much at this time to dissuade Europeans from worrying about NATO's weakness on the ground in the face of larger Soviet armies, the U.S. ambassador in Brussels, Robert Murphy, proposed a major address by the president reaffirming the commitments the alliance had already made. He then should make a resounding statement of U.S. solidarity with Europe when the MDAP appropriations request for fiscal year 1951 came up later in the spring. In the meantime, the publicity campaign should be modest, concentrating on exposing the neutrality sentiments as "a will-of-the-wisp." Ambassador Murphy also speculated about cloaking the North Atlantic Council with greater powers, but only if the department was prepared to go in this direction. He was doubtful if the Senate would look favorably on this approach.[39]

Charles Bohlen's comments from Paris were ambiguous. On the one hand, he felt that the danger of a revival of neutralism was exaggerated. On the other, he offered cogent reasons for such neutralism as did exist. It boiled down to a recognition that in the short run, French public opinion could not see how they could defend themselves from Soviet ground forces. He went on to note that 40 percent of France's military potential was being spent in Indochina. Furthermore, the French worried about the reliability of their British ally as much they did about the inadequacy of U.S. military aid; the psychology of 1940 with its defeatist undertones, he felt, and its sense of betrayal by the British was still alive. Bohlen's rather tepid recommendation was to emphasize the successful preventive nature of the Atlantic Pact. He believed that the Soviets had "a healthy respect for the power of this country which holds back the Russians," and "that it is this conviction of the over-all strength of America which is the principal factor currently preventing the Russians from launching a war."[40]

None of these American responses relieved Europeans of their fears or suspicions. Auriol noted Chauvel's bitter comment: He would prefer being put in chains to abandoning independence for the sake of American aid.[41] There was a touch of paranoia about pronouncements of this sort. Suspicions of American motives grew out of a perception of a secret annex to Article 7 of the bilateral agreements, which dealt with export controls of potential war materiel to the Soviet bloc. While the article was omitted from the published texts, it originally included a secret annex demanding each country's adherence to the principle of export control. But an informal U.S. consultative group in Paris determined that there was enough progress made in the development of export controls that it was unnecessary for the United States to force a secret agreement on its allies. This understanding obviously was intended to prevent further conflict between the United States and its European allies over their differing views on export controls.[42]

The issue became public on January 31, 1950, when the *New York Times* reported the existence of a "secret annex." An article by Sydney Gruson, writing from London, claimed that the secret annex was proposed after Europeans objected to the language in the original draft of the bilateral agreements. The State Department tried damage control, noting that Gruson must have seen a first draft of the agreement, a preliminary working draft prepared only for discussion that was not included in the final version.[43]

That there was an outcry from the Communist press as well as from suspicious allies was only to be expected. The secretary-general of the Norwegian Foreign Office anticipated negative commentaries, but felt that consultations about export control should have been a military matter that properly excluded information to the public. He deplored the sensational journalism that created tensions between the United States and its European partners. Repercussions in Washington, however, were minimal. The Senate Foreign Relations Committee was satisfied that there were no secret agreements. In fact, one senator felt that the provision covering East–West trade should have been included publicly in the bilateral agreement.[44]

In any event, the State Department's official position was that a secret minute of negotiation was not an agreement and not so considered under Article 102 of the UN Charter. Besides, as Ambassador Murphy noted from Brussels, it was generally known that an informal multilateral organization met in Paris from January 9 to 29 under the auspices of the OEEC to deal with the broad question of East–West controls over transmission of strategic materiel to USSR or its satellites. This meeting concluded with the Belgian suggestion that East–West trade controls be handled by multilateral means. "So there would seem to be no reason not to put a bold face on [the] matter and say that of course we and like-minded western nations are concerned with stopping flow of strategic materials behind the Iron Curtain and that we are taking steps to this end."[45]

No matter how vigorous U.S. efforts were to put the matter of a secret annex to rest, they were bound to feed the neutralist mood that was affecting Europe, especially France, in the winter and spring of 1950. The influential *Le Monde* captured the spirit of the newspaper, which, in the eyes of the American embassy, always sought a neutral path between the United States and the USSR, balancing anti-American with anti-Soviet articles. But the balance tilted more against the former than the latter. The journal was "regularly lukewarm toward any policy of [the] French Government which seemed to follow ours." In essence, the editors judged that the Americans were always tempted to sacrifice Europe in the event of war. The U.S. plan for restoring an invaded Europe consisted of reconquering Europe following Soviet occupation. Small wonder that the Communist *Humanite* chose to echo *Le Monde*'s conviction that the United States was ready to turn its back on Europe.[46]

Le Monde's editorial position on neutrality did not go unanswered in France. The prominent intellectual, Raymond Aron, unleashed a strong attack in the more conservative *Figaro,* in which he condemned the doctrine of neutralism as illusory, a form of "subtle defeatism," that endangered Europe's security. The argument that the Soviets would respect European neutrality, he contended, was a fallacy. Detaching itself from the United States would only whet the aggressors' appetite for Western Europe's industrial resources. But Aron's appeared to be a minority voice in the winter of 1950. *Le Monde* was able to exploit the view of Gen. Pierre Billotte, former chairman of the French delegation in the UN Military Staff Committee, noting NATO's failure to ensure the security of Europe.[47]

The issue of neutrality debated in such influential newspapers inevitably attracted the attention of U.S. diplomats, but it did not surface as a serious challenge to NATO until the first anniversary of the treaty on April 4, 1950. Harriman may have contributed to NATO's complacency, saying on that day that he had no feeling that there was a wave of neutrality. Instead, he saw only a latent danger that should be counteracted. Nevertheless, to have the issue reopened on this date by Jean-Jacques Servan-Schreiber, a persuasive young journalist writing for *Le Monde,* was troubling. It spoiled the outpouring of self-congratulations that NATO's foreign ministers expressed in a message to Secretary of State Acheson: "Much valuable work had been done during the past year and a sound organization has been established to carry out the common task."[48]

Actually, Servan-Schreiber's article was not a diatribe against U.S. leadership. Rather, it was a wake-up call to Europeans to recognize that the faith of Europe in the guarantee of America's protection had failed. Security is an illusion, and the delivery of Sherman tanks, artillery, and even B-29s from surplus American stocks did not change the situation. Soviet military power at this juncture in time could not be stopped should it be deployed. In this context, neutrality may have been the least of bad solutions. Yet he recognized that neutrality itself may well be insufficient. A Europe isolated from the United States would be even more vulnerable to Communist pressures.[49] His was a reflection of Europe's malaise a year after the signing of the North Atlantic Treaty.

Impact of the Superbomb

The H-Bomb Decision

The strength of neutralism's appeal lay in Europe's sense of impotence in the face of new elements in the contest between the United States and the Soviet Union. The Communists had caught up with the Americans by detonating an atomic device in the summer of 1949, and they had the technological capacity to move ahead with the more powerful hydrogen bomb. While cables from London and The Hague backed Harriman's view that an information campaign disparaging the notion of European neutralism would be effective, a more pessimistic judgment emerged from the State Department. Assistant Secretary of State for Public Affairs Edward W. Barrett suggested that waning public enthusiasm was "a symptom of a deeper problem: belief that the military strength of Russia vis-à-vis the U.S. had increased markedly." This sentiment arose from such factors as Russia having the A-bomb, the conviction that the Soviets could develop the H-bomb as well, and the fact that their land armies were many times stronger than the combined Western ground forces. Not only did NATO lack the power to turn Russian forces back, but Europeans feared that the United States was not really intending to build up the necessary power to cope with Soviet aggression. The few recommendations Barrett made to buck up the allies were not sufficient to counter his sober evaluation of the situation in the winter of 1950.[50]

The foregoing commentary did not exactly echo *Le Monde*'s despair expressed a few weeks earlier when the newspaper claimed that American strategists had not taken the Soviet A-bomb into account. But they were not far apart. *Le Monde* charged that the Americans were busy drawing up paper divisions as though these could stop Soviet troops. That Europe would be invaded and overrun did not affect U.S. planning, which consisted of reconquering Europe only after Europe was destroyed. The implication was that the West was powerless to resist the atom bomb, let alone the more powerful hydrogen bomb. It required Albert Einstein specifically identifying the hydrogen bomb as the instrument capable of annihilating all life on earth before the H-bomb itself merited headlines in French newspapers. Barrett's cable captured the essence of France's hope that neutralism could be an alternative to a doomed alliance.[51]

The dark cloud of Soviet nuclear power inevitably determined the course of action the Truman administration took in the winter of 1950, irrespective of the challenge of European neutralism. The surprising Soviet development of the atomic bomb at least two years before U.S. intelligence's estimates, along with the concurrent success of Communist China in pushing Chiang Kai-Shek out of the mainland, exerted irresistible pressures for U.S. counteraction. The links between the two Communist states were undeniable: on January 10, 1950, Jacob Malik, the

Soviet delegate to the United Nations, dramatically walked out of the Security Council to protest its refusal to seat Communist China in place of the Republic of China, now in Taiwan. A month later, on February 14, the USSR signed a Treaty of Friendship, Alliance, and Mutual Assistance with its Chinese ally. In this same period, successful Soviet espionage became evident when the British arrested a prominent German exile, Klaus Fuchs, a central figure in Anglo-American atomic energy research. In this heated atmosphere Sen. Joseph R. McCarthy (R-WI) launched a reckless campaign accusing the Truman administration of harboring Communists in various U.S. agencies.[52]

Still, countervailing issues stood in the path of a precipitate military response to the series of new challenges that had arisen in the fall of 1949 and increased in the winter of 1950. Among them was President Truman's concern for keeping the Defense budget under a $13 billion ceiling. Furthermore, the decision to build an H-bomb exposed divisions within the administration that had been kept in check as the Atlantic alliance and the MDAP were being designed. Not that dissonance within the ranks was lacking in 1948 and 1949. The dissenting voices of George Kennan, then director of the Policy Planning Staff, and his fellow Soviet expert, Charles Bohlen. counselor of the State Department, were always audible but never decisive in the decision-making process. Kennan reluctantly acquiesced in the treaty and left the office in February 1950, while Bohlen remained in his post until his departure to the American embassy in Paris later in 1950. There was always some uneasiness in the ECA about the militarization of U.S. foreign aid. Granted that foreign policy would affect the economies of the Marshall Plan beneficiaries, key figures in the program, such as Averell Harriman, supported both NATO and MDAP. Potentially more divisive was the behavior of Secretary of Defense Louis Johnson, envious of Acheson's leadership and protective of the Truman Defense budget ceiling, who was ready to challenge the State Department's primary role in NATO and the MDAP at every opportunity. But Acheson was fortunate to have an ally in Gen. Omar Bradley, the chairman of the Joint Chiefs of Staff, whose position on military aid had played a positive role in congressional debate over the MDAP.

The decision to go ahead with building the hydrogen bomb opened new fissures within the administration. Propelled into action by the Soviet success with its atomic bomb, the president appointed a special National Security Council committee on November 10 composed of Acheson, Johnson, and David E. Lilienthal, chairman of the Atomic Energy Commission, to advise him whether the United States should "undertake the development and possible production of 'super' atomic weapons." There was no doubt that the president was troubled by the responsibility of unleashing such destructive force. He was also uncomfortable with the pressures in favor of such a program, and certainly listened to arguments on both sides. He found himself in "a situation that I don't like to be put in bluntly." He liked it even less when the Alsop brothers accused the administration of dealing with "issues of life and death . . . in dingy committee rooms," where vital issues "have been far too long concealed from the country." The president told Sen. Brien McMahon (D-CT), chairman of the Joint Committee on Atomic Energy, that "I don't know where the 'Sop Sisters' got their information but evidently somebody thinks it is proper to talk to such lying scoundels . . . I don't."[53]

It was too late to put the issue back into "Pandora's Box" (the title of the Alsop article). Two months earlier, on October 30, 1949, six members of the General Advisory Committee of the Atomic Energy Commission, including Harvard University President James B. Conant and J. Robert Oppenheimer, former director of the atomic bomb project at Los Alamos, had signed a statement asserting that the hydrogen bomb "might become a weapon of genocide." Their position was directly opposed to that of Atomic Energy Commissioner Lewis L. Strauss's campaign "to get ahead with the super," as he put it in a letter to his fellow commissioners on October 5. "By an intensive effort, I am thinking in terms of talent and money, comparable, if necessary, to that which produced the first atomic weapon." Strauss, a protegé of Herbert Hoover who rose from his position as assistant to Herbert Hoover in World War I to prominence as a New York banker in the 1920s and as a rear admiral in World War II, took pride in his hawkish minority position on the Atomic Energy Commission. On November 25 he recommended that the president proceed "with the development of the thermonuclear bomb, at highest priority subject. . . ."[54]

Strauss was not alone in his views. He had powerful allies in the Defense Department and in Congress. Sen. Brien McMahon (D-CT) had already weighed in on the subject, noting that a subcommittee of his Joint Committee was "unanimous in believing that we should get ahead as quickly as possible." From the scientific community Strauss had allies in Ernest O. Lawrence and his colleagues at the Berkeley Radiation Laboratory, and in Edward Teller and some of the scientists at Los Alamos. While Secretary Johnson would not be enthusiastic over any initiative outside his control, the Defense establishment lined up with Admiral Strauss. Secretary of the Air Force W. Stuart Symington judged that the Soviet atomic success raised the question of the survival. Only fear of retaliation would prevent the Soviet Union from using whatever it had in its arsenal, including a superbomb.[55]

Still, Strauss had doubts about winning over the president. The many distinguished opponents of the H-bomb detected a sympathetic ear in the secretary of state. When Lilienthal asked, "Why can we not spend a few months for an intensive and realistic reexamination of the worsening of our position as a result of our preoccupation with atomic weapons? It seemed to me that this was a far wiser course than to make a decision, prejudicing the reexamination. . . ." He noted that the secretary of state "found little in what I said with which he would disagree." But Acheson also recognized that congressional pressures for a decision, combined with those from the Defense establishment, prevented deferment of the issue. As he told Adm.

Sidney W. Souers, consultant to the president on National Security Affairs, "I had about reached the position that we should advise the President to go ahead and find out about the feasibility of the matter but that we should be quite honest and say that in advising this action, we are going quite a long way to committing ourselves to continue along that road. However, after considering drawbacks and advantages, adding and subtracting, that it seemed to me the position we should take." The matter was settled at a meeting on January 31, 1950.[56]

Actually, the balance had been tipped before this meeting. An impatient Louis Johnson had sent a memorandum from General Bradley directly to the president in support of the production of the H-bomb, and the president expected a resolution at that meeting on January 31. Lilienthal's personal objections notwithstanding, the president accepted Acheson's judgment that delaying nuclear research would not deter the Soviets from continuing their program. Experience with the adversary in the Cold War suggested that efforts to accommodate with the Russians on the bomb would be fruitless. A dispirited Lilienthal joined Acheson and Johnson in a unanimous recommendation that the president direct the Atomic Energy Commission to continue its work on all forms of atomic weapons, including the so-called hydrogen or superbomb. Lip service at least was given to a goal of a satisfactory plan for international control of atomic energy.[57]

NSC 68

The way was now clear for rapid development of the H-bomb. Paul H. Nitze, who replaced Kennan on January 1, 1950 as director of the Policy Planning Staff in the State Department, had an outlook much closer to Acheson's than that of his predecessor. Nitze had moved quickly and happily from a successful career on Wall Street as a young man into the more exciting world of Washington. A prominent figure in the Strategic Bombing Survey of World War II, he brought a keen intellect into both the Defense and State departments in the course of his long public career. Acheson felt he "was a joy to work with because of his clear, incisive mind" in implicit contrast to Kennan's contemplative brilliance, marred, as he saw it, by indecisiveness.[58]

Nitze's assets became evident in the conception and development of NSC 68. Having Acheson's ear, he enjoyed an initiative in dealing with the Defense Department that he maintained throughout the preparation of NSC 68. When the National Security Council assigned him to the chairmanship of a joint State–Defense ad hoc study group, he grasped the opportunity—and burden—of shaping a policy that could have major budgetary implications. While the secretary of defense and the Joint Chiefs were seemingly content to accept the budget ceiling of fiscal year 1950, even as they supported the development of the H-bomb, Nitze pointedly disagreed with the secretary of defense.[59]

Had Secretary Johnson not alienated most of his colleagues in the Defense as well as the State Department in asserting the authority of his office, he might have been a more formidable opponent of Nitze's position, as expressed in NSC 68. An ambitious West Virginia lawyer who had seen action in World War I and served as national commander of the American Legion, he had been an active fund-raiser for fellow Legionnaire Harry Truman in 1948 and was arguably the president's most loyal aide in holding the line on defense spending when he was appointed secretary of defense in April 1949. Johnson shared Truman's prejudices against the navy and displayed more zeal than the president in cutting down the navy's role in national defense to preserve the budget's ceiling.[60]

Johnson's myopic view of the Defense establishment had repercussions in his dealings with the State Department, and especially with Secretary Acheson. For him, NATO was an irrelevance, a needless cost that Western European defense imposed. Johnson resented the MDAP as a potential infringement on his authority. As secretary of defense, he reluctantly admitted that "foreign military assistance is an integral part of our foreign policy, and as such primary responsibility belongs to the secretary of state." But he pointed out to the president that his department would have most responsibility for operating the program, and as such "I deem it most important that the policy direction emanating from the Department of State come from an administrator located at the highest possible level within that Department, preferably above that of an Assistant Secretary of State and be to and through my office."[61]

If there was a touch of megalomania in this letter, it would not have surprised Acheson. He observed in his memoirs that Johnson underwent a brain operation in his later years. Acheson's references to Johnson as a collaborator in the making of American foreign military policy were usually sarcastic. He frequently pounced on what he perceived as Johnson's many errors of judgment. Unquestionably, his most egregious behavior was exhibited in the notorious meeting on March 22, 1950 in Nitze's Planning Office room in the State Department when Johnson vented his resentment at being summoned to a meeting without his authorization and to give a report to the president without his involvement. His outburst shocked his colleagues as he, in Acheson's words, "stalked out of the room." Refusing subsequently to have any connection with the NSC project, he left the completion of the document to Nitze, with Maj. Gen. James H. Burns as the Pentagon's liaison with the State Department. While it was a shocking experience, it permitted the State Department to complete the project in a remarkably short time.[62]

Notwithstanding the clash between Acheson and Johnson, the divisions between the two departments were not as deep as Johnson's outburst indicated. A consensus existed on the working level. Burns and Air Force Maj. Gen. Truman H. Landon of the Joint Strategic Survey Committee worked harmoniously with

Nitze and his colleagues on the State Department's Policy Planning Staff. The sec-retary of defense did not carry the department with him; the Nitze group's prod-uct appropriately was identified as a State–Defense Staff Study.[63]

Consciousness of impending doom accelerated the pace of Nitze's group. The document that it produced predicted that the Soviets would have atomic parity with the United States in the near future. The Soviet Union's image in NSC 68 ap-peared as an implacable hostile force "animated by a new fanatic faith" and devel-oping "increasingly terrifying weapons of mass destruction." Only by moving with the speed and scale of the Manhattan Project of World War II could the United States cope with the growing threat. The year of maximum danger was 1954, no longer in an indeterminate future. To cope with this reality, the United States would have to build up its political and economic as well as its military strength to retain the confidence of its allies in the free world. Such was the message of this pessimistic document.[64]

After discarding continuation of current policies, NSC 68 considered a num-ber of ways to meet this Communist challenge, including a preventive war that might destroy the Soviet economy in a single massive blow. However, it not only found such action morally "repugnant" but also susceptible to failure given the vastness of the Soviet Union. An alternative approach of reviving isolationism was equally unacceptable. Removing U.S. forces to the Western hemisphere might also assign its NATO allies to the fate of a Nazi Eurasia that had been prevented only by victory in World War II. Nor did a renewed effort to invigorate peace negotiations offer any better prospect of success in dealing with the Communist adversary. Four years of failed talks pointed to the futility of this path. Only when the United States and its allies had acquired the strength to equal and surpass that of the Soviets could negotiations have a chance of success. NSC 68 concluded that there would be no way to make ourselves inoffensive to the Kremlin except by complete submission to its will.[65]

After eliminating potential alternatives, the authors decided that the only re-course left was a massive reordering of U.S. economic priorities. To build the mili-tary strength necessary for the nation's security, the United States could devote half of its gross national product to military purposes—expenditures for U.S. military hardware, foreign military production, and investment directed to defense-sup-porting industries. In sounding this alarm, it enveloped the NATO allies in its dark vision of the future. Europe must do its part by increasing its ability to help deter attack and make it more difficult for the Soviet armies to overrun the continent. A gloomy future was in prospect: "Unless the military strength of the western Euro-pean nations is increased on a much larger scale than under current programs and at an accelerated rate, it is more than likely that those nations will not be able to op-pose even by 1960 the Soviet armed forces in war with any degree of effeciveness."[66]

That the cost of implementing the NSC 68 would be enormous did not appear in the sixty-page document. If it had, the relatively mild reaction of the president might have been quite different. Truman responded to the report submitted by the executive secretary of the NSC with a request that it provide more information. "I am particularly anxious that the Council give me a clearer indication of the programs which are envisaged in the reports, including estimates of the probable cost of such programs." He wanted to know how the Bureau of the Budget, the Council of Economic Advisers, and the secretary of the treasury envisioned the economic and budgetary implications of NSC 68. In the meantime, he did not want any changes in the current programs. Nor did he want publicity of the report without his approval. In effect, he rejected the specific conclusion that the president direct the NSC "to coordinate and insure the implementation of the conclusions herein on an urgent and continuing basis for as long as necessary to achieve our objectives."[67]

That the document itself did not offer any clues about eventual costs "was not an oversight," as Acheson observed. The details would have thrown out the $12.5 billion current budget. Such a prospect would not have affected the JCS's and the army's backing of the NSC 68. Not that they envisioned the "massive" changes of $35 billion to $40 billion, which were the study group's preliminary projected annual appropriations. They thought in terms of $4 billion or $5 billion more than they had been receiving, for which they would be grateful. Nitze's calculations, realized after the outbreak of the Korean War, were more realistic. As he put it at a Princeton conference in 1953, "When we tried to make up our own mind as to what the order of magnitude of the effort required was, we came [to] this conclusion . . . of fifty billion a year. Now we didn't dare put any such in the paper itself. There is no figure in the paper itself. This was impossible. We never could have gotten these concurrences."[68]

Nitze was right. If NSC 68 had included estimated costs, it would have been dead on arrival at the president's desk. His erratic behavior notwithstanding, Secretary Johnson was more in tune with the president than Acheson or Nitze. Johnson had signed on to the NSC 68 in the same spirit that Truman had accepted it. It would be put under advisement on the assumption that the current program was working. The budgetary limitations that Truman had decreed for the Defense establishment would remain in effect. Johnson's fidelity to the president's conception of national security may have been the reason why Truman did not fire him after the blowup in Nitze's office.

To The Hague

Combatting Neutralism

America's NATO partners may have been unaware of the detailed negotiations within the Truman administration, but the many leaks in the press and the resulting commentaries from Congress were no secret to the allies. The militant language that emerged from U.S. supporters of the H-bomb exacerbated the fears of those Europeans who saw neutralism as their best way out of the Cold War. In the wake of the U.S. decision to build the H-bomb, France's President Auriol was convinced that a meeting of the four major powers was indispensable. Jean Chauvel, head of the foreign office at the Quai d'Orsay, agreed, in light of the damage that the superbomb issue had inflicted on the credibility of the Atlantic alliance.[69]

The volatile mood of the NATO allies, stimulated by the H-bomb's effect on European neutralism, required positive acts on the part of NATO's leadership to counter disillusionment and demonstrate progress in building Europe's defenses. The administration's concentration on NSC 68 diverted attention from the roles of allies, who presumably would be the beneficiary of America's accelerated arms buildup. So much of the administration's energy in the weeks between the decision to build the hydrogen bomb and the issuance of NSC 68 seemed to have left the allies out of the picture. There was no consultation with any of them, not even the British, although the document repeatedly associated the allies with the United States in coping with the Communist challenge. The question, then, is how the allies reacted to what was essentially a solipsistic program.

The record suggests that the European partners made little distinction between the H-bomb and NSC 68. They had little information about the latter, and such as they had would be conflated with the superbomb itself. Its impact for much of Europe was to keep neutralism alive on the assumption that the building of the American military might provoke a war in which Europeans would be the first victims. At best, a sophisticated diplomat such as Jean Chauvel would observe divisions in America over the wisdom of a buildup and wonder if the decision was genuine. Like his American counterparts, Chauvel noted that funds for developing the bomb had not yet been sought. But he also recognized that the protection promised under the treaty was no longer available after the U.S. monopoly on the atomic bomb was broken. He felt that time was working in favor of the Soviets.[70]

The continuing uncertainties over the state of the alliance in the winter of 1950 made plans for a meeting of the Defense Committee at The Hague on March 31 all the more urgent. To counter the public pessimism in Europe, the State Department and the EEC came up with a number of approaches. An obvious and familiar one was to emphasize that MDAP and NATO were essential components of U.S. foreign policy. Ambassador David K. E. Bruce in Paris wanted to use every opportunity to hammer home to the European public that the significance of military assistance lay not in the statistics it publicized, but in its contribution to the common task of preventing aggression.[71] But no matter how true this assertion was, it was too passive to satisfy European critics.

More specifically, the administration had to impress on the allies that the MDAP was not limited to supplying weapons. Rather, it had to demonstrate that the MDAP in no way contradicted the priority of European economic reconstruction. The formidable figure of Sir Stafford Cripps, Britain's Chancellor of the Exchequer, was an obstacle to U.S. attempts to assure the allies of the compatibility of military aid and economic reconstruction. In essence, Cripps resented America's interference in the settlement of European problems, and was put off by the "schoolboy lectures" he felt regularly subjected to by American officials. Cripps offended Harriman by his charge of American dictation to the Organisation for European Economic Co-operation (OEEC), the organization that would carry the weight of reconstruction after the Marshall Plan ended. Harriman felt that Cripps, "petulant and arrogant," should not be allowed to undermine U.S. support of European integration. At The Hague meetings of the major NAC committees at the end of March, Cripps failed to have defense expenditures frozen at the present ceilings at a time when Bradley and Harriman were studying financial ways of supporting higher military expenditures without jeopardizing the European economies.[72]

There were other distractions as the Defense ministers prepared to assess the progress of Defense measures since their last meeting in December. To respond to European interest in new negotiations with the Soviet Union, or at least to make a pretense of respecting this element of European neutralism, State Department officials considered reviving Article 43 of the UN Charter. This would involve giving substance to a UN military presence that would enforce the collective security objectives of the world organization. They did not anticipate a favorable response from the USSR, nor even wanted one. The Soviets, they assumed, would be worried about the implications of invoking Article 43. "The strongest factor in militating against Soviet acquiescence in such a proposal," according to one official, "is not the fear that once the forces created might be used against the USSR, but rather the basic distrust of Kremlin leader in the reliability of Soviet forces outside Soviet borders." The advantage of such a proposal for the United States was that Article 43 might focus world attention on Soviet intransigence as well as discourage Europeans from initiating new parleys with the Soviets.[73]

Ultimately, the State Department judged that there was "definitely no imperative necessity" to take the initiative at this time on Article 43. Among other problems, it would open the United States to the accusation this was solely a propaganda ploy without any possibility of realization in light of the realities of the Cold War. Only if the allies raised the issue should the United States consider it. Despite this advice from the director of the Office of European Regional Affairs (RA), the Office of British Commonwealth and Northern European Affairs (BNA), which had circulated the idea, still found the idea tempting, but not enough to put the matter before the secretary of state.[74]

A more promising collaboration with NATO allies emerged from discussions within the administration over the sharing of U.S. technology and military information to promote standardization of equipment within the alliance. This was a major point of contention with U.S. military representatives who had reservations about giving away classified information and materiel to potentially untrustworthy allies. The State Department made a strong case in favor of such action, based in part on the possibility of European allies producing inferior equipment under the AMP program because of their lack of access to advanced U.S. technology. If the decision was positive, the question then was whether NATO planning should include territories of France, Britain, and the Netherlands outside Europe. The State Department's answer again was affirmative, on the assumption that bases in those territories served NATO's interests.[75]

Actually, sharing critical information, always excepting atomic weaponry, was already in progress. The United States and Britain agreed on January 27, 1950 to release their classified military information relating to published technical and tactical training doctrine to other NATO allies. But the U.S. military stood in the way of implementing this policy. The French military attaché in Washington expressed his dissatisfaction with the Pentagon's refusal to provide him with certain classified materials. He was fobbed off with a requirement to go through proper channels, in this case through the Joint American Military Advisory Group (JAMAG) in London, before his request could be considered. It was no surprise that this treatment of the French military attaché in Washington goaded Defense Minister René Pleven to retort that France may be forced to develop prototypes of weapons that might be better produced elsewhere.[76]

Pleven revived familiar resentment over France's inferior status in the Anglo-Saxon–dominated alliance. French suspicions were never far below the surface. They never accepted repeated U.S. assertions that the Combined Chiefs of Staff of World War II had been terminated when the war ended. In August 1949, the question of reviving the Combined Chiefs did arise at a meeting of U.S. and British chiefs of staff, but it was agreed that "although close collaboration between the U.K. and U.S. should continue, this collaboration should be carried on under a different arrangement than the Combined Chiefs of Staff." Understandably, the Chiefs wanted to tell the press that the matter was not discussed at their meeting in London.[77]

Ambassador Bruce in Paris was well aware of Pleven's ruffled feelings and was disturbed over the apparent inability of the Americans, Canadians, and British to divulge details about their latest weapons to the French. The ambassador did alert Secretary Johnson to the seriousness of the issue, but the Defense response, while agreeing in principle with exchanging military information with the allies, still recommended that Pleven continue to submit French request for details on specific U.S. items through General Kibler's JAMAG in London rather than communicate directly with Pleven, as the State Department preferred. This response once again exposed Johnson's tin ear in interpersonal relations.[78]

The Defense Department remained uncomfortable with extensive sharing, noting that the procedure for handling French requests for technical information would continue to be handled through JAMAG in London. It was unhappy with a special agreement with the French, if only because the other allies would quickly learn about the discriminatory policy. Defense professed to fear a bottleneck developing in London if it did not discourage a flood of requests. It recommended instead a piecemeal, nation-to-nation approach.[79]

Although Najeeb Halaby, director of Defense's Office of Foreign Military Affairs, was open to the State Department's argument that sharing not only information but bases as well with NATO partners would promote a better feeling of unity, the allies themselves had reservations about disclosing detailed information about their own programs. Their reasons were varied and usually reasonable. Military considerations predominated: there was reluctance to expose deficiencies in their existing forces; there were also political reasons—they would be divulging information not available to their own parliaments, as well as economic—hesitation about making financial commitments that might affect their future economic viability. Perhaps the primary problem, according to Edwin M. Martin, director of the State Department's Office of European Regional Affairs, was the continuing inability of "twelve sovereign nations [to] work completely as one unit and trust each other with their secrets." And as long as the United States refused to extend to its allies "top-secret development and production information the reluctance of others to provide is difficult to criticize."[80]

It was in this unsettled state of the alliance that the Defense ministers were to meet at the end of March. The dangers of neutralism, mistrust among the allies, and resentment against the senior partner were beyond the scope of the Defense ministers' mission. What they conceivably could do was to take stock of what had been accomplished in the four months since their last meeting and to narrow the gap between the military production plans of the MPSB and the means to finance them through the DFEC.

Defense Committee Meeting: March 30–April 1, 1950

There were no great expectations of solving all NATO's difficulties in the first meeting of NATO's Defense Committee since December 1, 1949. It was the occasion to see what such important subordinate elements—the Regional Planning Groups, the DFEC, and the MPSB—had produced since the fall. Their sessions would precede the formal sessions. A successful meeting at The Hague would set the scene for celebrating NATO's first anniversary on April 4.

But how much progress could the ministers realistically identify? The modest flow of military assistance in April deserved some publicity, but it was obvious that the amount of aid in the ports of allies was too little to assure any ally of NATO's ability to defend the West against a Soviet attack. The working groups had been in constant motion since the year began and if they did nothing else, NATO's first secretary-general, Lord Ismay, could subsequently say that "the habit of working together was growing sensibly. So far so good."[81]

But was this good enough? The groups' failure to proceed beyond drawing up lists was blamed on the distance between the DFEC's need to know just what military production estimates were from the MPSB and the MPSB's dependence on estimates of what the member nations were prepared to spend on the equipment identified by the board. That the MPSB was headquartered in London and the DFEC in Rome did not promote either harmony or progress. That the State Department considered the MPSB the agency to deal with MDAP matters and the DFEC to deal primarily with NATO matters further stymied collaboration between two vital NATO bodies. As of March 22, a week before the Defense Committee meeting, neither the regional groups nor the Standing Group had developed a list of equipment requirements. As NATO scholar Wallace Theis observed, "the various lists, studies, and reports compiled during 1949 and 1950, however, led only to more lists, studies, and reports."[82]

The fate of the AMP and with it the prospects for offshore procurement was a major example of the troubles facing the alliance. U.S. officials had high hopes that Western Europe's use of MDAP funds would yield not only vitally needed goods but would also lead to a Europe weaned from U.S. surplus weaponry and confident enough to move toward the goal of standardization. All these developments would proceed presumably without damaging the economic revival that the Marshall Plan had sparked. No administrator was more devoted to the Atlantic alliance than Maj. Gen. Lyman L. Lemnitzer, director of military assistance in the Pentagon in 1950 and a true believer in its future. He was dismissive of those who felt that the AMP and standardization of weaponry were the quick and easy solution to the defense of the West. Years after he retired as Supreme Allied commander, Europe, he mused at length about the hurdles facing standardization:

> One of the things that annoys me is that everybody who comes along, whether he is a minister of defense in Europe, or secretary of defense here, says that we could get at least the same defense we recently get in NATO with a 25 percent reduction if we standardized. And they just glibly say it like that. I'm trying to get some realism into this so-called standardization today, but the difficulties of standardization are not well understood. When we got the first $1.1 billion, we allocated about $100 million for offshore procurement and immediately ran into all sorts of standardization problems. The initial one was that the blueprints of American firms were not readable by Europeans. We were first going to standardize tank construction; it looked to be the easiest. When we got into

it, it was impossible: the screw threads, the caliber of armaments, the electronics, everything in a tank was on a different basis. Really we had an awfully hard time getting the program underway. We had the machine tools, yes, but it was difficult to translate them into production know-how. And in many cases proprietary rights were also involved. The program came along very very slowly.[83]

Slowness was not a particular drawback in the eyes of the State Department. It was to be expected, as Acting Secretary James W. Webb informed U.S. embassies in NATO Europe: "Although work in NATO toward standardization necessarily will continue over a long time, standardization considerations are important at this time . . . particularly for AMP projects supported by MDAP funds." While Webb did not sound complacent about the rate of progress of standardization, it was obvious that there was no urgency about the pace; no crisis with the Soviet Union was expected before 1954.[84]

The ministers assembling in The Hague could not be expected to resolve long-term problems in a two-day session. What the Defense Committee could do was to provide ammunition for the State Department to justify the continuation of the MDAP at congressional hearings. In advance of the meeting of the Defense ministers, both the MPSB and the Military Committee displayed confidence that progress was being made toward a coordinated NATO production program and that an integrated defense plan was in place. In fact, the Military Committee "unanimously agreed that planning had progressed more rapidly than had been expected due in large measure to the outstanding work of each of the five regional planning groups." And at a meeting of American ambassadors in Rome on March 2–24, it was agreed that NATO's successes should be publicized to deprive the USSR of any credit for its "peace" campaign.[85] The U.S. Congress should have been sufficiently impressed to move ahead with legislation renewing the MDAP. It was, even though the U.S. military leadership held doubts about NATO's military advances.

General Bradley, speaking for the U.S. Joint Chiefs to the Standing Group a week before the meeting in The Hague, exposed the inadequacy of the force requirements submitted by the Regional Planning Groups. These were unrealistic and needed drastic revision if the medium-term defense objectives were to be achieved. He judged that "the basic reason for the impracticability of the present plan arises from the fact that it was developed within the Regional Groups purely on a requirements basis, and without due regard for reasonably anticipated availabilities."[86]

Dirk Stikker, the Dutch foreign minister, accurately identified NATO's situation in the weeks before the meeting at The Hague. He was "outwardly optimistic," but worried about the gradual deterioration of the essence of the alliance, namely, the absence of a sense of unity in NATO as it worked to secure a common defense. National priorities superseded NATO objectives as the ministers, particularly the finance ministers, were fully occupied with their own internal problems.[87]

He was right to worry. As the report of the Rome conference pointed out, too few of the promises were being fulfilled. Lt. Col. Charles H. Bonesteel, executive director of the EEC, gloomily noted that as of January 1, 1951, it was unlikely that more than 30 percent of the army, 20 percent of the navy, and only 5 percent of the tactical air force programming would be fulfilled. And the day before the ministers met at The Hague, Bonesteel, in a personal letter to John Ohly, deputy director of the ECC, pondered the question of how to raise 50 divisions maybe at a cost of $30 billion without straining European resources, soon to be aggravated by the cessation of the Marshall Plan. The physical capacity to fulfill the objective was available if West Germany's resources could be tapped. He feared that the demands on the civilian economies would be so great that the public would react to the call for sacrifices "like ostriches burying their heads in the sand." Sacrifices would be accepted only if there was "a realistic chance that they can provide success."[88]

The Defense Committee approved the recommendations of the Military Committee on April 1, essentially ignoring the disconnects between the DFEC and MPSB and between what the MPSB intended to supply and the costs of the programs planned. The ministers unanimously approved the Medium-Term Defense Plan as expected given the abandonment of the short-term plan. British Minister of Defence Emanuel Shinwell told the House of Commons that the Defense Committee had approved reports from the Military Committee and the Military Production and Supply Board on the progress made in planning for the common defense based on plans drawn up by the Defense Committee in December 1949. The next stage would be the NATO summit in May, where the foreign ministers would examine how much progress had been made in implementing those plans. While asserting that he and his fellow ministers "have no illusions about the task that lies before us," Shinwell seemed satisfied with the overall direction the alliance was taking.[89]

Winston Churchill, then leader of the Opposition, dismissed Shinwell's account by asking rhetorically and sarcastically, "Isn't it lamentable with all this well-turned official verbiage, and with all these meetings of great consequence between the most important people of the world that so little progress should have been made in . . . the much more than 12 months which have elapsed since the Atlantic Pact was signed?" While Churchill's skepticism was more on the mark than Dutch Minister W. F. Shokking's claim that Western Europe could now live without fear of foreign conquest, or Louis Johnson's claim that the alliance had moved from the planning stage to "realistic" action, it would have been more appropriate to measure progress since December rather than April 1949. The results were still very modest but understandable. Shinwell did admit that the allies would have "to give effective force and content to the strategic plans to which we have, in principle, assented."[90]

It was obvious even to the most optimistic of participants that NATO's problems could not be resolved at the Defense Committee level. The AMP program

and the links between the DFEC and MPSB needed the attention of the North Atlantic Council. And they needed more forceful intervention by the United States
to combat persistent European neutralist sentiments. Matters, according to Assistant Secretary of State Perkins, were growing worse "as there appears to be a
tendency for certain friendly non-Communist Europeans to believe that despite
all our efforts to build up the strength of the western world . . . , the gap between
the strength of the Soviet Union and the weakness of the western powers is actually widening in favor of the Soviet Union, and that time, is in fact, working in
favor of the latter." Only at a meeting of the highest level of the alliance could they
find ways of reversing this trend, and this should be at the forthcoming summit in
London.[91] The two previous NAC meetings primarily centered on organizational
issues and strategic objectives. The end product of the May sessions, he hoped,
would be realistic measures to resolve many of the problems now troubling the
allies. Perkins made these observations before the Defense Committee met at The
Hague. Its proceedings only confirmed his recommendations.

6

To London

April–May 1950

Spring Challenges

The many holes in the foundations of a viable NATO defense program could not be filled in the Defense Committee sessions at the end of March, and there were no illusions among NATO planners—civilian or military—that they would be. It was expected that problems would be kicked up to the next level, the forthcoming NAC meeting in mid-May, when the foreign ministers would gather in London. Most of these issues were fundamental and wide-ranging—the unsettled linkage between the MPSB and DFEC, the uneasy relationship between NATO and the WU, the faltering efforts toward European integration, the continuing European resentment over American unilateralism, and the obstacles in exploiting German resources for NATO purposes. The foregoing do not exhaust the list but raise the question of whether NATO could meet these challenges—or needed to meet them.

The Medium-Term Defense Plan (MTDP)

The Medium-Term Defense Plan agreed upon at The Hague meeting provides a case in point. The MDTP, after all, was the most visible achievement of the Military and Defense committees meeting at the end of March. But how realistic was a plan that anticipated ninety active and reserve divisions, along with the specific numbers of 1,705 antiaircraft batteries and 8,820 aircraft to be in place by 1954? Where would the funds and equipment come from? How the forces were to be equipped and paid for was left for another time.[1] All that the committees had done at The Hague was to look over the pooling of national resources derived from hasty Regional Planning Groups without taking into account the impact of such a buildup on the economic stability of the member countries. These were not insignificant issues, but from the U.S. point of view, the need to impress Congress with sufficient accomplishments to justify continuation of the MDAP trumped all other considerations.

On paper at least, the reports seemed to confirm genuine progress in developing the MTDP. Reviewing the work of the recent NATO meeting, on April 7 State

Department officials found that "the vicious circle as to whether military planners should first spell out and cost a detailed plan or whether Finance Ministers should first establish a financial ceiling calling for further military planning appears at last to have been broken." But the evidence supporting this assertion was thin. Regional Planning Groups were to compile lists of equipment deficiencies and let the MPSB know the costs of production. Actually, the MPSB did have preliminary lists of available capacity for military production, but these were just a compilation of national lists unrelated to any coordinated NATO defense plans. Finance ministers were to "immediately study available capabilities for additional military expenditures." Instead, they turned to the Defense Committee for its estimate of costs in meeting requirements for defense of the West.[2] There was a promissory note in each of these activities, with one committee passing the buck to another.

The major achievement of the MDAP and the DFEC was to disparage the British Finance Minister Sir Stafford Cripps's demands for giving absolute priority to economic recovery by setting a financial ceiling for military planning. They agreed in principle that an effort to secure more funds for military purposes was necessary "without any implication that the Finance Ministers would be obligated to meet whatever figure might be supplied by the military planners."[3]

This caveat rendered meaningless any serious effort to fulfill MTDP goals. Just a few days earlier, the Dutch indicated that the new coordinated defense plan would cause serious problems in the Netherlands. Problems in Indonesia diverted so much of that nation's military budget that only U.S. additional aid would permit the Netherlands to contribute to the plan.[4]

Each of the European allies claimed cogent reasons for evading the requirements, sufficient for Field Marshal Montgomery, chairman of the Western Union's Commanders-in-Chief Committee, to blurt in his customary blunt fashion that the "defence of Europe was a façade." Actually his language was milder than usual as he blamed the problem on defects in the French military system in which "there was no strong, able and competent man in command of the French Army." His feud with de Lattre de Tassigny was obviously still alive as Ambassador Douglas noted in his letter to Acheson. It was also obvious that the allies were still caught up in the "vicious circle."[5]

In partial recognition of the problem of winning over Congress to military assistance in fiscal year 1951, John O. Bell, assistant director of MDAP, recalling that Congress had required a formal bilateral agreement from each country seeking military assistance, speculated about eliminating the need for these requests. He would allow more flexibility in providing equipment in the future. Flexibility was all the more important when the FMACC recognized that there was little use in discussing estimates of fiscal year 1951 AMP plans "in view of the apparent desires on the part of officials of the various governments to avoid any implications of commitments." Given this situation, the FMACC would have to make unilateral estimates for the

1951 program, risking "a very adverse reaction in Congress." But would Congress have reacted more favorably if the bilateral agreements were cancelled? The answer, as usual, was to establish another working group to study all aspects of the situation, including the reprogramming of unexpended AMP funds.[6]

To circumvent these obstacles the FMACC resorted to rationalizations, observing that the Defense Committee had set a goal in The Hague meetings "for development of physical means for defense and determining the base line (forces available on July 1, 1950) from which to progress toward the goal." The committee judged that the priorities outlined there were "sufficient for initial measures in increasing defensive capacity." As defense capacities increase, more definite priorities will be developed. On April 17 the Pentagon seemed satisfied that, as the Defense Committee put it, "a first approximation of the goals" had been established.[7]

The committee was even more extravagant in its estimation of progress when it presented NATO's accomplishments to the Bureau of the Budget at the end of the month. While still only "a first approximation" of an integrated defense program, the report recognized that rapid development of European military production projects should not have been expected. But the DFEC and MPSB had reviewed the fiscal year 1950 and fiscal year 1951 AMP programs and found that "the projects were soundly conceived, filled high priorities deficiencies and were within the realm of financial feasibility." No wonder that the FMACC evaluated these developments as a substantial accomplishment in the first six months of operations.[8]

The State Department's list of NATO achievements was more modest than the FMACC's. It looked upon the first approximation of the force estimate to support the strategic plan for NATO defense as "a start." It emphasized that further and more rapid progress was necessary, declaring that "it is of the utmost importance . . . that the cost of the plan be determined as soon as possible so that it can be intelligently considered within NATO and by the respective governments." This was not a resounding endorsement of MTDP's progress.[9]

The U.S. judgments about the state of the alliance were rarely in synch with those of its transatlantic partners. European plans for building their own defenses were predicated on how much assistance, as in the AMP, they would receive from the United States. The Americans, for their part, wanted only to cover dollar deficits that rearmament required, leaving the majority of the burden for Europeans to carry. NATO Europe hoped to have Uncle Sam make up its internal deficits, as well as assume the new costs stemming from implementation of the plan. On such matters as European integration, Britain remained apart from the continent; on the United States' demand to rearm Germany, the French remained unreconciled.[10]

There were contradictions within the American position rivaling the dissents among the European allies. How seriously did the U.S. NATO planners take their own statements about progress? Less than three weeks after celebrating the breaking of the "vicious circle," the State Department revived the term, and then concluded its report with familiar circular reasoning: "Progress in defense planning is handicapped by a kind of vicious circle in which the military and production side of the Treaty Organization calls for financial guidance in their planning, while the financial and economic side calls for equipment needs and the cost before determining financial and economic availabilities."[11]

Another report, prepared by JAMAG in response to a suggestion on April 21 by Ambassador Douglas to Gen. Thomas T. Handy, the senior U.S. military representative for MDAP in Europe, led to a compilation of information about the effectiveness of the armed forces of the major European allies. It was initially intended for Acheson's use at the May NAC meeting in London, and then expanded for congressional hearings on MDAP in early June. The results confirmed the pessimism connoted in the vicious circle syndrome. They undercut the rosy evaluations and optimistic expectations that both the State and Defense departments sent out in this period. The armed forces of Britain, France, Germany, and Italy were inspected, and none of them was judged to be in shape for successful resistance to a Soviet assault. The best case that could be made for each of the three countries was that MDAP would mitigate some of the deficiencies, although the study recognized that they "can only be partially rectified through the medium of MDAP." The restrained praise of the military leaders of the four countries for their support to NATO military planning and to MDAP itself was balanced by condemnation of their governments for their failure to give "necessary practical backing, especially in the financial field, to the implementation of plans developed by the NATO."[12]

If there should be doubts about the accuracy of the JAMAG's assessment, Lord Ismay dispelled them in the report of the first five years of NATO's history. The military situation in May 1950, according to his account, was bleak: "international tension all over the world had in no way relaxed and in Europe the military situation was fraught with danger. To the west of the Iron Curtain the members of the Atlantic alliance had about fourteen divisions on the Continent and less than 1,000 aircraft. These divisions were of varying quality both in training and in equipment and several were below strength. They were not controlled by any single authority and arrangements for their effective command in case of war would have had to be hastily improvised."[13] Since Ismay's pronouncements were written after the outbreak of the Korean War, it was a wake-up call that did not come until after the May meeting. Understandably, his description of the state of NATO's defenses was darker than those on the scene in the spring of 1950.

Transatlantic Gaps

Balanced Collective Forces vs. Balanced National Forces

The gulf between the transatlantic allies was broader and deeper than arguments over who would pay for the costs of rearmament. European uneasiness over key elements in the strategic concept was never far beneath the surface. It was expressed whenever the question of balanced forces came up. This was never an issue for the United States. It always meant balanced "collective" forces, whereby each member would assume for the common good those tasks it was best able to undertake. In this context Americans would assume responsibility for supplying strategic aircraft while Europeans would provide ground forces. While balanced collective forces were at the center of the alliance, they signified to Europeans unbalanced forces for their armies or navies. Smaller nations would be wholly dependent on NATO's collective power to come to their aid in the event of a crisis. Could they count on an instant response when Article 5, at U.S. insistence, offered no guarantee of immediate assistance?

The issue of balanced national forces versus balanced collective forces was a sore point with many of the allies, not least with the United States, but U.S. legislators as well as its military continued to complain about diversions from the integrated balanced collective ideal. As the chairman of the Senate Armed Services Committee observed at hearings on the extension of the MDAP in June 1950, "We had evidence today that Holland was embarking on an expansion of its navy, the old tradition when Holland was in naval command of the whole world, nearly, being revived, and it seems to me that they ought to be discouraged, because they can use those funds and resources much better in some other ways."[14]

While Americans tended to see Europe's parochial obsession with its national forces as a matter of national pride, NATO Europe saw it as vital to survival in the event of a crisis. When the United States introduced a resolution at the NATO Council meeting of May 16, Acheson was surprised to find objections to the recommendations urging members to "concentrate on creation [of] balanced collective forces rather than balanced national forces."[15] The subject certainly was not new. It was implicit in the strategic concept, and explicit in America's vision of a defensible Europe. The MDAP fundamentally was designed to help Europeans develop specialized strengths that would serve the common welfare of the alliance. But Norway's Lange wanted to omit any negative reference to balanced national forces from the resolution. The principle was sound, he agreed, but only if each country could be assured that balanced collective forces could defend it. In the case of vulnerable Norway, neighboring the USSR, Lange wanted a guarantee that surrendering part of its military would not leave the country unprotected.[16]

Norway was not alone in its discomfort. The Netherlands, always conscious of its navy, agreed with the principle of balanced collective force, but asked for consideration of particular situations. This theme resonated with the continental allies. France, as its foreign minister, Robert Schuman, claimed, supported the main aim, but observed that other members had commitments outside the NATO area. There was a psychological factor involved that led Italy's Carlo Sforza to favor Lange's and Schuman's positions. Bevin had no problem with the principle or even the language except that it was too brief to cover the needs of individual countries' peacetime needs. Belgium's Paul Van Zeeland thought that the clause containing balanced collective forces could be deleted without compromising the principle.[17]

Acheson's response was to assert that the resolution—and its language—went to the heart of NATO's problems. He felt that the issue was the most important before the council, and would not consent to abandoning the language. He won over his colleagues by admitting that there would be occasions when national forces would be needed to cope with particular situations. Nor did he intend to imply that national forces should be sacrificed if they were needed to deal with other parts of the world where members had commitments. These clarifications permitted Norway to approve the wording that Acheson felt was crucial to the welfare of the alliance. The issue evolved from a problem over principle to a matter of drafting acceptable language. The compromise, if it was that, did not affect the contrast between "collective" and "national" when the resolution appeared in the final communiqué. The resolution received a unanimous vote in the North Atlantic Council, although Acheson acknowledged in his memoir that it "was still a rather vague concept."[18] Only because it was vague, and hence innocuous, was there unanimity in the alliance.

Two weeks later Secretary Acheson took the opportunity given him at a special joint session of Congress to speak definitively about balanced collective forces. When he was asked what effect adding such potential new members as Turkey or Spain would have on achieving such a force, he responded that bringing new countries into the Atlantic community was a "wholly separate question" and went on to explain that "balanced collective forces means that each country does what it can do best, and that it does not duplicate what every other country is going to do, so you concentrate on the mission which is assigned to a particular country as part of the whole collective defense." The allies' willingness to accept the American position reflected the influence a superpower could exert. NATO's failure to achieve balanced collective forces in 1950 reflected the limits of a superpower's authority.[19]

The nub of the problem was the allies' unwillingness to do more than simulate acceptance of U.S. demands. Despite Acheson's apparent adamancy on the subject in his discussions with the allies, alternatives had long been suggested, notably the U.S. increasing its own forces and inclusion of German resources in the event the forces asked for did not materialize. But there was no rush to take up other alternatives; the sense of urgency was lacking in the spring of 1950.[20]

NATO and the WU

That an uneasy relationship between NATO and the WU would continue into 1950 was only to be expected. The Brussels Pact was a year older than NATO, and indeed was an important building block in the creation of the Atlantic alliance. The committee structure established under the Western Union was a model that NATO adopted with few changes. Ultimately the WU was subsumed under NATO. But the WU was exclusively a European organization, comprising the core members of NATO, and as such sought special treatment from the senior partner. Much of the activity of WUDO, the military arm of the Brussels Pact, was designed to impress its American counterpart, to demonstrate the European entity's entitlement to American military assistance.[21]

WU's survival after 1949 was due in part to its potential contributions to the defense of the West. Granted that it was a rump version of the alliance, largely dependent on the benevolence of the superpower, but its key members—Britain and France—were the major partners of the United States. As such, Britain in particular carried weight in NATO that it otherwise would not have enjoyed. It was understandable that the United States would count on the Western Union, as it developed after 1948, to be the kernel of a unified Europe that NATO was seeking. The WU in this context would be the advance agent in the defense of Western Europe. Given the productive experience of collaboration in World War II, Britain was expected to be the primary factor in meshing WU experience with NATO objectives.

But, as noted, the special relationship did not necessarily produce Anglo-American harmony. Whether the issues were Britain's sterling crisis or its reluctance to unite with the continent or its resentment over its junior status in the alliance, friction was always in the background of their relationship. France's grievances were sharper as it harbored lingering suspicions of an Anglo-American conspiracy to control the alliance at its expense. While France shared with Britain discomfort with America's superior role in NATO, its primary problem was disagreement with both Britain and the United States over Germany's future.

Arguably, France had more serious difficulties with its British partner in the Western Union than with the United States in NATO. Still nursing memories of Britain's abandonment in 1940, the French felt that Britain's presence in the continent was crucial to counter rising German influence. Their pique over the "special" relationship was genuine enough, but, as noted in Chapter 5, it was of less importance than Britain's unwillingness to accept a genuine union with the continent, the lynchpin of France's sense of security. The United States understood French concerns and tried with mixed success in 1950 to push Britain into the continent.

The pressure was always qualified because the American—and British—vision of the Atlantic community differed markedly from that of the French. As Kenneth Younger, Bevin's principal deputy, wrote in his diary, "We and the Americans want to start building up an Atlantic Community which includes but transcends Western Europe, while the French still hanker after a European solution in which the only American function is to produce military and other aid. The difference is important because it stems from two quite different concepts. Bevin has no faith in the solidity or efficiency of France or Belgium, and believes Western Europe will be a broken reed, and will not even attract the loyalty of European or impress the Russians, unless it is solidly linked to North America. I think this is realistic though depressing." Field Marshal Montgomery's feud with General de Lattre in WUDO seemed to support this depressing theme. His frequent tirades against France, emphasizing its military deficiencies, reflected contempt for the capabilities of all his continental allies.[22]

Younger may have been exaggerating what journalist Don Cook called "the Great Dichotomy of the North Atlantic Alliance."[23] France wanted far more than military aid from the United States. It wanted ties that could not be easily broken—with Britain as well as with America—solid links that would permit concessions to Germany otherwise impossible to make. In this context Britain's position in the continent was also the guarantee France needed to promote Franco-German harmony.

But as much as France needed Britain by its side, it did not want British domination of the Western Union. De Lattre sought a substantial British land force on the continent but not under the imperious Montgomery. The French preferred an executive board with leaders from the different member nations working in concert. The alternative would be a single supreme commander who inevitably would have to be an American. They took umbrage over the possibility that Britain would offer only air and naval units while the rest of Europe would provide infantry. This prospect, attributed to a casual remark by U.S. Gen. Lucius Clay, provoked French Minister of Defense René Pleven to say "if that should be United States official policy, I would not remain another instant as Defense Minister."[24]

Although the internal state of affairs within the WU appeared to be in disarray in May, Ambassador Douglas, in a conversation with Montgomery, judged that the five WU countries, all members of NATO, were much further advanced in defense planning than NATO itself, "that the WU countries had a more identical attitude toward the problems of the defence of Europe than some of the other members of NAT[O]." There was greater clarity in the Brussels Pact's Article IV, obligating each of them to go to war immediately if any one of them were attacked, than in the treaty's Article 5 where the obligation "is not so precisely or clearly defined." Moreover, the advances the WU had made in the development of infrastructure facilities, according to Douglas, represented an achievement that the United States could honor by committing U.S. funds to a common pool.[25] Perhaps Montgomery's complaint that the defense of the West, in the hands of the WU, was only on paper needed some revision.

By mid-June the WU powers appeared to have earned the confidence that Lewis Douglas had expressed in May. The WU was able to come up with £38 million for financing the infrastructure program, which would support such high-priority facilities as airfields, communications, and headquarters. At the May summit the financial assets available for infrastructure were estimated at only £20 million. In light of this genuine progress without MDAP aid, Douglas recommended encouraging WU members to solve their financing problems among themselves before relying on the MDAP. It was important, however, that WU plans all fit a NATO context and that MDAP aid would be given only to meet regional requirements.[26]

WU's progress in meeting the challenges of European defense, in the face of internal bickering, had been anticipated in the April meeting of WU's Consultative Council. The foreign ministers were expected to settle down to the main business of how the five powers would share the cost of joint defense arrangements. In the past year each of the five governments paid the costs of its own contingents, which the French felt tended to make the common defense effort more expensive for France than for its allies. According to *The Times* of London, the French would ask the WU to pool the total expenses and have the costs distributed in proportion to the financial resources of each member. Although the British claimed not to be opposed to the principle of pooling expenses, they would suggest that the fairest way would be simply to fix the percentages each country should bear. If a facility should be of particular advantage to the country in which it was located, the share of cost could be weighed according to the extent of the benefit the host country received.[27] What would be noteworthy about the forthcoming discussions in April was the willingness of the parties not only to move ahead, but to do so without the rancor displayed on too many occasions in the past.

In the long run, the Western Union should function in harmony with the larger and more powerful Atlantic alliance, which included all its members. In the short run, mutual suspicions too often surfaced to create transatlantic tensions. While it made sense for American officials at least to observe, if not participate in, the proceedings of WU's Consultative Council at its April meeting in Brussels, Bevin disagreed. He rejected Gladwyn Jebb's recommendation that Douglas be invited to meet with the council. Douglas wanted to make the point that the United States reminded the ministers to take no actions that would prejudice NATO decisions. He advised that should sensitive issues be raised, they should be postponed until they had been examined in the NATO context.[28]

Bevin's attitude unduly disturbed Douglas. The ambassador found a sympathetic response from René Massigli, France's ambassador to the United Kingdom, and particularly from Gladwyn Jebb, the British delegate on the Consultative Council. Massigli told Douglas that Bevin was no longer chairman of the Consultative Council and that his wishes were not necessarily those of the council.[29]

When the council met in informal session on April 17, Douglas was warmly welcomed by its chairman, Belgium's Van Zeeland. The U.S. ambassador won assurance that WU's actions would not reduce options available to NATO. Specifically, the council promised that WU's force objectives would be coordinated with those of NATO's Standing Group; that infrastructure projects would not be financed at the expense of AMP programs; and that there would be no recommendations for ceilings on defense projects.[30] Acheson hoped for a positive response from the council, but still instructed Douglas to oppose any action giving priority to the WU over NATO. The secretary of state was particularly concerned about the council recommending measures that went counter to NATO's core concept of balanced collective defense, a position fully shared by Douglas.[31] On the surface, the issue of both U.S. presence at important WU meetings and the substance of the council's decisions were in accord with NATO's (read the United States') interests, but implementation was another matter. The gap between balanced collective and national forces remained wide.[32]

Interaction between WU and NATO officials was limited. The United States may have won a seat at a WU table, but reciprocation was not accorded to WU's secretary-general in the following month. When he asked if he could be present as an observer at the forthcoming meeting of the North Atlantic Council, Bevin thought it might be useful because of the special relationship between the two organizations. It was not special enough. The State Department worried about setting a precedent for representatives of outsiders, especially the Regional Planning Groups, to attend meetings.[33]

After the WU's Consultative Council met on April 16, Douglas was not unhappy to report that the WU backed off from a recommendation to create new machinery for ensuring a close permanent liaison between the WU and NATO. This would be discussed at the May summit meeting. The WU agreed to let NATO's Standing Group be the medium to coordinate its target forces with NATO's as well as review WU's infrastructure projects. Douglas seemed relieved to postpone the roles of the two organizations until sometime in the future.[34]

In his long personal memorandum to Secretary Acheson on May 18, Ambassador Douglas recommended that it might be wise and appropriate to have unofficial American observers sitting at all levels of Western Union's committees. U.S. observers were already serving unofficially in some of the working groups, and Douglas himself earlier had sat with the Consultative Council, as noted, to consider questions of concern to the United States. Still, he was not certain that this procedure was adequate for the long run. Regularizing the arrangement might give rise to charges that the United States was being partial to the Western Union at the expense of NATO members outside the WU.[35] The connections between NATO and the WU remained unsettled in May 1950, even as U.S. officials recognized WU's contributions to the defense of Europe.

"The Atlantic High Council for Peace"

Implicit in the uneven connections between NATO and the WU was the need for some higher body or individual leader to integrate the many political and economic strands in the expanding Atlantic alliance. Actually, the term "integration," according to Paul-Henri Spaak, was "foreign to European usage." He preferred to consider it as the "organization" of Europe, a word less loaded with implications disturbing to the British, who had to be lured when not prodded into identification with the continent.[36] The semantic distinction did not stop Americans from urging their allies to integrate their resources. This, after all, was at the heart of balanced *collective* forces.

Generals Lemnitzer and Alfred Gruenther speculated in mid-March about the benefits of further integration of military forces in NATO. It would not only generate solidarity in the alliance, but could also be a vehicle to harness West Germany to NATO without increasing its capacity for aggressive behavior. Reluctantly they dismissed the prospect as feasible only under stress of war or as a by-product of substantial political federation. They wistfully hoped that in the near future a NATO command organization might be created to advance integration, but assumed that such a change would take place only in an emergency. In the meantime the "present clash of nationalities" made this an unlikely prospect.[37]

Actually, ideas of political and economic integration had been circulating among the French in this period, although not quite in the form the Americans preferred. The influential political commentator, Jean-Jacques Servan-Schreiber, had explicitly suggested a path to integration in his critical essay on the weaknesses of the Atlantic alliance, published on the first anniversary of the North Atlantic Treaty. As noted in Chapter 5, he had positive as well as negative observations. Dismissing neutralization as ultimately too dangerous, he felt that a Europe isolated from the United States would be even more vulnerable to Soviet intimidation than it was at present. What, then, was the direction he advocated for the West? Ideally, he hoped for a genuine Atlantic union comprised of the United States and Western Europe, with a single parliament and a single economy. He saw the American union as that ideal, but confessed it would be too difficult to adapt the American model to his larger vision. He proposed an alternative in the form of what he called an "Atlantic Cominform." The term evoked not only a Soviet-dominated Eastern Europe but also an organization that would carry the Atlantic Pact beyond its military ambitions to embrace a common polity and a common economy. Integration should apply not just to Western Europe but to the entire Atlantic world, including the United States. The OEEC, the Council of Europe, Western Union, and NATO existed with no hierarchical system to enable collective decisions. His "cominform" would replace the American-controlled Marshall Plan and create an entity to which each member would donate a percentage of its budgets.[38]

This version of a unified West was quickly taken up by Premier Georges Bidault under the name of the High Atlantic Council for Peace. He claimed that Servan-Schreiber had encouraged him to launch the proposal, although he sourly noted that the journalist subsequently turned against the idea when it failed.[39] Bidault, always quick to defend himself, had a mercurial personality with a distinguished record of public service. A hero of the French resistance in World War II, he was foreign minister from January 1947 to July 1948 and a key figure in the formation of the Dunkirk Treaty and the formation of the Brussels Pact. Along with Ernest Bevin, he had been instrumental in enticing the United States into the Atlantic alliance, though he was convinced that he did not receive enough credit for his achievements.[40] By October 1949 he was premier and head of the moderate Catholic party, Mouvement républicain populaire, where he was once again a major force in the Atlantic community.

At the moment his High Atlantic Council was just a title. The permanent committee, half European and half American and Canadian, was not clearly identified beyond his belief that it would not need a representative from each member nation. Although the ideas had been in circulation for some time in Washington and London, his foreign minister, Robert Schuman, had not been informed about the proposal until he returned from his vacation, and the U.S. ambassador to France suspected mixed motives on the premier's part. Bidault felt himself "the forgotten man" in the development of the Marshall Plan. The new plan would prop up his reputation with the French public and France would gain the prestige in the international scene it currently lacked. If, as Servan- Schreiber pointed out in Le Monde, the West needed a "third man" in the image of Churchill in 1949 and Marshall in 1947 to lead the way, that man could be Bidault.[41]

When Bidault delivered his speech at Lyon at the opening of the Thirty-second Lyon International Commercial Fair on April 16, the details of the plan were just as hazy as speculations about it had been. Bidault was conscious of the shortcomings of his proposal and made a point of explaining to Ambassador Bruce the reasons for his action. Recognizing that the unification of Europe was not feasible in the short term, he looked for a dramatic approach to spur the European allies to exert greater mutual efforts that would bring the United States into full partnership. He was convinced that only in this circumstance would the British wholeheartedly join.[42]

Bidault emphasized how important the British factor was for France: "France is in the difficult position of not being able to live with England or without her." And given how busy the European foreign ministers were running from conference to conference, they were too distracted to give the time needed to supervise the implementation of the programs NATO had launched. This was one of the reasons, he said, why he proposed the establishment of a small group of select men who would address themselves uninterruptedly to such questions. Furthermore, he assured Bruce that Foreign Minister Schuman was in complete agreement with him, and would draft a program to be delivered to Acheson as a basis for discussion when he visited London in preparation for May's summit. Bidault presented himself as a man with no pretensions who simply wished to move the alliance forward.[43]

Secretary of State Acheson obviously was anxious to find out just what Bidault wanted out of the "Atlantic High Council for Peace," and suggested that he would offer cautious sympathy for the idea when Bidault came to London. He mused that American participation might be a vehicle to bring Germany more intimately into the Atlantic community, but Acheson was basically doubtful about a new organization "merely for organization sake" when existing agencies were available to enlarge their functions. He saw the potential of Bidault's proposal capturing the imagination of the allies, but while he valued continuous high-level coordination among the major powers, he opposed bringing the smaller nations into anything comparable to the Standing Group. He wondered if Bidault had in mind a new organizational machinery or expansion of the functions of NAC. Behind these reservations lurked a suspicion that John Foster Dulles nurtured about the effect on West Germany. Dulles saw no prospect of France admitting Germany into whatever new configuration Bidault was seeking for the alliance.[44]

There were other suspicions as well that were rarely articulated in official correspondence. Was the idea of establishing new machinery for embracing political and economic collaboration a disguised move, as Norwegians feared, to gain more authority for the Big Three? Or was it another way of forcing America to share its wealth? France had been the most vocal critic of American bilateralism in its dealings with the allies. If NATO were genuinely on the road to integration, pooling the resources of all its members, most notably its American member, would resolve many of Europe's economic problems. Bidault, of course, did not emphasize this element in his High Council, but that would be a consequence of merging economic and financial with the political and military aspects of the alliance. This implication was clear to Clermont-Ferrand's *La Montagne* when it observed that Bidault's plan would make the American budget "a veritable Atlantic budget."[45]

It was left to Maurice Ferre, Washington correspondent of *Le Monde,* to make clear to his readers why the United States would not adopt the Bidault plan. He felt that the superpower "considers paradoxical that the old continent of Europe, while continuing to solicit financial and economic aid, should attempt to include the United States in a European organization that would superimpose itself on American sovereignty." Bruce granted that reactions to the proposal had been negative in the U.S. press, but felt that French doubts about its effectiveness might be a more basic reason for the lack of enthusiasm in Europe as well as in America.[46]

Certainly European leaders were not impressed with the Bidault plan. The Netherlands' Foreign Office dismissed it as "wishy-washy" and believed that the response to the problem lay in strengthening existing NATO organizations and creating a permanent full-time secretariat when the foreign ministers gathered in London in mid-May. When the U.S. ambassador in Oslo talked with members of the Storting, he found that Norway was already on record in support of increased authority for the North Atlantic Council and felt that there was no need to impose an additional political body on NATO's framework. They were inclined to view Bidault's High Council as a typical French bid for publicity as well as an attempt to steal the limelight from the British on the eve of the London meeting.[47]

Given the obvious benefits that France would enjoy from Bidault's plan, it is worth noting the Quai d'Orsay's reservations about his ideas. According to a Foreign Office source, the Cabinet had not cleared the speech and expected only generalities from the premier at the fair. If the source was accurate, Bidault's colleagues resented his unilateral behavior. Foreign Minister Robert Schuman felt that there were already enough planning bodies in NATO, and that what was needed was a person of high stature, assisted by a staff, to "ride herd on the various member countries with a view to seeing that agreed plans are implemented." Bidault had just this goal in mind, encased in an elaborate superstructure with himself as the person to do the riding.[48]

From the American perspective, Robert Schuman, an Alsatian raised in imperial Germany, was an easier person to work with than the prickly Bidault. Although a member of the Mouvement Républicain Populaire (MRP), like Bidault, his low-key aspirations for French rapprochement with Germany meshed with those of the United States. Ambassador Bruce recognized the delicacy of the situation, but did not touch on the political tensions that would topple Bidault's fragile coalition on June 24, 1950. Schuman, who survived the change of government, was a steadier manager of France's foreign affairs.[49]

President Auriol gave a personal as well as political tone to his distaste for Bidault's High Council. But it was not just an old Socialist berating the leader of a rival party and using any weapon at his disposal to denigrate the proposal. Auriol was incensed that a premier would intrude on the territory of the Foreign Office by launching a plan without appropriate authority. Bidault's mixing of economic, political, and military responsibilities of other European bodies, he felt, would mark the end of the Council of Europe, the end of the Brussels Pact, and even the end of the United Nations. He did not envision Europe winning equality with America. Rather, if the plan were implemented, it would make America the head of all of Europe, an unpalatable prospect for the French president.[50]

International Working Group, April–May 1950

Preparatory Talks: Article 2

As the date for the NAC meeting approached, it was clear that new mechanisms for coordinating the alliance would be discussed, even if they were not quite what Bidault had in mind. The foreign ministers of the United States, the United Kingdom, and France assembled in London before the council meetings after lower echelon preparatory talks, beginning on April 24, were completed. These were to deal in the first week with broad general subjects and in the second week with such specific subjects as Germany, Southeast Asia, and China. Acheson was scheduled to arrive in Paris on May 7 for talks with Schuman, and then on May 9 and 10 with Bevin. He would meet with both Schuman and Bevin on May 11. The council would convene on May 15–17 if all its members agreed.[51]

The thrust of NATO's activities in 1950 had been building the organization's defenses through coordination of the MPSB and DFEC, along with a recognition that a stronger central authority was needed to manage coordination of all the organization's activities. Yet these were not the primary focus of the International Working Group (IWG), chaired by the State Department's Edwin M. Martin, director of the Office of European Regional Affairs. Its draft agenda for NAC as of May 2 only alluded to "the possible creation of some additional central machinery" as a stepping-stone to more important issues, such as the expansion of Article 2 to promote closer economic collaboration among the allies and the promotion of public information activities, which would lead NATO publics to a better understanding of the alliance's missions. Special attention would be paid to the IWG's report on the establishment of an Ocean Shipping Planning Board. Reviews of the reports of the DFEC and Defense Committee were included, but only as a formality.[52]

It was understandable that Canadians would seize the opportunity of the forthcoming NAC meeting to focus again on their belief in the importance of Article 2, which Acheson had denigrated as unnecessary during treaty negotiations in 1949. This could be the time to use Article 2 to eliminate international economic conflicts. Shortly before the convening of the NAC in London, Canada's minister of external affairs, L. B. Pearson, appearing before the Rotary Club in Belleville, Ontario, on May 2, was quoted as saying, "I hope that at this meeting we shall do more than create a military alliance. I hope we shall begin a social and economic process that will produce a North Atlantic democratic union that will be above and beyond our sovereign states."[53]

American indifference notwithstanding, Canada won some European support for Article 2. The Norwegian Foreign Office, for example, saw it as an opportunity to develop the full possibilities of the Atlantic Pact. Emphasis on political and economic objectives of the alliance would remind the members—and its Communist adversaries—that NATO was more than a military organization. Expansion of Article 2 would be a unifying force in the Atlantic community. Inevitably, the U.S.'s role in this circumstance would be diminished, which would be a bonus to its supporters. The Italian government also expressed interest in immediately strengthening economic as well as political collaboration in NATO. While its foreign office had not yet formulated specific recommendations, it wanted to see a dramatic forward step toward broadening the scope of the alliance.[54]

If there was an implied rebuke of the senior partner in these commentaries, it was relatively mild. No dramatic steps were taken at the NAC sessions in May. Supporters of Article 2 could take limited satisfaction in noting that it was cited in the communiqué, but only as the fifth and last task of the council. It agreed to "consider what further action should be taken under Article 2 of the Treaty, taking into account the work of existing agencies in this field."[55]

Preparatory Talks: Ocean Shipping Planning Board

The prominence given to the proposed Ocean Shipping Planning Board in the sessions of the International Working Group—and later the ministerial meetings—was an example of misplaced priorities. The subject certainly was important enough for the allies to list it among matters to be concluded at the NAC meeting. A mechanism had to be put in place to coordinate the distribution of vital supplies from the United States to its allies. The U.S. Joint Chiefs of Staff recognized in February that the current plan of using U.S. ships exclusively for transporting MDAP end items would leave a shipping deficit in a future emergency.[56]

Membership of the board became a subject of controversy. The United States, joined by France, Italy, Belgium, and Canada, felt it appropriate that the planning board be situated in NATO. Britain, supported by the Scandinavian allies, the Netherlands, and Portugal, wanted the alliance to encourage participation by non-NATO maritime countries. It had in mind the sensitivities of the Commonwealth nations. The United States, however, felt that expansion would weaken the organization. The U.S. view prevailed.[57]

This did not end all controversy as the British contested the American preference for the Ocean Planning Group to be located in Washington for effective liaison with the Standing Group. The United States agreed to leave the decision to the board, without prejudice to its position, a concession to Britain's concern about its position as a maritime power. Presumably, British pride was assuaged when the United States recommended that the NAC approve holding the first board meeting in London.[58]

When NAC met on May 15 and 16, it included in the sixth and last paragraph of its communiqué the establishment of the North Atlantic Planning Board for Ocean Shipping without reference to non-NATO nations. Representatives of the participating nations would compose the board, which was charged with maintaining close collaboration with other NATO bodies involved with merchant shipping.[59] Granted that the subject once again raised differences between the United States and Britain, was it significant enough to occupy as much of the IWG's time as it did in the months preceding the NAC meeting?

Preparatory Talks: Spain, Turkey, Indochina

The three allies on the Standing Group were anxious to have their delegates introduce issues seemingly extraneous to the alliance and to Western Europe, but important to constituencies within their military communities. Spain was a prime example. The United States, or at least the Joint Chiefs of Staff, clearly indicated that Spain should be discussed in the May foreign ministers' meeting. They urged military cooperation with Franco's Spain either bilaterally or as a future member of NATO. If Secretary Acheson could not place Spain on the agenda, it should be considered in connection with the general subject of strengthening the North Atlantic area. The strategic interests of the United States—and NATO's as well—required a Spanish role if France and the Low Countries were to be protected against a Soviet attack. At stake were bases that Spain's geographic position on the Mediterranean could provide the alliance. The Joint Chiefs asked that some way be found to overcome the political objections of the United Kingdom and France.[60] Despite their passionate advocacy, Spain was not on the May agenda. Franco's fascist history remained the obstacle.

Even less likely a subject for serious study was Turkey's request to be a member of a regional pact connected with the alliance. Britain expressed interest as it had in the past in some sort of eastern Mediterranean defense arrangement that would include Egypt as well as Turkey. The subject might have surfaced in the May sessions given France's favorable reaction to the idea. But both the British and the French wilted in the face of U.S. opposition. Assistant Secretary George C. McGhee, of the State Department's Bureau of Near Eastern Affairs, recommended that if this matter were raised by the British or French, they should be informed that the United States was not in a position to consider any security pact in the Mediterranean or Near East at present. The U.S.'s position was sufficiently negative to remove the subject from further tripartite discussions.[61]

A more plausible addition for the May meeting was the linking of Indochina to NATO's concerns. The French delegation vigorously championed the connection and made it a subject of exhaustive bilateral and trilateral talks in the weeks leading up to the May summit. The views of the three powers were clearly set out and were clearly divergent. The one point of agreement, admittedly an important one, was that Communist penetration of Southeast Asia, and particularly Indochina, ultimately endangered the security of the United States as well as Britain and France. The British were sympathetic to stating publicly that the allies would oppose any attempts from within or without to overthrow the government of Indochina. No specific mention of Communism would be contained in the statement, as Bevin hoped for India and Pakistan to endorse the linkage. They were worried, however, about the appearance of colonial powers ganging up in support of the French position.[62]

To win over the allies, France sought to have them look at Southeast Asia as a whole. While claiming that Indochina's situation was critical, its problems differed more in degree than in kind from other Southeast Asian countries. By expressing solidarity with the French in Indochina and the British in Singapore, the allies would strengthen resistance of the entire area to Communism. Such a tripartite statement, however, would take too much time since Britain would have to clear it with Commonwealth governments. The United States, for its part, was willing to announce that MDAP funds had been made available to help equip the armies of the French Union, and cautiously suggested that it would recommend that MDAP funds already appropriated be made available for continuing aid to these forces. Ambassador at Large Philip C. Jessup, head of the U.S. delegation in London, thought that a special presidential statement prior to the tripartite meeting in London might also be useful in bucking up French morale.[63]

Massigli, speaking for France at the tripartite subcommittee on Southeast Asia, sounded an alarm on May 4. The U.S. position was unacceptable to France. The amount of aid projected was grossly inadequate to maintain French and British forces in the area. Consequently, Massigli was instructed to dissociate himself from any joint document drafted in the preparatory talks. When Jessup pleaded with him to accept a statement on points of common agreement, Massigli refused, claiming that he had to wait until Schuman had taken up the matter with Acheson and Bevin in London.[64]

It was obvious that the French were trying to turn over the responsibility for Indochina's defense to the American partner. The United States refused. Granting that the security of Southeast Asia was of strategic importance to the United States, its delegates at every level of the talks felt that the French and British had primary responsibilities in the area. The U.S. function would be to defend Southeast Asia by diplomatic action against further Communist encroachment, and to grant military aid to that end, but no more. Jessup recognized that "certain French government circles" would "have us accept [the] principle of financial responsibility for Indochina war," as observed in inspired press stories coming out of France. He pointed out to Schuman that there had been no change in U.S. policy in Indochina since November 1949, and the limits of U.S. involvement had been constantly reiterated since then. Acheson made it clear to the French foreign minister that the United States felt that all it could do was add to, but not substitute for, France's efforts.[65] The NAC communiqué of May 18 made no reference to discussions about Southeast Asia, let alone any decisions on the subject.

Preparatory Talks: Germany

The future of the Federal Republic's relations with NATO, however, should have been a centerpiece in the preliminary tripartite talks in April and in the full NAC meetings in May. Germany was uppermost in the minds of French officials, and not far behind in those of American officials. Trouble developed, as it had since the end of World War II, over France's overriding conviction that while Germany's resources should be harnessed by the allies, it should not be in a position to develop a centralized nation-state with an economy and polity that could pose a potential threat to the security of Europe. French public and official opinion would identify the German menace equal to that of the Soviet. By contrast, while the United States would understand and even share, to a lesser degree, France's concerns about a resurgent Germany, its leaders increasingly made German manpower as well as economic resources a vital factor in deterring Soviet aggression. The perceived need for German resources explained the United States' pressure for concessions to German sovereignty, which France vigorously resisted. Britain's reluctance to commit itself fully to the continent stiffened France's opposition to any form of German rearmament. Only if Britain became a full partner of France on the continent would that country feel secure enough to yield to U.S. pressures.

As early as April 6, Ambassador Franks emphasized that Britain associated itself with the Europeans in excluding Germany from the agenda of the London meetings. No solution to a German role in an integrated defense would be possible unless the overall economic problem, particularly the dollar-gap situation, was resolved. Franks had in mind competition with German manufactures as well as U.S. tariff policies. These concerns did not preclude examining the possibilities of utilizing German industrial production in the service of the MTDP, considering that present production in western Germany was 98 percent of 1936 levels. As far as a future German relationship with the treaty was concerned, Britain wanted to exclude any reference to that possibility until Germany joined the Council of Europe.[66]

Once the IWG's sessions began, Acheson weighed in with the observation that the present Occupation Statute was inherently unstable. To move ahead, the United States wanted a continuing German contribution to Western defense in the form of items other than implements of war. For the United States' part, he said, over the next two years the allies should progressively remove all controls except those relating to basic security requirements, the right to maintain troops in western Germany, and the right (if necessary) to assume supreme authority. These changes not only would give Germans a sense of participating in cooperative efforts to strengthen the West economically and defensively, but also encourage the French to adopt a constructive instead of a restrictive approach to German problems. The inflammatory question of German rearmament circulating in Washington did not appear in the cable. Nor did the slightly less flammable subject of France's fifty-year lease on the Saar's coal mines.[67]

The first round of bilateral talks on Germany on May 4 touched gingerly upon issues sensitive to France. The British and Americans deferred to the French preference to wait until the Occupation Statute was reviewed before relaxing eco-

nomic restrictions. Some of the Franco-American tensions were lowered by the
American assertion that—persistent rumors notwithstanding—rearming Germany was not part of U.S. policy.[68]

Although the three allies could present a united front on maintaining the West's
position in Berlin, differences between British and American as well as British and
French approaches to Germany made for considerable U.S. discomfort. The British seemed ready to restore German control of foreign affairs, but were not ready
to release controls on foreign trade. They envisioned Germany as a full member
of NATO within two years, giving Adenauer a police force that would become the
core of future German armed forces. It disturbed Henry A. Byroade, director of
the State Department's Bureau of German Affairs, that relaxing controls without
asking for greater commitments would tie Germany financially and economically
to Britain. American cautions about proceeding too rapidly were not shared in
Britain. As for the negative impact on France, Sir Ivone Kirkpartrick was quoted as
saying that France was "no damn good" and indicated that Germany would make
a better partner.[69]

Displays of temper did not characterize recommendations made to the foreign
ministers in the tripartite foreign ministers' meetings on May 11 and 12. Southeast
Asia and Germany were extensively discussed, and then were essentially pushed
aside. The tripartite discussions of May 9–11 on Germany centered on the U.S.
support of "progressive restoration of control to Germany over its own affairs and
rights of an independent state," but avoided any mention of a military role that
the Joint Chiefs advocated. The officials came up with innocuous conclusions that
included support for German membership in the Council of Europe and a long-
range program for relaxation of controls. The use of the adjective "progressive"
was ambiguous enough to be acceptable to all the allies. The occupation regime
would remain in place, and no plans were made for a separate peace treaty with
the Federal Republic.[70]

The Schuman Plan

Even if a consensus could have been reached on the totality of the German relationship to NATO, which might merit a celebration in the communiqué, the surprising
intrusion of France's Schuman Plan would have short-circuited the process. As the
foreign ministers were preparing to travel to London, René Massigli announced
on May 9, the second day of Acheson's bilateral talks with Bevin, that the French
government had proposed joint utilization of the coal and steel resources of France
and Germany. The new organization under this plan would be "open to all countries that wish to participate in it."[71] With a stroke of a pen the prospect of pooling
the mineral resources of two old adversaries upended the cautious recommendations emanating from ministerial conversations in Paris and London. Tying the

heavy industries of France and West Germany together appeared to be a means of making future wars between the two countries impossible.

Such was the aspiration of the French economist Jean Monnet, who inspired the program that Foreign Minister Robert Schuman refined under his own name. While the plan took Acheson unawares, he knew of it before it was unveiled in London. Stopping in Paris en route to London, Schuman disclosed the plan to the secretary of state, asking him to keep it secret until his Cabinet was informed. This meant that the Schuman Plan was sprung on Bevin without advance warning, chilling Anglo-American relations for the moment as the British foreign secretary speculated about a Franco-American plot to exclude Britain from a grand design. Bevin, recovering from a serious operation, was understandably out of sorts. He accused Acheson of going to Paris to put the finishing touches on the plan while he was kept in the dark.[72]

In fact, the secretary of state was embarrassed by his promise to keep silent. He was also suspicious. Was this, as he asked in the Princeton sessions in 1953, "the damnedest cartel I had ever heard in my life?" Or was this proposal of a rapproche-ment between France and Germany a giant step toward the economic integration of Europe? Acheson chose to take the positive view offered in the French govern-ment's announcement that the plan was "a first step in the federation of Europe, and will change the destinies of those regions which have long been devoted to the manufacture of munitions of war, of which they have been the most constant victims." Dulles was even more supportive, pointing out to the secretary that "the proposal is along lines which Secretary Marshall and I thought about in Moscow in 1947 but which we did not believe the French would ever accept."[73]

Bevin was always suspicious of France's intentions, and certainly shied away from the word "federation," but Britain reluctantly accepted the coal and steel community while refusing to join it. The United States was prepared to see in the Schuman Plan a fulfillment of its own hopes for European unity and to effect this incrementally rather than through an overarching grand scheme. Monnet himself underscored this point by contrasting his plan with the grandiosity of Bidault's Atlantic High Council.[74]

Foreign Minister Schuman, never known for his eloquence, nonetheless im-pressed his colleagues at the tripartite foreign ministers' meeting on May 12 with his observation that while the plan on its surface appeared to be essentially eco-nomic, its purpose was more political than economic. This emphasis diverted attention from those critics who saw a special French advantage in their access to German steel. Adenauer responded favorably, noting that with the pooling of Saar coal, one cause of Franco-German tension would be removed.[75]

Acceptance of the Schuman Plan was followed by German acceptance of the invitation to join the Council of Europe. Both fitted Adenauer's conviction that the plan and the Council of Europe were part of a growing cooperation of Europe on a federative basis. Although Britain remained cool to the plan, the other members of the Western Union rallied around the program. But in light of the Schuman Plan's impact on Anglo-French relations and momentarily on Anglo-American relations, its absence from the final NAC communiqué was inevitable.

The Medium-Term Defense Plan in May 1950

Vital as Germany was to the future of Western defense, it was set aside by the foreign ministers. As the communiqué indicated, implementation of the Medium-Term Defense Plan (MTDP) and establishment of some kind of permanent political body within NATO were the key elements in the NAC deliberations in London. These seemingly were the most manageable, if not the most significant, problems that the allies could settle in the spring of 1950.

Given what had been accomplished since the fall of 1949, time should have been on NATO's side in pursuing the medium-term defense goals. The U.S. ambassadors' meeting in Rome in March thought it would be highly useful if the U.S. study of MTDP requirements could come up with a total bill before NATO completed its report on this subject to the DFEC. But it did not seem to bother the ambassadors that it may take a minimum of three or four months for NATO to come up with that bill. There was no sense of urgency in official communications of the ECC in London in this period.[76]

This was evident in the inability of the U.S. representatives on the Standing Group to help the MPSB and DFEC achieve rapid refinement of the MDTP. The best that could be hoped for would be sufficient information by the fall of 1950 to move ahead with the Standing Group's program. Certainly in the spring of 1950, none of the committees was prepared to take any action. Consequently, General Bradley recommended that the State Department hold a conference "to determine if the North Atlantic Treaty plans are likely to be a suitable basis for arriving at long range United States policy and budgetary decisions." This JCS memo indicated low expectations for the results of the NAC summit in London. It indicated, too, that there was no immediate need for meeting the MTDP requirements.[77]

The U.S. Defense Department had already signaled its understanding that a downward revision of the first approximation of force requirements for the MTDP would require a serious revision of the DFEC's estimate of defense costs. The JCS in effect conceded that the allies would be unable to meet the requirements projected at The Hague in March. In this context Secretary Johnson warned Acheson to be wary of any commitment in London that would raise undue expectations. As for the question of a new body within the organization, the Joint Chiefs refrained from any judgment until they had more complete information on its composition, organizational structure, and functions.[78]

Implicit in the U.S. judgments about the state of the MDTP was the familiar criticism of the European allies' foot-dragging on their contributions to Western defense. Both the State and Defense departments agreed to hold off on further commitments to the allies until they demonstrated that they "have done their utmost" to energize self-help and mutual aid among themselves. "It would be unrealistic," Acting Secretary of State Webb asserted, "particularly from the point of view of Congress and our military establishment to call for such US commitment (as might seem implied) before our NATO partners have done their part."[79]

Once again the United States called on its allies to show concrete evidence of movement toward a balanced collective force. The phrase "balanced collective," along with "integrated," served as slogans regularly invoked in America's dealings with its European partners. Balanced collective force was at the heart of the resolution the United States proposed to the North Atlantic Council at its May meeting, but caveats recognizing that economic recovery was the best defense against the Communist threat usually accompanied the warnings. They clouded the clarity of the statement Acheson made on May 8 that "the ability to raise additional military expenditures must be judged not only in the light of economic and financial conditions but equally in light of the needs for Defense." Europeans would pay more attention to the caveats than to the warnings.[80]

The substance of the bipartite and tripartite talks among the senior officials of the American, British, and French foreign ministries essentially avoided specific ways to advance the MDTP largely because they were not going to be provided in the immediate future. Not that the core problem of costing the defense programs was absent from the working groups' discussions. But fear of excessive burdens on the economies of the allies inhibited the United States from pushing them too hard, even as it sought to shift the weight of at least some of the defense expenditures onto the shoulders of the allies. Ambassador at Large Philip C. Jessup, head of the U.S. delegation in London, did consider a way out of the dilemma by suggesting that the communiqué note the United States' willingness to share technical and scientific developments within a new organization that would encourage increasing European military budgets without jeopardizing the health of their economies. But this was only a thought negated by recognition that "certain fields would obviously be excluded." The fields, of course, dealt with atomic matters, excluded by Congress from any sharing with the partners. But any public statement promoting such an organization "would seem to indicate all too clearly that we have not been cooperating in this field."[81]

It was then that drafts of U.S. resolutions giving the NAC's stamp of approval to a DFEC request for a detailed estimate of finances laying out priorities were too controversial to appear in the final communiqué. A French draft recommended that the cost of increasing production of materiel and equipment "should be equitably distributed between the different participating programs."[82] Trying to define "equitably" alone was enough to remove the wording and the issue from the table.

Fourth Session of the North Atlantic Council: May 15–18, 1950

At the conclusion of their London session, the ministers addressed what Lord Ismay subsequently regarded as a substantial achievement: namely, "that the problem of adequate military forces and the necessary financial costs *should be examined as one, and not as separate problems.*" That he italicized what should have been obvious showed how limited NATO's aspirations were. The most that NAC could do was to urge "their governments to concentrate on the creation of balanced collective forces in the progressive build-up of their defence of the North Atlantic area, taking at the same time fully into consideration the requirements for national forces which arise out of commitments external to the North Atlantic area." In effect, the second half of that sentence nullified the recommendation of the first.[83]

There was no alternative to waffling. As the Norwegian ambassador made clear to Acting Secretary Webb shortly after the conference ended, Norway's geographic connection to the Soviet Union required a "balanced national force." Norway feared that U.S. constitutional requirements in the event of a Soviet attack "might delay a declaration of war and precious hours [would] be lost." Webb conceded that the achievement of balanced collective forces had an "evolutionary implication." The United States also tacitly accepted the ritual professions of solidarity on the part of the smaller members of NATO as their foreign ministers used the occasion of the summit to expound their special interests. Italy spoke on delicate Yugoslav relations with NATO, Portugal on the inclusion of Spain in NATO, and Canada on the expansion of Article 2.[84]

What was left for the ministers to address was the issue of a central command to coordinate and direct the course of the alliance. It was a major preoccupation in the IWG preceding the summit. Bidault's proposal for a High Council provided the framework for discussion that resulted in the NAC's one notable decision, namely: the creation of a Deputies Council. The French took a distinct position on the central machinery, which was not fully shared by their allies. They favored the establishment of a high-level permanent group to coordinate financial and military problems between meetings of the council. The group should have a fixed location and be composed of ambassadors stationed in that country. It should be prepared to meet at any time, in continuous session if necessary. Moreover, they insisted on a strong figure as secretary-general, along the lines of the Bidault proposal. British delegates resisted the idea of a powerful secretary-general, suggesting instead an interim council with deputy foreign ministers in permanent session. They felt that the volume of work would be too great to be handled by ambassadors. They also worried about excessive power in the hands of an executive outside their control. The U.S. delegate on the IWG shared these concerns, but agreed that the need for some central machinery to ensure consideration of interrelated questions that had tended to fall between too many stools trumped dangers of its encroachment on the authority of existing bodies. But he doubted if a full-time representative was necessary.[85]

It was apparent that all the allies were convinced that some central machinery was essential. They could also assent to the Canadian observation that its specific functions must be carefully discussed by the council before an organization was put in place. Where consensus failed was in the assignment of powers to the new post. It initially fell apart over the French preference for a strong secretary-general and the British distaste for a strong executive. One compromise was a concept of a weaker executive committee, made all the weaker by the elimination of "executive" from the draft of the text at Britain's initiative.[86]

U.S. ambivalence contributed to the stalemate. On the one hand, the State Department had long favored the prospect of deputies acting in place of the ambassadors. On the other hand, the United States was uncomfortable with officials of lower rank than ministers acting in their name. They might cheapen the prestige and influence of the council. There remained too many areas needing clarification, such as uncertainty about the authority that a new permanent commission would have to issue formal directives to the Defense Committee. Might it even exercise the right under Article 9 of the treaty to establish subsidiary bodies on its own?[87]

The Joint Chiefs added their own reservations, asking for more detailed information about how the new body would function, and ultimately deciding that the military implications of a Deputies Council made it "most unwise to enter hastily into specific details as to what new central machinery shall accomplish." They feared the possibility of the Deputies Council giving the civilian side of NATO undue control over military matters. In the meantime, they determined that the French resolution on behalf of a strong executive was unacceptable in any form.[88]

The State Department's position was closer to the British than to the French on the powers of a new coordinating body. There would be no secretary-general or secretariat and no new commission. Each member nation would appoint a deputy to its representative on the council to act with full authority at council meetings when the foreign minister was not present. The strengthened council would establish "the necessary organization responsible for coordinating activities of the alliance, including all the committees that has been established since the fall of 1949."[89] But when the twelve nations met on May 14, their communiqué omitted any reference to a new organization. The Deputies Council would study, recommend, and exchange views on relationships among the agencies and support plans for defense of the North Atlantic area. NAC judged that the combined resources of the member nations, "if properly coordinated and applied," were sufficient "to ensure progressive and speedy development of adequate military defence without impairing the social and economic progress of these countries."[90] In brief, the council produced a toothless rendition of both the ambitious agenda of the Bidault proposal and the scaled-back French version presented in the preparatory sessions.

Assessments of the London Meeting

What took much of their time in the tripartite sessions were efforts to resolve differences between the American, the British, and the French positions on NATO objectives with respect to the military buildup. They had difficulty, too, with NATO's posture toward the Soviet adversary. While there were no major differences in substance, Massigli, speaking for France, regarded the American position as too much of a crusade, even a "declaration of cold war," while Philip Jessup, for the United States, contended that the American position was a "declaration of hot peace." Whether this was a distinction without a difference was a matter of tone, but it touched the essence of the mindsets of Americans and Europeans. The latter perceived the United States as too aggressive, pushing NATO into war, while Americans regarded Europeans as too passive, too ready to concede ground to the Soviet adversary.[91]

Debate over the language of the resolutions to be issued in London was a subject of intense debate, arguably to the exclusion of other more vital issues. The United States felt that the British and French drafts were too wordy and repetitive to create the desired impact on public opinion. Both sides were anxious to recapture the psychological initiative in the Cold War from the Soviet peace offensive, but were always wary of going out on a limb. While there was an uneasy consensus in the bilateral talks about the unlikelihood of the Soviets launching a war in the next few years, there was enough uncertainty to undermine predictions. The issues of disarmament and Soviet nuclear advances were not addressed. Resolutions on sensitive areas of Southeast Asia and, in particular, Germany, were avoided. The result inevitably was a blend of drafts that ensured blandness. The single achievement hailed by the allies—the creation of a Deputies Council—was so watered down that it was unlikely to be an effective agent of NAC.[92]

Two weeks after the London meetings adjourned, the State Department's Division of European affairs summarized the contents of the communiqué, identifying the establishment of the Deputies Council as the chief achievement. The council should also be commended for addressing the problem of adequate military forces and the necessary financial costs to pay for them as a single problem, not separate ones. American interests were expressed by the mention of balanced collective forces in the communiqué, even though it had to be coupled with an understanding that requirements for national forces arising from commitments outside the North Atlantic area had to be taken fully into consideration.[93] In reality, the fourth session of the North Atlantic Council evaded the most difficult issues facing the alliance. Those they did deal with were either relatively marginal to the future of NATO or were so stripped of content as to be meaningless.

Yet NATO felt it had reason to be satisfied with the results of its London meeting. *New York Times* columnist Harold Callender reported that the summit conference set up a new sense of unity in which the United States solidly integrated itself with Western Europe. He marveled that "the mere agreement on the machinery for creating such unity in the use of resources for a common end is something that sovereign nations, including the United States, would have found fantastic just a few years ago." Dean Acheson and Averell Harriman, though less effusive, shared some of this elation. Harriman claimed some years later that the meeting laid the foundation for putting the O in NATO. Acheson, in retrospect, thought that "perhaps what we all felt at London was something more basic—an act of will, a decision to do something. We had planned and adopted resolutions long enough. Even though the most modest plans seemed hopeless of achievement, the time had come to start trying. At London we fashioned the first crude tools."[94]

7

The Shock of June 25, 1950

NATO after the May Meeting

NATO leaders did not anticipate the outbreak of the Korean War little more than five weeks after the London meeting adjourned, even though evidence of potential conflict could have been detected if they had been on NATO's radar. Asian issues occasionally surfaced in NATO deliberations in early 1950, but they seemed only peripherally related to the European arena. That war on the rim of East Asia would have a major impact on NATO's development was not an issue that seemed relevant to the allies. In this context they could proceed along the relatively relaxed lines outlined in London.

The Amended Mutual Defense Assistance Act of 1949

Little change followed from the summit meeting in London. The glacial movement of the alliance toward a more efficient and more effective organization was accepted without argument. Certainly extending the MDAP for another year was not considered a problem in early June. Its extension was never in question, even as its purposes were debated in congressional committees. And it was a low-key operation compared with the passions raised less than a year before when it required news of a Soviet atom bomb to move Congress to action.

President Truman recommended the authorization of additional funds as an amendment to the Mutual Defense Assistance Act of 1949 on June 1, and hearings before the joint Senate Committees on Foreign Relations and Armed Services were held on June 2, 4, 6, and 15. After joint executive sessions, a bill was reported out on June 21, incorporating the recommendations of the two committees.[1]

The billion-dollar figure for NATO did not faze the committee members. Some differences within the administration and Congress did arise at the hearing on June 5, but not over the amount. Acheson was convinced that the annual cost of military aid would have to rise beyond the additional aid for 1950. He felt "that we are a long way from having an adequate security force for the North Atlantic."

Johnson disagreed. When asked if there would be annual requests for aid, he assured the senator that after 1952, the request would not exceed the amount the administration was then asking, and it would decrease in the future.[2]

Paul Hoffman, as administrator of the ECA, was understandably upset by Senator Lodge's proposal to take ECA monies to help pay for arming Europe. It was a minor flurry; the senator backed off within a week. Hoffman claimed to fear that the Soviets would use the insertion of funds programmed for economic recovery as proof of NATO's aggressive designs.[3]

The risk of Europeans using U.S. funds and equipment to compete with American manufactures provoked discussion at the hearings. General Bradley encountered resistance to the administration's plans to help Europeans start their own industries, which would relieve the United States of the need to provide end products to them. To advance this project, Bradley would liberalize the aid program by substituting the term "production tools" in place of the more restrictive "machine tools." The senators recognized the benefits to be gained from encouraging Europeans to make weapons themselves and so decrease the size of appropriations the United States would have to make in the future, and yet they wanted to ensure that no money would be used to build new factories. While Chairman Tom Connally agreed to some liberalization of the definition of machine tools, he and the committee would keep the term intact.[4]

The deliberations accompanying the extension of the MDAP were exactly that—deliberate. There was no need to hurry. Even as Acheson informed Congress that NATO's military buildup was insufficient to meet an immediate Soviet challenge, he was as willing as Johnson to see a crisis in the future, not in the present, although his future was longer than that of the secretary of defense. Reviving NSC 68 was not on either of their horizons.

Deputies Council

Granted that the most visible indications of the *O* in NATO after Korea was the creation of new and permanent organs of the alliance, the psychological preparation for drastic changes had long been in evidence. The Deputies Council itself was essentially a substitute at the lowest possible denominator for recommendations that surfaced in the first six months of 1950. It was the result of compromise among the many NATO constituencies, a compromise that elicited little enthusiasm in the wake of the May meeting in London.

The Deputies Council got off to a slow start for some obvious reasons. Prominent among them was the question of relations between this new office and the array of committees in the NATO firmament as well as those in the U.S. State Department's hierarchy. Within the State Department, a staff member of the United Nations office felt that the relation of the deputy to chiefs of diplomatic missions were not clear, and suggested that the deputy conduct operations with the member nations' foreign offices through chiefs of missions, with Douglas in London as "Deputy to the Deputy." Other ideas were floated, creating a second deputy to the deputy in the United States, possibly at Cabinet level. Even more ambitious would be an additional undersecretary of state for military affairs.[5]

Perkins, the assistant secretary of state for European affairs, and Webb, acting secretary of state, seemed agreeable to a relationship between the deputy and Douglas similar to Harriman's with Bruce in Paris. Diplomatic contacts with foreign offices would be handled through chiefs of mission, with Douglas "designated as Deputy to the Deputy." But the secretary of state followed Perkins's advice that no mention of this idea be made at the time. The State Department was able to keep the Defense Department from having a military adviser assigned to the U.S. deputy. The Pentagon wanted assurance that military planning would not be under civilian control. "We threw [a] big bucket of cold water on the idea," according to Acheson's assistant, Lucius Battle. JAMAG should be sufficient to defend the military's interests.[6] It was obvious that there was considerable uncertainty in the United States about the role of the new deputy.

The Europeans added to the confusion. Britain weighed in with the idea of a "provisional" appointment until a decision on a candidate had been made. Canada opposed this arrangement since it would leave the impression that NATO was in no hurry to appoint deputies. Delays over the American choice distressed some allies. Canada, Belgium, and Italy all refused to name their choices until the United States had made its decision.[7]

Europeans assumed that the chairman would be an American, an assumption unquestioned by the U.S. State Department, and that the person designated would be a figure of prominence. They were mistaken. Not until two days before war erupted was the American choice made official, and even then the American deputy, Charles M. Spofford, a New York lawyer, was in no rush to take up his assignment; he had to clean up affairs before leaving for London, notably raising funds for the Metropolitan Opera. He was scheduled to arrive in Washington on July 5 for a briefing. He would not meet with the other deputies until July 31. It was not surprising that the allies were pressing for a provisional appointee until the deputy was in place.[8]

What the allies wanted was "a high level man of high competence," as Assistant Secretary of State Perkins assured British minister Derek Hoyer Millar, and that this was the U.S. objective. Former Undersecretary of State Robert A. Lovett would have been an ideal candidate had his health permitted. Equally important from the allies' perspective was quick action. When the choice was finally announced, the Dutch were disappointed that Spofford was a comparatively unknown New York businessman, and consequently the deputy position would suffer from a loss of status. Acheson was needed to mount a spirited defense of Spofford: "I don't know of anyone who could do the job better than he can do it and of very few who could do it as well."[9]

In his absence at the first meeting of the Deputies Council—ironically, on June 25, 1950—Spofford was unanimously elected as permanent chairman of the council. At its second meeting, held on June 26, the ministers acknowledged that North Korean aggression "illustrated clearly how urgent and important is the work of this Council."[10] What it was prepared to do in aid of the United States was not at all clear. Certainly, the State Department's unhurried pace in selecting a U.S. deputy, and then dispatching him to London only after he had tidied up his many obligations at home, seemed to confirm the judgment that no meaningful organization existed before June 25.

But NATO's rapid transformation in the last six months of that year was not a product of spontaneous combustion. Appointment of a coordinator to pull together the many committees the council had established was a frequent subject of discussion prior to the May summit meeting. Bidault's High Council for Peace may not have been a solution the allies would accept in the spring of 1950, but it spawned serious discussions about a central authority, even a central command, that NATO needed to pursue—that American goal of balanced collective forces.

While no figure lobbied for the post of coordinator with the exception of Bidault, who saw himself as the appropriate candidate for the leader of his High Council for Peace, names were bandied about informally in all the NATO circles. That General Eisenhower would become the Supreme Allied commander by the end of the year would have seemed logical to the diplomats in London in May. Nor would Lord Ismay's selection as secretary-general seem out of order as civilian coordinator of the organization after the Lisbon NAC meeting in February 1952. Ismay had been Churchill's chief of staff in World War II. None of these names, however, appeared in the May communiqué following the London meetings. Only the creation of the Deputies Council passed for a major reorganization of the alliance. But these possibilities were in NATO minds, ready to be put into place if a crisis demanded them.

The apparent dissolution of the Brussels Pact as it faded into the body of a revitalized NATO in the wake of the war seemed to be a fitting termination of the Western Union. It was designed, after all, to lure the United States into an entangling alliance, and it had succeeded in that purpose. There was no longer any need for the continuing existence of the Brussels Pact. Its major components—financial, economic, and military supply committees—had been adopted by NATO in its first year, and the infrastructure program it had initiated played an important part as NATO's integration progressed after June 25, 1950. Actually, the WU did not dissolve; it survived as a relic, to be revived when it suited NATO's purposes in the next generation.

The German Question

No issue roiled emotions more within the NATO community than the question of Germany's relations with the West. World War II had happened only five years before the Korean War, and the wounds from that conflict were still too raw to be settled in the way the senior ally wanted. France was the primary figure in limiting as much as it could the Federal Republic's revival as the major actor in Western Europe. Its opposition in the broadest sense was over the establishment of a strong central government. More than any of the allies, France was responsible for the federal character of West Germany, keeping power in the hands of the individual *Laender*. More narrowly, it sought to prevent Germany from resuming control of the Ruhr Valley, the source of German industrial strength. Even more important was a continuing and apparently successful effort to separate the coal-rich Saar from Germany. Memories of three invasions governed their actions, and fear of a revived Germany, bent on revenge, kept French emotions at a high level.

The United States lacked the visceral distrust of German intentions, even as the American high commissioners shared French concerns over a revival of Nazism and economic overtures to the Soviet bloc. But the American eye pragmatically was on the service the Germans could provide the Atlantic alliance. U.S. spokesmen consistently dwelled on the resources, including military, that Germany could bring to the alliance. The U.S. military were the most ardent supporters within the Truman administration of rearming West Germany to benefit the common cause. The Americans welcomed steps that would hasten the process of returning Germany to the West, and their backing of German membership in the Council of Europe was an earnest sign of their aspirations.

But Acheson recognized that important as it was to bring West Germany into the West as quickly as possible, it would take time to work out the many problems associated with the process. Even as he appreciated the value of using West Germany's industrial capacity to remedy deficiencies in NATO Europe, he advised "the greatest discretion before getting too involved" in the political and financial problems associated with this project. He would not expect any action for several months. No sense of urgency was to be found in Acheson's communications before the Korean War.[11]

Britain stood somewhere between the American and French positions on the Federal Republic. Wary of Germany becoming an aggressive economic competitor, Britain was not anxious to relax the allies' controls of its foreign trade. Yet Britain was less patient than the United States over the slow pace of German integration into the West. Adenauer's police force could become the core of a German military contribution to NATO, and in fact Britain saw no reason why West Germany should not become a member of the alliance within two years. British ambivalence toward Germany was a factor in continuing French resistance to German integration. Not that Britain was committed to immediate German membership in NATO in the spring of 1950. Gladwyn Jebb advised in the Tripartite Preparatory meetings that no indication of any change in status should be given until Germany was in the Council of Europe.[12] It was one step at a time.

The Schuman Plan, unveiled on the eve of the May foreign ministers' conference, opened a path to softening, if not resolving, the old Franco-German conflicts. But British discomfort, along with U.S. uncertainty about its direction, meant that the Schuman Plan itself would not settle the problem in mid-May. No mention of the German question can be found in the NAC communiqué. In fact, Henry A. Byroade, director of the Bureau of German Affairs, felt that the London meeting "did not unfortunately throw a great deal of light on NATO and Germany."[13]

The Germans did not always help their cause. When Adenauer pressed hard for a German paramilitary police to cope with the Soviet arming of East German police, he seemed to feel it was an obligation of the allies to accept his proposal for a force of 25,000, equipped with light arms. The High Commission was thinking of a force of only 5,000 police. In a fit of pique, Adenauer earlier had withdrawn the appointment of a consul general to New York. The chancellor contended that if the State Department declined to allow the consul to live in Washington, he would not accept a secondary location in New York. Adenauer was always sensitive to a perception of a slight.[14]

A similar sense of entitlement was evident when German industrialists in April toyed with the idea of establishing their own trade relations with the East despite NATO's restrictions. Ruhr industrialists were reported to have given extensive credits to Soviet-zone concerns at a time when East Germany was shipping few goods to the Federal Republic. The Socialist deputy president of the Bundestag, Carlo Schmid, suspected that the Ruhr magnates were prepared to deal with the Communists just as they did with the Nazis. Only a few days after the May summit, West Germans were reported to seek an end to the ban on steel shipments to the Soviet zone.[15]

Speaking to Ruhr leaders on June 19, U.S. High Commissioner John J. McCloy lashed out at the nerve of these industrialists seeking outlets for their production in the Soviet zone while complaining about high occupation costs, high taxes, and the dismantling of German plants. When the president of the Essen Chamber of Commerce blamed the refugee problem on the Roosevelt and Churchill wartime agreements, McCloy reminded his audience: "Don't forget high taxes are the result of German aggression. Don't forget who started this war. Whether or not you gentlemen here are responsible personally for it, remember the war and all the misery that followed it—including your own—was born and bred on German soil and you must accept the responsibility."[16]

These expressions of discontent with the NATO allies might have been expected. A recovering Germany sought authority commensurate with its size and potential power to have a foreign ministry of its own, to remove prohibitions on foreign capital investments in Germany, and to possess the same freedom to export their manufactures that other beneficiaries of the Marshall Plan enjoyed. None of these goals was achieved in May. Yet the chancellor was well aware of how important Germany was to the alliance when he asserted in an interview on May 6 that "our aim is and must be to save Western Europe from the dangers of communism and to contribute our share to the accomplishment of this task."[17]

Although Adenauer was disappointed by the silence on Germany at the NAC meeting in London, his argument was sufficiently persuasive to win concessions after the meeting. Actually, the three foreign ministers of the United States, Britain, and France signaled their intentions before the May meeting. They issued a declaration on May 7 to "draw up a plan intended to liberate the Federal Republic by stages from controls to which she is still subject, in order to give her the greatest possible measure of sovereignty compatible with the basis of the occupation regime." A week after the NAC adjourned, the foreign ministers repeated the promises it had made on May 7.[18]

In early June the Federal Republic won the authority to negotiate and conclude international treaties without the approval of the High Commission. International treaties made by Bonn would be valid unless specifically vetoed by the occupying powers.[19] France was one of the three members of the High Commission to validate this policy. Adenauer cited the Schuman Plan as a bridge not only between France and Germany. It would also lead to a third force of a united Western Europe that would bridge the gap between the United States and the Soviet Union.[20] France appreciated both ideas. Such was the relationship between Germany and the NATO allies in the days before the outbreak of the Korean War. Despite spasms of suspicion on both sides, prospects for continuing the integration of Germany into the West were bright.

The O in NATO

The Mutual Defense Assistance Program: Summer 1950

Given the dramatic changes after June 25, the impression of the alliance becoming an organization after the outbreak of war is understandable. Following the North Korean invasion, the MDAP was in a position to expand rapidly, with the infusion of monies poured into it. The fourteen months preceding the war witnessed the groundwork of expansion of the MDAP, which would not have been possible if it had begun from scratch on June 25.

All the elements of the program were in place. What was needed was the incentive to increase the size of the military aid, not its scope. The Korean War provided that incentive. On August 2 the president asked Congress for an emergency bill of $4 billion to take into account the new dangers facing the alliance as a consequence of the Korean War.[21] While the MDAP bill of 1949 required detailed congressional examination, the emergency bill—two months later and more than three times the size of the original—was tacked on to a supplemental appropriations bill after very little study. The panicky action of August makes a striking contrast with the calm reaction of the administration's proposal in June.

The Deputies Council after June 25

The creation of the Deputies Council may have been a weak compromise before the Korean War, but stronger alternatives were fully recognized before the outbreak of that conflict. When Secretary of Defense Johnson was asked about an integrated command in early June, he had no problem replying that "no such command has been set up as of this time, and none is contemplated in the immediate future." Sen. H. Alexander Smith (R-NJ) wondered if, in the event of war, each member would control its own forces rather than have them decided on by an integrated command that "will tell us, 'this is your share.'" Johnson had a pious answer: "No, sir. If the time ever comes, and God forbid it does, that will solve itself." He underlined this point by noting that "if trouble should come, there would eventually, of course, be an overall command."[22]

The time came far sooner than Johnson had anticipated. Although the problem did not solve itself, there were enough solutions on the shelf for the allies to manage it. Supreme Allied commands were established six months after the war began, and in February 1952 the office of the secretary-general took over many of the functions of the Deputies Council. As for the Western Union, it did not dissolve; it survived as a relic, only to be revived when it suited NATO's purposes, especially in moving West Germany into the alliance in 1955.

The German Question after June 25

The Korean War should have blown away whatever obstacles still stood in the way of integrating the Federal Republic into the alliance. Its resources and manpower were needed as never before in NATO's post-Korean War expansion. The war did have that effect, but not as quickly or as smoothly as the Truman administration wanted. French objections in particular held up German membership in NATO for four years, and even then its entry into the organization had to be through the backdoor of an enlarged Brussels Pact.

Of all the changes brought about by the Asian crisis, the role of Germany was the most difficult to resolve, even though the German role in the defense of Europe had been part of almost every discussion in NATO circles since the signing of the North Atlantic Treaty. Like military assistance and the reorganization of the

NATO structure, there was no question that in the long run, the Federal Republic would have significant roles to play in NATO's history, not least of them was its participation in the termination of the centuries-old division of Western Europe.

The O in NATO?

The new NATO landscape after June 25 could not contain remedies for all the problems that afflicted the alliance in its first year. France's long-standing suspicions of Anglo-American intentions, the smaller powers' resentment over their exclusion from the decision-making process, Britain's uneasiness over its place in the "special relationship," America's impatience with Europe's sluggish responses, and Europe's dissatisfaction with American domination of NATO all remained issues to be confronted throughout the Cold War. But the conventional wisdom of the alliance becoming an organization only as a by-product of the Korean War is misplaced. The O was in NATO from its inception, ineffective and inchoate though its manifestations often were.

8

Conclusion

The sixtieth anniversary of the signing of the North Atlantic Treaty was an occasion for NATO officials, journalists, and scholars to reflect on the alliance's past, present, and future. What resulted from pundits' projections and conference deliberations in the weeks leading up to the anniversary was a judgment of the past that excluded NATO's history before the Korean War. The distinguished British military historian John Keegan listed the nations that signed the treaty on April 4, 1949, and then immediately moved from April 1949 to December 1951 and February 1952, respectively, to observe that "the treaty appointed an American to be commander of NATO forces but a European to be secretary-general, with policy to be decided by a council of ministers."[1]

These appointments, emerging from NAC meetings and affected by the consequences of the Korean War, implied that whatever events took place between 1949 and 1951 were forgotten or not worth mentioning. Members of a high-level NATO conference at a British Foreign Office retreat in January 2009 had no memory of the first strategic concept unveiled in January 1950, although the conference was devoted to examining the history of all NATO strategic concepts to guide NATO policymakers as they prepared for a new strategic concept in 2010. Only one of the participants recalled that there was a strategic concept before the Korean War.[2]

This monograph has sought to fill significant blanks in 1949 and 1950 that NATO officials and analysts alike have largely ignored. The creation of the alliance, however, was not one of the blanks. The European allies breathed a collective sigh of relief when the treaty was signed on April 4, 1949. And in the United States, with the exception of the dwindling band of isolationists, the nation hailed the ending of the isolationist tradition as it recognized the necessity of devising new means to cope with the menace of Soviet-inspired Communism and to fashion a new order in the Old World that would open the way to a united states of Europe.

Toward this end, the United States, Canada, and their European allies crafted what Harlan Cleveland, U.S. permanent representative in NAC from 1965 to 1969, called "a transatlantic bargain."[3] In its simplest form, the bargain involved a U.S. commitment to rebuild, economically and militarily, a Western Europe devastated by World War II. In exchange for abandoning its traditional abstention from European political and military affairs, Europe would have to take steps to abandon its traditional divisions and integrate its resources on every level. The sheer magnitude of the mutual obligations received widespread attention on both sides of the Atlantic and within the Communist bloc as well. But the Korean War's impact on the development of the organization marginalized the prewar history of NATO. This period deserves reevaluation.

There was nothing automatic about the cooperation expected under the treaty, and NATO's experience in its first year showed how fragile the bargain was. U.S. military aid was a prime example of strains that signatures on documents could not conceal. After prolonged Senate debate in the summer and early autumn of 1949 during which American suspicions of Europe were fully exposed, the United States finally granted aid, but under conditions that undermined transatlantic solidarity. Before funds could be released, a strategic concept had to be identified that displayed the inferior position of the European allies in NATO: the United States would supply strategic air power, while the continental allies would supply troops on the ground. Unhappy allies also had to accept humiliating arrangements allowing American officials in each nation's capital to oversee the utilization of the aid. The United States did try to soothe feelings with some success in Paris by removing the word "adviser" from the name of the supervising team, and limiting diplomatic privileges for its counterpart in London.

There was a contradiction inherent in U.S. insistence on bilateral negotiations in areas sensitive to the Europeans, while requiring that European defense be centered on balanced collective forces, with each member serving the organization according to its special assets. Secretary of State Dean Acheson repeatedly demanded that Europeans overcome their parochial obsession with balanced national forces and accept integration of their military as a price for the aid the United States was offering. The MAP, after all, was designed to help the European allies develop specialized strengths to serve the common welfare of the alliance. The Europeans professed to agree with the objective, at least in principle, but feared that an imbalance in their own national forces might leave them unprotected in the event of an attack. Doubts persisted throughout this period that the United States would come to their defense quickly enough. Only their own "balanced" forces, encompassing all the military branches, could provide the necessary assurance.

Just as the United States managed to overcome European objections to bilateral requirements—bases in exchange for aid—Europeans were able to evade American demands for integration of their military forces. A communiqué from the London meeting of NAC on May 18, 1950 gave lip service to balanced collective forces without abandoning Europe's concerns for national forces. The council "urged their governments to concentrate on the creation of balanced collective forces . . . taking at the same time fully into consideration the requirements of national forces. . . ."[4] More directly, the allies succeeded in persuading the United States to scrap its short-term defense plan, which would have initially relinquished the continent to the enemy in the event of war. It was replaced by the MTDP, which covered Western Europe to the Rhine.

None of these adjustments to the bargain satisfied every party. Tensions between the donor and the recipients were alive throughout the fourteen-month period before the North Korean invasion. They ranged from French resistance to Anglo-American pressures for concessions to West Germany to outbreaks of neutralism in Europe fueled by doubts about the constancy of the American commitment to Europe's security. But despite the many transatlantic frictions, NATO's infrastructure was in place before the Korean conflict—the system of mutual assistance, the host of committees under the authority of the council, and the beginning of a more centralized governance.

The Korean War was not needed to convert the alliance into an organization. It already existed on June 25, 1950. While the progress of NATO's development was often improvised and usually untidy, "the first crude tools" of the organization, as Dean Acheson noted, had been cast by the end of the London meeting of the council.[5]

The seeds of major changes in the form of Supreme Allied commanders and a civilian coordinating body could be found in negotiations during the winter and spring of 1950, and as rocky as it was, the path to Franco-German rapprochement was visible in the acerbic exchanges among the allies in this period. So, too, was the direction NATO's enlargement would take when NATO accepted Greece and Turkey in 1952 and the Federal Republic of Germany in 1955. Preparations had been made before the war. As for the O in NATO, its origins can be located in the text of the treaty in Article 9, under whose wing new responsibilities were justified.

Historiographical Reflections

In my study of the origins of NATO, *NATO 1948: The Birth of the Transatlantic Alliance* (Lanham, Md.: Rowman & Littlefield, Inc., 2007), I was able to provide a historiographical essay on the subject. No such essay is possible for NATO before the Korean War. Scholars have touched on the period, but only cursorily in monographs covering NATO's sixty-year history. For the most part they have concentrated on specialized studies in such areas as the Suez crisis of 1956 and France's withdrawal from the military structure of the organization in 1956. Those that do examine NATO before the Korean War have been official U.S. military studies—my *A Community of Interests: NATO and the Military Assistance Program, 1948–1951* (Washington, D.C.: Office of the Secretary of Defense, Historical Office, 1980); Steven L. Rearden's *History of the Office of the Secretary of Defense: The Formative Years, 1947–1950* (Washington, D.C.: Office of the Secretary of Defense, Historical Office, 1984); and Kenneth W. Condit's *The History of the Joint Chiefs of Staff: The Joint Chiefs of Staff and National Policy, 1947–1949* (Wilmington, Del.: Michael Glazier, Inc., 1979). Chester J. Pach Jr.'s thorough study of U.S. military assistance, *Arming the Free World: The Origins of the United States Military Assistance Program, 1945–1950* (Chapel Hill: University of North Carolina Press, 1991), complements the foregoing monographs. Lord Ismay, NATO's first secretary-general, wrote an official history of the organization's first five years, *NATO's First Five Years 1949–1954* (Paris: NATO Information Service, 1954), and understandably concentrated on his tenure, which began in 1952. Only a few pages were given to the first year, and then primarily to identify NATO's committee structure and strategic concept.

Robert E. Osgood, whose pioneer history of NATO in 1962, *NATO: The Entangling Alliance* (Chicago: University of Chicago Press, 1962), recognized the importance of NATO's early years, as did another political scientist, Timothy P. Ireland [*Creating the Atlantic Alliance: The Origins of the North Atlantic Treaty Organization* (Westport, Conn.: Greenwood Press, 1981)]. Osgood lacked access to documents of the period while Ireland consulted only printed materials. Journalist

Don Cook's sprightly history of the formative years, *Forging the Alliance: NATO: 1945–1950* (London: Secker and Warburg, 1989), lacked documentation. More sophisticated was historian Melvyn P. Leffler's *A Preponderance of Power: National Security, the Truman Administration, and the Cold War* (Stanford, Calif.: Stanford University Press, 1992), which is a comprehensive examination of U.S. security policy in the Truman years. NATO rated space in this able study, but not in the context it warranted. David Calleo's provocative *The Atlantic Fantasy: The United States, NATO, and Europe* (Baltimore: Johns Hopkins University Press, 1970) had a light touch on everything NATO. Although he was not particularly interested in NATO's first year, he confidently asserted that Korea was responsible for converting NATO from a "transitional mutual assistance treaty into an integrated military alliance, run by the United States" (pp. 25–26). Douglas L. Bland's *The Military Committee of the North Atlantic Alliance: A Study of Structure and Strategy*(New York: Praeger, 1991) offered a Canadian perspective on a major committee formed in NATO's first year. The impact of the Korean War was minimal in this monograph. Wallace J. Thies's *Friendly Rivals: Bargaining and Burden-Shifting in NATO* (Armonk, N.Y.: M. E. Sharpe, 2003) gave little attention to prewar NATO, but his perceptive evaluation of the bargaining process showed that it was present from the beginning of the alliance.

It is worth noting that most of the scholarship on NATO has been produced by political scientists, not by historians. Some have been sensitive to the historical context; others have been more interested in NATO's contribution to alliance theory rather than in assessing NATO's place in the larger scheme of things. Some years ago I remarked about the lack of interest among American historians in the history of the alliance, and speculated about its reasons ["After Twenty-five Years: NATO as a Research Field," *AHA Newsletter* 12 (November 1984): 6–7]. The absence of documents was undoubtedly a factor, but more important was a sense that NATO was subsumed under the Truman Doctrine as part of the machinery mobilized to cope with the Soviet challenge. Primary materials are no longer a problem, and yet NATO as a significant part of American diplomatic history in the last half of the twentieth century still has not attracted a corps of NATO scholars. This situation may be changing as a new generation of historians have turned their attention to détente and the Helsinki agreements in the 1970s. It is unlikely, however, that they will include NATO before Korea as a fruitful subject for exploration.

European scholars, by contrast, have been active and productive contributors to NATO scholarship. NATO study centers flourish in Florence, Oslo, Potsdam, and Zurich. They recognize the significance of the Atlantic alliance in the history of Western Europe since World War II. NATO before Korea, however, has not figured prominently in these centers. Regrettably, the monumental three-volume project, edited by Gustav Schmidt [*History of NATO: The First Fifty Years* (New York: Palgrave, 2001)], did not pay serious attention to NATO before Korea.

Almost every scholar active in NATO studies contributed to the project. Of the three chapters devoted to "The Promise of Alliance: The Origins and Meanings of NATO," one was a perceptive view from a Canadian perspective, with no reference to the pre-Korean period; a second and equally well-written chapter covered the security crisis of the late 1940s, but did not go beyond the Washington Exploratory talks of 1948; the third, oddly, dealt only with the Atlantic Congress of 1959. Ironically, it may be a European, the prominent French historian, Pierre Melandri, whose book *Les Etats-Unis face l'unification de l'Europe, 1945–1954* (Paris: Editions à Pedone, 1980) best captured the essence of the fourteen months between the signing of the treaty and the outbreak of the Korean War. He clearly illuminated "le terrible effet" of that war.

In brief, it is hard to escape the judgment that the period from April 4, 1949 to June 25, 1950 remains a neglected chapter in NATO's history.

Appendix A

The North Atlantic Treaty,

Washington, D.C.—4 April 1949

The Parties to this Treaty reaffirm their faith in the purposes and principles of the Charter of the United Nations and their desire to live in peace with all peoples and all governments.

They are determined to safeguard the freedom, common heritage and civilisation of their peoples, founded on the principles of democracy, individual liberty and the rule of law. They seek to promote stability and well-being in the North Atlantic area.

They are resolved to unite their efforts for collective defence and for the preservation of peace and security. They therefore agree to this North Atlantic Treaty:

Article 1

The Parties undertake, as set forth in the Charter of the United Nations, to settle any international dispute in which they may be involved by peaceful means in such a manner that international peace and security and justice are not endangered, and to refrain in their international relations from the threat or use of force in any manner inconsistent with the purposes of the United Nations.

Article 2

The Parties will contribute toward the further development of peaceful and friendly international relations by strengthening their free institutions, by bringing about a better understanding of the principles upon which these institutions are founded, and by promoting conditions of stability and well-being. They will seek to eliminate conflict in their international economic policies and will encourage economic collaboration between any or all of them.

Article 3

In order more effectively to achieve the objectives of this Treaty, the Parties, separately and jointly, by means of continuous and effective self-help and mutual aid, will maintain and develop their individual and collective capacity to resist armed attack.

Article 4

The Parties will consult together whenever, in the opinion of any of them, the territorial integrity, political independence or security of any of the Parties is threatened.

Article 5

The Parties agree that an armed attack against one or more of them in Europe or North America shall be considered an attack against them all and consequently they agree that, if such an armed attack occurs, each of them, in exercise of the right of individual or collective self-defence recognised by Article 51 of the Charter of the United Nations, will assist the Party or Parties so attacked by taking forthwith, individually and in concert with the other Parties, such action as it deems necessary, including the use of armed force, to restore and maintain the security of the North Atlantic area.

Any such armed attack and all measures taken as a result thereof shall immediately be reported to the Security Council. Such measures shall be terminated when the Security Council has taken the measures necessary to restore and maintain international peace and security .

Article 6 (1)

For the purpose of Article 5, an armed attack on one or more of the Parties is deemed to include an armed attack:
- on the territory of any of the Parties in Europe or North America, on the Algerian Departments of France (2), on the territory of or on the Islands under the jurisdiction of any of the Parties in the North Atlantic area north of the Tropic of Cancer;
- on the forces, vessels, or aircraft of any of the Parties, when in or over these territories or any other area in Europe in which occupation forces of any of the Parties were stationed on the date when the Treaty entered into force or the Mediterranean Sea or the North Atlantic area north of the Tropic of Cancer.

Article 7

This Treaty does not affect, and shall not be interpreted as affecting in any way the rights and obligations under the Charter of the Parties which are members of the United Nations, or the primary responsibility of the Security Council for the maintenance of international peace and security.

Article 8

Each Party declares that none of the international engagements now in force between it and any other of the Parties or any third State is in conflict with the provisions of this Treaty, and undertakes not to enter into any international engagement in conflict with this Treaty.

Article 9

The Parties hereby establish a Council, on which each of them shall be represented, to consider matters concerning the implementation of this Treaty. The Council shall be so organised as to be able to meet promptly at any time. The Council shall set up such subsidiary bodies as may be necessary; in particular it shall establish immediately a defence committee which shall recommend measures for the implementation of Articles 3 and 5.

Article 10

The Parties may, by unanimous agreement, invite any other European State in a position to further the principles of this Treaty and to contribute to the security of the North Atlantic area to accede to this Treaty. Any State so invited may become a Party to the Treaty by depositing its instrument of accession with the Government of the United States of America. The Government of the United States of America will inform each of the Parties of the deposit of each such instrument of accession.

Article 11

This Treaty shall be ratified and its provisions carried out by the Parties in accordance with their respective constitutional processes. The instruments of ratification shall be deposited as soon as possible with the Government of the United States of America, which will notify all the other signatories of each deposit. The Treaty shall enter into force between the States which have ratified it as soon as the ratifications of the majority of the signatories, including the ratifications of Belgium, Canada, France, Luxembourg, the Netherlands, the United Kingdom and the United States, have been deposited and shall come into effect with respect to other States on the date of the deposit of their ratifications. (3)

Article 12

After the Treaty has been in force for ten years, or at any time thereafter, the Parties shall, if any of them so requests, consult together for the purpose of reviewing the Treaty, having regard for the factors then affecting peace and security in the North Atlantic area, including the development of universal as well as regional arrangements under the Charter of the United Nations for the maintenance of international peace and security.

Article 13

After the Treaty has been in force for twenty years, any Party may cease to be a Party one year after its notice of denunciation has been given to the Government of the United States of America, which will inform the Governments of the other Parties of the deposit of each notice of denunciation.

Article 14

This Treaty, of which the English and French texts are equally authentic, shall be deposited in the archives of the Government of the United States of America. Duly certified copies will be transmitted by that Government to the Governments of other signatories.

1. The definition of the territories to which Article 5 applies was revised by Article 2 of the Protocol to the North Atlantic Treaty on the accession of Greece and Turkey signed on 22 October 1951.
2. On January 16, 1963, the North Atlantic Council noted that insofar as the former Algerian Departments of France were concerned, the relevant clauses of this Treaty had become inapplicable as from July 3, 1962.
3. The Treaty came into force on 24 August 1949, after the deposition of the ratifications of all signatory states.

Appendix B

Texts of Final Communiques, 1949–1974

TEXTS OF FINAL COMMUNIQUES
1949 - 1974

Issued by
Ministerial Sessions of
the North Atlantic Council,
the Defence Planning Committee,
and the Nuclear Planning Group

17th September, 1949

Washington

Chairman : Mr. Acheson, Secretary of State of the USA.

The Council agrees its terms of reference and organization. It creates a Defence Committee, a Military Committee and Military Standing Group as well as five Regional Planning Groups.

The Council established by Article 9 of the North Atlantic Treaty held its first session in Washington on September 17, 1949. Representatives of the Parties to the Treaty attending this first session were : For Belgium, the Minister of Foreign Affairs, M. Paul van Zeeland; for Canada, the Secretary of State for External Affairs, Mr. Lester B. Pearson; for Denmark, the Minister of Foreign Affairs, Mr. Gustav Rasmussen; for France, the Minister of Foreign Affairs, M. Robert Schuman; for Iceland, the Minister to the United States, Mr. Thor Thors; for Italy, the Minister of Foreign Affairs, Count Sforza; for Luxembourg, the Minister of Foreign Affairs, Mr. Josef Bech; for the Netherlands, the Minister of Foreign Affairs, Dr. Dirk U. Stikker; for Norway, the Minister of Foreign Affairs, Mr. Halvard M. Lange; for Portugal, the Minister of Foreign Affairs, Mr. José Caeiro de Matta; for the United Kingdom, the Secretary of State for Foreign Affairs, Mr. Ernest Bevin; for the United States, the Secretary of State, Mr. Dean Acheson.

The task of the Council is to assist the Parties in implementing the Treaty and particularly in attaining its basic objective. That objective is to assist, in accordance with the Charter, in achieving the primary purpose of the United Nations — the maintenance of international peace and security. The Treaty is designed to do so by making clear the determination of the Parties collectively to preserve their common heritage of freedom and to defend themselves against aggression while emphasising at the same time their desire to live in peace with all governments and all peoples.

It is in this spirit that the Foreign Ministers of the Parties have met in Washington and have taken steps to implement the Treaty. The meetings of the Council showed that all Parties are united in their resolve to integrate their efforts for the promotion of lasting peace, the preservation of their common heritage and the strengthening of their common defence.

The main purpose of the Council during this first session was to provide for its own future operation and, in accordance with Article 9, to establish a Defence Committee and such other subsidiary bodies as are deemed necessary to assist the Council in considering matters concerning the implementation of the North Atlantic Treaty.

Organization

The Council is the principal body in the North Atlantic Treaty Organization. In accordance with the Treaty, the Council is charged with the responsibility of considering all matters concerning the implementation of the provisions of the Treaty. Such subsidiary bodies as are set up under Article 9 of the Treaty are subordinate to the Council.

The organization established under the North Atlantic Treaty should be operated with as much flexibility as possible and be subject to review from time to time. The establishment of this machinery does not preclude the use of other means for consultation and co-operation between any or all of the Parties on matters relating to the Treaty.

Council

As regards its own organization, the Council agreed as follows :

As decided on April 2, the Council will normally be composed of Foreign Ministers. Should the latter be unable to attend, their places shall be taken by plenipotentiary representatives designated by the Parties. To enable the Council to meet promptly at any time the diplomatic representatives in Washington of the Parties shall be empowered to act as their Governments' representatives whenever necessary.

Terms of Reference

The North Atlantic Treaty shall constitute the terms of reference of the Council.

Time and Frequency of Sessions

The Council shall be convened by the Chairman and shall meet in ordinary session annually and at such other times as may be deemed desirable by the majority of the Parties. Extraordinary sessions under Articles 4 and 5 of the Treaty may be called at the request of any Party invoking one of these Articles.

Location of the Council Sessions

The location of each session of the Council shall be determined by the Chairman after consultation with the other members of the Council. For general convenience the ordinary annual session should be held at about the same time and in the same general geographical area as the annual session of the General Assembly. Other ordinary sessions should whenever practicable be held at some convenient location in Europe.

Chairmanship

Chairmanship shall be held in turn by the Parties according to the alphabetical order in the English language beginning with the United States. Each Party shall hold office from the beginning of the one ordinary annual session until the appointment of the new Chairman at the following ordinary annual session. If any Party does not wish to accept the Chairmanship, it shall pass to the next Party in alphabetical order.

Languages

English and French shall be the official languages for the entire North Atlantic Treaty Organization.

Permanent Co-ordination

Additional political bodies shall not be established unless and until experience has demonstrated their need. However, the existing informal arrangement for consultation between representatives in Washington of the Parties shall be maintained.

Defence Committee

The Council established a Defence Committee.

The Council reaffirmed that ensuring the security of the North Atlantic area is a primary objective of the North Atlantic Treaty and is vital to the security of each of the Parties. It is therefore of paramount importance that the Parties, separately and jointly, by means of continuous and effective self-help, and mutual aid, maintain and develop their individual and collective capacity to resist armed attack. The Defence Committee should therefore immediately take the requisite steps to have drawn up unified defence plans for the North Atlantic area.

As regards the organization of the Defence Committee, the Council agreed as follows :

The Defence Committee will be composed of one representative from each Party. These representatives will normally be Defence Ministers. In any case where this is not possible, another representative may be designated.

Terms of Reference

The Defence Committee shall recommend measures for the implementation of Articles 3 and 5 in accordance with general policy guidance given by the Council.

Time and Frequency of Sessions

The Defence Committee shall be convened by the Chairman and shall meet in ordinary session annually and at such other times as it may be requested to meet by the Council or as may be deemed desirable by the majority of the members of the Defence Committee.

Location

The location of each session of the Defence Committee shall be determined by the Chairman in consultation with the members of the Committee.

Chairmanship

Chairmanship shall be held in turn by the Parties according to the alphabetical order in the English language beginning with the United States. Each Party shall hold the office from the beginning of one ordinary annual session until the appointment of the new Chairman at the following ordinary annual session. If any Party does not wish to accept the Chairmanship, it shall pass to the next Party in alphabetical order.

The Council suggested to the Defence Committee the general outline of those subsidiary military bodies which it considered appropriate for the task of aiding the Defence Committee in recommending measures for the implementation of Articles 3 and 5 of the Treaty. The Defence Committee was invited, among other things, to consider the question of these subsidiary bodies in detail and to elaborate on the general provisions suggested by the Council for each body.

The Council suggested in general terms that the military organization should include the following :

Military Committee

The Defence Committee should establish a Military Committee composed of one military representative from each Party. These representatives should be Chiefs-of-Staff or their representatives. (Iceland, having no military establishment, may, if it so desires, be represented by a civilian official.)

Terms of Reference

The Military Committee should :

— provide general policy guidance of a military nature to its Standing Group;

— advise the Defence Committee and other agencies on military matters as appropriate;

— recommend to the Defence Committee military measures for the unified defence of the North Atlantic area.

Location

The Military Committee should normally meet in Washington.

Standing group

In order to facilitate the rapid and efficient conduct of the work of the Military Committee, there should be set up a sub-committee of that body to be known as the "Standing Group". The Standing Group should be composed of one representative each of France, the United Kingdom, and the United States.

Terms of Reference

The Standing Group, in accordance with general policy guidance provided by the Military Committee, should provide such specific policy guidance and information of a military nature to the Regional Planning Groups and any other bodies of the organization as is necessary for their work.

To achieve the unified defence of the North Atlantic area, the Standing Group should co-ordinate and integrate the defence plans originating in the Regional Planning Groups, and should make appropriate recommendations thereon to the Military Committee.

The Standing Group should recommend to the Military Committee those matters on which the Standing Group should be authorised to take action in the name of the Military Committee within the framework of approved policy.

It is recognised that it is the responsibility of individual governments to provide for the implementation of plans to which they have agreed. It is further recognised that it is the primary responsibility of the Regional Planning Groups to prepare plans for the defence of their respective regions. Subject to these principles, it is understood that before the Standing Group makes recommendations on any plan or course of action involving use of forces, facilities, or resources of a Party not represented on the Standing Group, going beyond or differing from arrangements previously agreed by the Party concerned, the Party should have the right to participate in the Standing Group in the work of formulating such recommendations. It is also understood that when communicating their regional plans to the Standing Group, the Regional Planning Groups should be entitled to have their plans presented and explained by any of their members and not necessarily by a member of the Standing Group.

Time and Frequency of Sessions

The Standing Group should be so organized as to function continuously.

Location

The permanent site of the Standing Group should be in Washington.

Permanent Representation

In order to maintain close contact with the Standing Group, a Party not represented thereon may appoint a special representative to provide permanent liaison with the Standing Group.

Regional Planning Groups

In order to ensure speedy and efficient planning of the unified defence of the whole North Atlantic area there should be established Regional Planning Groups on a geographical basis. It should be provided that :

1. Before any Regional Planning Group makes any recommendations affecting the defence of the territory or involving the use

of forces, facilities, or resources of any Party not a member of that Group, that Party should have the right to participate in the Group in the work of formulating such recommendations.

2. Any Group which considers that a Party not a member of the Group can contribute to the defence planning of that Group's region, can call upon that Party to join in the planning as appropriate.

Composition

Northern European Regional Planning Group

Denmark, Norway, and the United Kingdom.

The United States has been requested and has agreed to participate actively in the defence planning as appropriate.

Other Parties may participate under the provisions listed above.

Western European Planning Group

Belgium, France, Luxembourg, the Netherlands, and the United Kingdom.

Canada and the United States have been requested and have agreed to participate actively in the defence planning as appropriate. Other Parties may, and particularly Denmark and Italy will, participate under the provisions listed above.

Southern European-Western Mediterranean Regional Planning Group

France, Italy and the United Kingdom.

The United States has been requested and has agreed to participate actively in the defence planning as appropriate.

Other Parties may participate under the provisions listed above.

It is recognised that there are problems which are clearly common to the defence of the areas covered by the three European regional groups. It is therefore important that arrangements be made by the Defence Committee with a view to ensuring full co-operation between two, or if the need arises, all three groups.

Canadian-United States Regional Planning Group

Canada and the United States.

Other Parties may participate under the provisions listed above.

North Atlantic Ocean Regional Planning Group

Belgium, Canada, Denmark, France, Iceland, the Netherlands, Norway, Portugal, the United Kingdom and the United States.

The responsibilities for planning the defences in the North Atlantic Ocean cannot be shared equally by all members of the Group. On the other hand, these responsibilities can to some extent be divided along functional lines and allocated to those Parties who are best able to perform the respective defence functions. Therefore, the North Atlantic Ocean Regional Planning Group, when it meets, should establish a series of planning sub-groups related to specific functions of defence. The Group should determine on which sub-group or sub-groups each Party should sit, and the arrangements necessary to ensure co-ordination between these sub-groups in the interest of speedy and effective planning.

Terms of Reference

Each Regional Planning Group should :

— develop and recommend to the Military Committee through the Standing Group plans for the defence of the region;

— co-operate with the other Regional Planning Groups with a view to eliminating conflict in, and ensuring harmony among, the various regional plans.

Location

The Defence Committee should consider the question of the location of the Regional Planning Groups.

The Council recognises that the question of military production and supply is an integral part of the whole problem of the defence of the North Atlantic area. Consequently, there shall be established as soon as possible appropriate machinery to consider these matters. The details of organization of this machinery, terms of reference, etc. shall be studied forthwith by a working group which shall submit recommendations to the Defence Committee or to the Council.

The Council recognises the importance of economic and financial factors in the development and implementation of military plans for the defence of the North Atlantic area. Consequently, there shall be established as soon as possible appropriate machinery to consider these matters. The details of organization of this machinery, terms of reference, etc. shall be studied forthwith by a working group which shall submit recommendations to the Council.

18th November 1949

Washington

Chairman : Mr. Acheson.

The Council establishes a Defence Financial and Economic Committee and a Military Production and Supply Board.

The North Atlantic Council convened today in Washington in its second session. The Council considered and approved a report of the Working Group on the establishment of a "Defence Financial and Economic Committee" under the North Atlantic Treaty as follows :

Defence Financial and Economic Committee

In accordance with the decision of the North Atlantic Council on September 17, 1949, and in further implementation of Article 9 of the Treaty, there is hereby established a Defence Financial and Economic Committee. It shall be responsible for advising the Council on the financial and economic aspects of measures for the defence of the North Atlantic area.

The following general provisions shall govern the operation of the Defence Financial and Economic Committee :

1. The Defence Financial and Economic Committee shall be composed of a representative at Ministerial or similarly high level of responsibility from each signatory country. It shall report directly to the North Atlantic Council. It shall consult with the Defence Committee as appropriate.

2. The Committee and any subordinate bodies which it may set up shall establish and maintain close working relations with the North Atlantic military organization, and particularly the Military Production and Supply Board.

The Committee or its subordinate bodies shall provide them with guidance on all relevant economic and financial factors; shall obtain from them information on those requirements of defence programmes which are relevant to the consideration of economic and financial questions; and shall provide them with guidance on financial and economic arrangements to meet the requirements of defence programmes.

3.   The Defence Financial and Economic Committee is in particular responsible to the North Atlantic Council for the performance of the following functions, having regard for the principle of self-help and mutual aid in the field of military production and supply, and for the primary importance of economic recovery and continued economic stability :

(a) To develop in co-operation with the Military Committee (including the Standing Group) and the Military Production and Supply Board overall financial and economic guides to and limits of future defence programmes, including military production programmes, which North Atlantic Treaty countries as a group and individually should undertake within available financial and economic resources.

(b) To appraise the financial and economic impact on member countries of major individual defence projects formulated by the Military Production and Supply Board or the Military Committee (including the Standing Group), including consideration of financing problems and availability of raw materials, capital equipment, and manpower, and, on the basis of such review, make recommendations as to action on such projects.

(c) To recommend financial arrangements for executing military defence plans, and particularly financial arrangements for the interchange among North Atlantic Treaty countries of military equipment, surplus stocks, or materials and equipment to be used in producing military equipment.

(d) To measure and to recommend steps to meet the foreign exchange costs of imports of materials and equipment from non-member countries required by defence programmes under the North Atlantic Treaty.

(e) To consider, as may be found desirable and appropriate, plans for the mobilisation of economic and financial resources in time of emergency.

4.   The Committee may delegate to any Regional Defence Financial and Economic Committee which may be established by the governments of a Region any of its functions which, in its judgement, can be better performed by regional committees. Actions of regional committees under such delegations shall be under the general guidance of, and in accordance with the general policies laid down by the North Atlantic Committee, and shall be subject to its co-ordination and review.

5. The Committee shall provide itself with such subordinate bodies and staff assistance as may be necessary to carry out its functions. In particular, there shall be a permanent working staff in London, composed of qualified personnel representing interested countries to carry on the day-to-day work of the Committee and to which the Committee may delegate such of its functions as it deems appropriate. The Committee shall have a Secretary, with suitable assistance, to perform the secretarial and administrative functions.

6. The Committee shall meet at such times and places as shall be required. Its secretariat and working staff shall be located in London. The Committee shall decide its own rules of procedure. Chairmanship shall be held in turn by the Parties according to the alphabetical order in the English language beginning with the United States. Each Party shall hold the office for one year. If any Party does not wish to accept the Chairmanship, it shall pass to the next party in alphabetical order.

The Council took note of and approved the action of the Defence Committee in establishing a "Military Production and Supply Board". The Military Production and Supply Board has already met in London in its first session and has initiated a work programme which was summarised in a communiqué issued in London on November 2.

The directive issued by the Defence Committee in establishing the Military Production and Supply Board, and approved by the Council, is as follows :

North Atlantic Defence Committee Directive to the Military Production and Supply Board

In accordance with the decision of the North Atlantic Council on September 17, 1949, and in furtherance of Article 9 of the Treaty, there is hereby established a Military Production and Supply Board.

The following general provisions shall govern the operation of the North Atlantic Military Production and Supply Board :

1. The North Atlantic Military Production and Supply Board shall be composed of a representative at the sub-ministerial level from each signatory country. It shall report directly to the Defence Committee.

2. The Board shall establish and maintain close working relations with the appropriate military bodies set up under the Defence Committee. It shall look to them for information on military requirements and work with them to insure that, insofar as feasible, the military production and procurement programme supports defence plans effectively. The Board shall also work in close co-ordination with the military bodies on the promotion of standardisation of parts and end products of military equipment, and provide them with technical advice on the production and development of new or improved weapons. To facilitate the fullest co-operation and exchange of information between them on matters of joint interest, the Board shall establish and direct a suitably representative liaison group on a working level in Washington to work with the Standing Group.

3. The Board shall maintain close working relations with the finance and economic machinery to be established by the Council, and look to it for guidance on all relevant economic and financial factors.

4. The North Atlantic Military Production and Supply Board is responsible to the Defence Committee for the performance of the following functions, having regard for the principle of self-help and mutual aid in the field of military production and supply.

(a) The review of the military supply situation on the basis of data to be secured from the appropriate military bodies on military material requirements and on the current availability of military material to meet such requirements.

(b) The recommendation to the Defence Committee of ways and means of increasing available supplies where they fall short of requirements, either from production, surplus equipment or equipment economically capable of rehabilitation. In preparing such recommendations, account shall be taken of strategic factors, of physical capabilities of individual countries to produce military material, of the importance of securing maximum efficiency and integration of production, and of the guidance furnished by the finance and economic machinery with respect to financial and economic considerations.

(c) The promotion of more efficient methods of producing military equipment and of the standardisation of parts and end products of military equipment, including conservation in the use of strategic and critical materials, and including advice to the appropriate military bodies on the production problems involved in proposed new weapons or modifications in existing weapons.

5. The Board may delegate to any Regional Supply Board which may be established by the governments of a Region any of its functions which in its judgement, can be better performed by regional boards. Actions of regional boards under such delegations shall be under the general guidance of and in accordance with the general policies laid down by the North Atlantic Board, and shall be subject to its co-ordination and review.

6. The Board shall provide itself with such subordinate bodies and staff assistance as may be necessary to carry out its functions. In particular, there shall be, in addition to the liaison group in Washington, referred to in paragraph 2, a permanent working staff in London, composed of qualified personnel representing interested countries, to carry on the day-to-day work of the Board. The Board shall have a Secretary, with suitable assistance, to perform secretarial and administrative functions.

7. The Board shall meet at such times and places as may be required. Its secretariat and working staff shall be located in London. The Board shall decide its own rules of procedure. Chairmanship shall be held in turn by the parties according to the alphabetical order in the English language beginning with the United States. Each Party shall hold the office for one year. If any party does not wish to accept the Chairmanship, it is passed to the next Party in alphabetical order.

6th January 1950

Washington

Chairman : Mr. Acheson.

The Defence Committee's recommendations regarding the strategic concept approved.

The North Atlantic Council met today in Washington in its third session. The United States was represented by the Secretary of State Acheson, who is Chairman for the first year of the Council's operation. Representatives of the North Atlantic Treaty signatories were : For Belgium, Ambassador Silvercruys; for Canada, Ambassador Wrong; for Denmark, Ambassador de Kauffman; for France, Ambassador Bonnet; for Iceland, Minister Thors; for Italy, Ambassador Tarchiani; for Luxembourg, Minister Le Gallais; for the Netherlands, Ambassador van Kleffens; for Norway, Ambassador Morgenstierne; for Portugal, Ambassador Pereira; for the United Kingdom, Ambassador Franks.

The Council considered and approved recommendations agreed by the Defence Committee in Paris on December first for the integrated defence of the North Atlantic area. These recommendations embody the principles of self-help and mutual aid and will provide the basis for the common defence of the Parties.

15th-18th May, 1950

London

Chairman : Mr. Acheson.

Council Deputies established to meet permanently in London – Definition of "balanced collective forces" and of "progressive build-up of defence" – North Atlantic Planning Board for Ocean Shipping established.

At the fourth session of the Atlantic Council in London the Foreign Ministers of the 12 nations of the North Atlantic Treaty considered the principles on which their association is founded and the objectives toward which they are working.

They reaffirmed the adherence of their governments to the principles which inspire the United Nations Charter and their conviction that common action under the Treaty is an integral part of the effort which all free nations are making to secure conditions of world peace and human welfare.

They are determined that freedom, which is the common basis of their institutions, shall be defended against every threat of aggression or subversion, direct or indirect. Freedom means the independence of nations, the respect for spiritual values, and the dignity of man. Only a free society can guarantee to the individual, the benefits of economic and social betterment.

They are resolved to secure the economic progress and prosperity of the peoples of their countries and to promote the economic and social development of other peoples of the free world through close co-operation with each other and with other nations. To the immense resources of the free world, and its industrial and scientific development, the peoples of the North Atlantic Community bring the spiritual strength which comes from freedom.

Conscious of the strength and of the will to peace of their countries, the Ministers remain ready to seize any opportunity for achieving a genuine and lasting settlement of international problems: but for so long as some nations are not willing to co-operate on a basis of equality and mutual respect, they believe that the maintenance of peace and the defence of freedom require the organization of adequate military defence.

The nations of the Atlantic Council are accordingly resolved, by their united efforts, to build up a system of defence equipped with modern weapons and capable of withstanding any external threat directed against any of them.

The Council throughout its deliberations recognised that only through co-ordinated planning and joint effort could these objectives be achieved.

To this end the Council took the following decisions to improve the functioning of the North Atlantic Treaty Organization and to guide its future work.

1. They decided to establish, by the appointment of Deputies, mechanism to permit the Council fully to discharge its role as the principal and directing body of the North Atlantic Treaty. The full text of the Council resolution on this subject is attached.

2. The Council in this connection agreed on principles which should guide the work of the Deputies and of the other organizations of the North Atlantic Treaty.

3. The Council, having considered the reports of the Defence Committee, and the Defence Financial and Economic Committee, issued directives to guide them in their future work. These directives emphasise that the problem of adequate military forces and the necessary financial costs should be examined as one and not as separate problems.

In formulating their directives the Council proceeded on the basis that the combined resources of the members of the North Atlantic Treaty are sufficient, if properly co-ordinated and applied, to ensure the progressive and speedy development of adequate military defence without impairing the social and economic progress of these countries.

4. The Council recognising the indispensability of self-help and mutual aid among the Treaty Powers in making progress towards an integrated defence, and convinced that further mutual assistance is essential to rapid progress towards the strength required for the common security of the North Atlantic area, recommended that each Party make its full contribution through mutual assistance in all practicable forms.

5. The Council unanimously agreed that if adequate military defence of the member countries is to be achieved it must be along the lines of the most economical and effective utilisation of the forces and material at the disposal of the North Atlantic countries. They accordingly urged their governments to concentrate on the

creation of balanced collective forces in the progressive build-up of the defence of the North Atlantic area, taking at the same time fully into consideration the requirements for national forces which arise out of commitments external to the North Atlantic area.

6. In furtherance of Article 9 of the Treaty the Council established a North Atlantic Planning Board for Ocean Shipping to be composed of representatives of the participating countries concerned. This Board will report directly to the Council and will work in close co-operation with other bodies of the Treaty Organization in all matters relating to the factor of merchant shipping in defence planning.

The Ministers believe that the decisions they have taken here in London represent a marked advance towards the practical realisation of the objectives of the North Atlantic Treaty.

Resolution

The North Atlantic Council established in accordance with Article 9 of the Treaty has so far only met twice at the Ministerial level and on two other occasions when members of the Council have been represented by their governments' diplomatic representatives in Washington.

But under Article 9 the Council is the principal body of the North Atlantic Treaty. It is therefore the paramount duty of the Council to put itself in a position to exercise its full role as the central and most important of the various organs of the Treaty by taking the most effective steps to keep itself informed of all matters which fall within its competence, by taking the necessary decisions and by ensuring the execution of such decisions.

A year's experience has shown that on the political side the meetings of the Council have been too infrequent to permit a sufficient exchange of views on matters of common interest within the scope of the Treaty. On the military side the strategic concept of the Treaty has been adopted and a defence plan drawn up, and the corresponding estimate of the necessary forces is being established. The next step is to put these plans into effect by taking further measures in the direction of common defence, the division of financial responsibilities and the adaptation and development of the necessary forces.

In view of this situation, the Council will in particular undertake the following tasks :

(a) study the inter-relationship of the various programmes to support the plans for the defence of the North Atlantic area and ensure co-ordination of the work of the Defence Committee, the Defence Financial and Economic Committee, and all other bodies established under the North Atlantic Treaty Organization;

(b) recommend to governments the steps necessary to ensure that effect is given to the co-ordinated plans prepared for the defence of the North Atlantic area;

(c) exchange views on political matters of common interest within the scope of the Treaty;

(d) promote and co-ordinate public information in furtherance of the objectives of the Treaty while leaving responsibility for national programmes to each country;

(e) consider what further action should be taken under Article 2 of the Treaty, taking into account the work of existing agencies in this field.

To enable the Council effectively to carry out its responsibilities and to exercise them continuously, each government will appoint a Deputy to its Council representative. Each Deputy will be in a position to give whatever time may be necessary to ensure that the responsibilities of the Council are carried out effectively.

In the intervals between meetings of Ministers, the Deputies duly authorised by their respective governments, will be responsible, on behalf of and in the name of the Council, for carrying out its policies and for formulating issues requiring decisions by the member governments.

To assist the Council in fulfilling its responsibilities the Deputies, on behalf of their governments, shall select a Permanent Chairman from among their membership. With the advice of the Chairman, the Deputies shall establish a suitable full-time organization composed of highly qualified persons contributed by member governments. The Chairman, in addition to presiding at meetings of the Deputies, shall be responsible for directing the organization and its work.

Member governments will appoint their Deputies with the least possible delay in order that a Chairman may be selected, the organization established, and progress be made on the urgent problems before the Council. The Deputies, assisted by the Chairman and the organization to be created, should begin functioning in the very near future in order that tangible results may be achieved before the next meeting of the Ministers when the progress made will be reviewed. Without minimising the importance of any of the points listed above, first priority in the work of the organization should be given to points (a) and (b).

The Deputies will have their headquarters in London.

Notes

1. Origins of the Alliance

1. *Newsweek,* April 11, 1949, 19.

2. Ibid.

3. "Address of the President on the Occasion of the Signing of the North Atlantic Treaty, April 4, 1949," in *Public Papers of the Presidents of the United States, Harry S. Truman,* (Washington, D.C.: Government Printing Office, 1964), 196.

4. Theodore C. Achilles, "The Omaha Milkman," in *NATO's Anxious Birth: The Prophetic Vision of the 1940s,* ed. Andre de Staercke et al. (New York: St. Martin's Press, 1985), 30.

5. *America,* 81, no. 2 (April 1949): 56.

6. Dean Acheson, *Present at the Creation: My Years in the State Department* (New York: W. W. Norton & Co., 1969), 284.

7. *New York Times,* April 5, 1949, 2.

8. Ibid.

9. For background on Kennan's influence, see George F. Kennan, *Memoirs (1925–1950)* (New York: Bantam Books, 1969), chapters 11, 13, 14.

10. For background on European unity, see Walter Lipgens, *A History of European Integration: The Formation of the European Unity Movement* (Oxford: Oxford Univ. Press, 1972).

11. For background on eighteenth-century alliances, see Robert E. Osgood, *Alliances and American Foreign Policy* (Baltimore: Johns Hopkins Univ. Press, 1968); H. M. Scott, *British Foreign Policy in the Age of the American Revolution* (Oxford: Oxford Univ. Press, 1990).

12. Lawrence S. Kaplan, *NATO 1948: Birth of the Transatlantic Alliance* (Lanham, Md.: Rowman & Littlefield, 2007), chapters 1–3.

13. Memorandum by Secretary of State for Foreign Affairs, February 19, 1949, C.P.(49), 34, 1–2, CAB 129/32., National Archives, London.

14. Lawrence S. Kaplan, "The 'Atlantic' Component of NATO," in *The Long Entanglement: NATO's First Fifty Years* (Westport, Conn.: Praeger, 1999), 20–35.

15. Robert H. Ferrell, "Diplomacy without Armaments, 1945–1950," *The Romance of History,* ed. Scott L. Bills and E. Timothy Smith (Kent, Ohio: Kent State Univ. Press, 1997), 35–49.

16. For background on the origins of NATO, see Kaplan, *NATO 1948.*

2. Toward Ratification

1. U.S. objectives were clearly expressed in Arthur Vandenberg Jr., ed., *The Private Papers of Senator Vandenberg* (Boston: Houghton Mifflin Co., 1952), 400–4. Hereafter cited as Vandenberg Papers.

2. Trygve Lie, *In the Cause of Peace: Seven Years with the United Nations* (New York: Macmillan, 1954); see Lawrence S. Kaplan, *NATO and the UN: A Peculiar Relationship* (Columbia: Univ. of Missouri Press, 2010), 13–20.

3. "World Wide Security Found Only in World Wide Organization," address before the UN General Assembly, Lake Success, N.Y., April 5, 1949, *Vital Speeches of the Day*, 15, no. 13 (April 15), 415–16.

4. Charge in the Soviet Union (Kohler) to secretary of state, January 29, 1949, *Foreign Relations of the United States 1949* [hereafter cited as *FRUS 1949*], 4: 51–52, citing the statement of the Soviet minister of foreign affairs on the North Atlantic Treaty.

5. Memorandum of the Soviet government on the North Atlantic Treaty, March 31, 1949, in Alvin Rubinstein, ed., *The Foreign Policy of the Soviet Union* (New York: Random House, 1969), 268–69; ambassador to the Soviet Union (Panyshkin) to the secretary of state, March 31, 1949, *FRUS 1949*, 4: 264.

6. Preliminary position paper prepared by the staff of the U.S. delegation to the General Assembly, March 30, 1949, ibid., 2: 72–73.

7. Minutes of the Sixth Meeting of the U.S. delegation to the second part of the Third Session of the General Assembly, April 13, 1949, ibid., 2: 77–79.

8. *Current Digest of the Soviet Press*, May 3, 1949, pt. 14: 35–39.

9. UN General Assembly, 3rd sess., 2nd pt., 192nd plenary session, *Official Records*, April 13, 1949, 65.

10. Ibid., April 14, 78.

11. Quoted in *New York Times*, April 14, 1949, 4.

12. Gladwyn Jebb, *Memoirs of Lord Gladwyn* (New York: Weybright & Talley, 1972), 232; 193rd plenary sess., April 24, 1949, 80–81.

13. *Yearbook of the United Nations, 1948–1949*, 429.

14. George F. Kennan, *Memoirs 1925–1950* (Boston: Little, Brown, 1967), 427–28; Dean Acheson, *Sketches from Life of Men I Have Known* (New York: Harper Bros., 1960), 132.

15. Vandenberg to Prof. W. A. Young, April 15, 1949, italics included; Arthur H. Vandenberg Papers, Bentley Historical Library, Univ. of Michigan.

16. *New York Times*, April 15, 1949, 3.

17. North Atlantic Treaty *Hearings*, Senate Committee on Foreign Relations, 81st Cong., 1st sess., 3 parts, May 16, 1949, 4: 1121.

18. Robert J. Donovan, *Tumultuous Years: The Presidency of Harry S. Truman, 1949–1953* (New York: W. W. Norton & Co., 1982), 34.

19. U.S. Senate, 81st Cong., 1st sess., *Congressional Record*, 95, pt. 7 (July 5, 1949): 8819; Lawrence S. Kaplan, "NATO and the Language of Isolationism," *South Atlantic Quarterly* 57 (Spring 1958): 209–10.

20. North Atlantic Treaty *Hearings*, Senate Committee on Foreign Relations, 81st Cong., 1st sess., 3 parts, May 5, 1949, 2: 418.

21. Ibid., May 16, 1949, 3: 1007; see also E. Timothy Smith, *Opposition beyond the Water's*

Edge: Liberal Internationalists, Pacifists, and Containment (Westport, Conn.: Greenwood Press, 1999), 93–95.

22. North Atlantic Treaty, *Hearings,* Senate Committee on Foreign Relations, 81st Cong., 1st sess., 3 parts, April 28, 1949, 1: 97.

23. Dean Acheson, *Present at the Creation: My Years in the State Department* (New York: W. W. Norton & Co.), 281.

24. North Atlantic Treaty, *Hearings,* Senate Committee on Foreign Relations, April 27, 1949, 1: 85.

25. Ibid., April 28, 1949, 1: 136–37.

26. See ibid., May 16, 1949, 3: 1038 for an example.

27. *New York Times,* May 10, 1949, 3.

28. North Atlantic Treaty, *Hearings,* Senate Committee on Foreign Relations, April 29, 1949, 1: 191.

29. MAP-D-D/1, "Objectives of the Military Assistance Program," Policy Planning Paper Approved by FACC, May 15, 1949, *FRUS 1949,* 1: 314. In a change of title in April 1949, the FACC became the Foreign Military Assistance Coordinating Committee. See Steven L. Rearden, *The Formative Years 1949–1950* (Washington, D.C.: Office of the Secretary of Defense, 1984), 509–10.

30. Lawrence S. Kaplan, *NATO 1948: The Birth of the Transatlantic Alliance* (Lanham, Md.: Rowman and Littlefield Publishers, Inc., 2007), 154–56.

31. MC(49), 17th meeting, Military Committee, April 21, 1949, Whitehall, DG 1/6/38, Western European Archives, National Archives, London: MC(49), 19th Meeting, Military Committee, May 4, 1949, ibid.

32. Requests from the Brussels Treaty Powers to the United States Government for Military Assistance, April 5, 1949, *FRUS 1949,* IV: 285–87; reply of the United States Government to the "Request from the Brussels Treaty Powers for Military Assistance," dated April 5, 1949, ibid., April 6, 1949, 287–88.

33. Rearden, *The Formative Years,* 496.

34. *New York Times,* April 26, 1949, 1; MAP D-G/14, Military Rights Question, May 20, 1949, *FRUS 1949,* 1: 311–12.

35. Rearden, *The Formative Years,* 497.

36. North Atlantic Treaty, *Hearings,* Senate Committee on Foreign Relations, April 27, 1949, 1: 60.

37. Ibid., 4: 288; see fn32.

38. Vandenberg Papers, italics included, 479.

39. North Atlantic Treaty, *Hearings,* Senate Committee on Foreign Relations, April 27, 1949, I: 16.

40. Rearden, *The Formative Years,* 504.

41. *New York Times,* May 3, 1949, 6.

42. *Congressional Record Daily Digest,* 81st Cong., 1st sess., vol. 95, pt. 18, June 6, 1949, D358.

43. Vandenberg Papers, italics included, 498; memorandum by the director of the Policy Planning Staff (Kennan) to the acting secretary of state, June 1, 1949, *FRUS 1949,* 4: 301.

44. *Congressional Record—Senate,* 81st Cong., 1st sess., vol. 95, July 11, 1949, pt. 7, 9205.

45. *New York Times,* July 23, 1949, 1.

46. Ibid., July 24, 1949, 1.

47. Ambassador to France (Jefferson Caffery) to the secretary of state, April 7, 1949, *FRUS 1949*, 4: 288–89; April 27, 1949, ibid., 4: 297.

48. *Le Monde*, July 24, 1949, 1.

49. René Massigli, *Une comedie des erreurs, 1943–1952* (Paris: Plon, 1978), 139; Vincent Auriol, *Journal du Septennat, 1947–1957*, July 20, 1949, 7 vols. (Paris: A. Colin, 1970), 3: 300.

50. *New York Times*, July 28, 1949, 3.

51. Secretary of state to the Embassy in France, August 10, 1949, *FRUS 1949*, 4: 318.

52. Parliamentary Debates (Hansard), House of Commons, *Official Report*, Session 1948–49, May 12, 1949, Fifth Series, vol. 464: 2037; ibid., 2035.

53. Auriol, *Journal du Septennat*, April 22, 1949, 3: 207.

54. "Le Pacte et L'Allemagne," *Le Monde*, June 28, 1949, 1.

55. See list of papers agreed to by the foreign ministers of France, the United Kingdom, and the United States, April 8, 1949, *FRUS 1949*, IV: 177–85.

56. Acheson, *Present at the Creation*, 291–301; William H. Hitchcock, *France Restored: Cold War Diplomacy and the Quest for Leadership in Europe, 1944–1954* (Chapel Hill: Univ. of North Carolina Press, 1998), 112.

57. Hervé Alphand, *L'Étonnement d'etre, 1939–1973* (Paris: Fayard, 1977), 213.

58. Report of the Senate Committee on Foreign Relations, June 6, 1949, Department of State *Bulletin* 20, June 19, 1949, 787–94; U.S. Senate Committee on Foreign Relations, The Vandenberg Resolution and the North Atlantic Treaty: *Hearings Held in Executive Session*, Historical Series, 81st Cong., 1st sess., June 2, 1949, 270–71.

59. Parliamentary Debates (Hansard), House of Commons, *Official Report*, Session 1948–49,May 12, 1949, Fifth Series, vol. 464: 2062–63.

60. North Atlantic Treaty, *Hearings*, Senate Committee on Foreign Relations, April 28, 1949, l: 201; April 29, l: 281; April 27, l: 61.

61. Ibid., April 29, 1949, l: 281–82.

62. *New York Times*, July 24, 1949, 1.

63. Parliamentary Debates (Hansard), House of Commons, May 12, 1949, 2027–28; 2038.

64. *Congressional Record—Senate*, 81st Cong., 1st sess., vol. 95, pt. 15, May 21, 1949, A4533.

65. Ibid., pt. 13, April 26, 1999, A2399; ibid., pt. 12, March 26, 1949, A1573.

66. *Keesing's Contemporary Archives: Weekly Diary of World-Events, 1948–1950*, May 21–28, 2004, vol. VII: 10004.

67. Parliamentary Debates (Hansard), House of Commons, May 12, 1949, 2022; *Times* (London), May 13, 1949, 4; ibid., June 8, 1949, 4.

68. *Keesing's*, June 11–18, 1949, 10012, 10042; *New York Times*, July 23, 1949, 2.

69. *Keesing's*, July 30–August 6, 1949, 10140.

70. Ibid., July 23, 1949, 10130.

71. Ibid., July 9–16, 1949, 10098; ibid., July 30–August 6, 1949, 10146; ibid., March 26–April 2, 1949, 9893, ibid.; *New York Times*, June 10, 1949, I: 4; ibid., August 25, 1949, 3.

72. *Keesing's*, July 30–August 6, 1949, 10143.

73. Ibid.; *New York Times*, July 28, 1949, 3.

74. *Keesing's*, 10154; *New York Times*, July 22, 1949, 13.

75. *New York Times*, June 3, 1949, 4.

76. *Congressional Record—Senate*, 81st Cong., lst sess., vol. 95, pt. 8, July 20, 1949, 9784.

77. Ibid., July 21, 1949, 9915–16.

78. Ibid., 9916; ibid., July 11, 1949, 9206.

3. Mutual Defense Assistance Program

1. Steven L. Rearden, *The Formative Years: 1947–1950,* vol. 1 of *History of the Office of Secretary of Defense,* ed. Alfred Goldberg (Washington, D.C.: Historical Office, Office of the Secretary of Defense, 1984), 490.

2. Ibid., 505.

3. Chester J. Pach Jr., *Arming the Free World: The Origins of the United States Military Assistance Program, 1945–1950* (Chapel Hill: Univ. of North Carolina Press, 1991), 20–21; Melvyn P. Leffler, *A Preponderance of Power: National Security, the Truman Administration, and the Cold War* (Stanford: Stanford Univ. Press, 1992), 285–86.

4. Edwin G. Nourse, "The Impact of Military Preparedness on the Civilian Economy," April 5, 1949, *Vital Speeches of the Day* 15, no. 4: 429.

5. Pach, *Arming the Free World,* 216; memo from Kennan for the secretary of state and the undersecretary of state, April 14, 1949, *Foreign Relations of the United States 1949* [hereafter cited as *FRUS 1949*], I: 282; record of the secretary's meeting, April 15, 1949, ibid., 283–84.

6. Quoted in *New York Times,* June 20, 1949, 13.

7. Policy paper approved by the FACC by July 1, 1949, "Relationship of the Military Assistance Program to U.S. Strategic Interests," *FRUS 1949,* I: 347–48.

8. Quoted in *New York Times,* July 23, 1949, 2.

9. Quoted in ibid., June 16, 1949, 5.

10. *Congressional Record—Senate,* 81st Cong., 1st sess., vol. 95, pt. 7, July 8, 1949, 9100.

11. *New York Times,* June 24, 1949, 2; *Le Monde,* June 24, 1949, 1.

12. *Congressional Record—Senate,* July 21, 1949, vol. 95, pt. 8, 19885–86; quoted in Department of State *Bulletin,* August 8, 1949, vol. 21, 196.

13. Letter from Vandenberg to Lippmann, July 18, 1949, underlined, Bentley Historical Library, Univ. of Michigan, Ann Arbor.

14. Letter from Lippmann to Vandenberg, July 22, 1949, ibid.; Edward J. Sparks, chargé, American embassy, Copenhagen, August 28, 1949, 840.20/8/1849, RG 59 National Archives and Records Administration (NARA), College Park, Md., comments on the impact in Denmark of James Reston's column on Danish vulnerability in "Vulnerable Danes . . . ," *New York Times,* August 7, 1949, 3.

15. Letter from Lippmann to Vandenberg, July 22, 1949, Bentley Historical Library; letter from Acheson to James K. E. Bruce, U.S. ambassador to France, Acheson Papers, Box 65, Harry S. Truman Library, Independence, Mo.

16. Quoted in *New York Times,* August 7, 1949, 1.

17. The National Security Act of 1947 as amended by Public Law 216, 81st Cong., 1st sess., August 10, 1949, replaced the National Military Establishment (NME) with Department of Defense, Title II, Sec. 202 (a) and conferred new powers on the chairman, JCS, Title II, Sec. 211(a). See Alice C. Cole et al., eds., *Department of Defense: Documents on Establishment and Organization* (Washington, D.C.: Historical Office, Office of the Secretary of Defense, 1978), 87, 94.

18. Military Defense Assistance Program of 1949, *Hearings,* HR, Committee on Foreign Affairs, July 29, 1949, 19; Military Assistance Program, *Hearings,* Senate Committees on Foreign Relations and Armed Services, 81st Cong. , 1st sess., August 9, 1949, 49.

19. Quoted in *New York Times,* July 31, 1949, 1, 2.

20. Ibid., August 7, 1949, 2; Senate Committees on Foreign Relations and Armed Services, 81st Cong., 1st sess., *Hearings,* Mutual Defense Assistance Act, Bradley testimony, August 10, 1949, 89.

21. Lawrence S. Kaplan, "An Unequal Triad: The United States, Western Union, and NATO," in Olav Riste, ed., *Western Security: The Formative Years* (Oslo: Norwegian Univ. Press, 1985), 107–8.

22. Lemnitzer interview, March 21, 1974, 10–12, Historical Office, Office of the Secretary of Defense, Washington, D.C.

23. Rearden, *The Formative Years,* 469; U.S. Delegation to the Western Union.

24. Lemnitzer to Wedemeyer, Department of the Army, 4, August 1, 1948, CCS 092. RG 218, NARA.

25. DELWU 5, July 26, 1948, ibid.

26. Quoted in third meeting of WU Chiefs of Staff Committee, October 26, 1948, DG 1/6/36, WEU Archives, Brussels.

27. MD (50)12, Montgomery to WU secretary-general, July 7, 1950, DG1/1/56, ibid.

28. See Bradley testimony, fn20.

29. Special Message to the Congress on Need for a Military Aid Program, July 25, 1949, *Public Papers of the Presidents, Harry S. Truman,* 398.

30. HR, Committee on Foreign Affairs, 81st Cong., 1st sess., Mutual Defense Assistance Act, *Hearings* on HR 5748, July 28–29, 1949, Acheson testimony, 98ff; Johnson testimony, 45ff; Bradley testimony, 69ff; Dean Acheson, *Present at the Creation: My Years in the State Department* (New York: W. W. Norton & Co., 1969), 310.

31. Rearden, *The Formative Years,* 505.

32. Letter from Vandenberg to Carl M. Saunders, editor of the *Jackson Citizen-Patriot,* August 1, 1949; rell 5, Bentley Historical Library, Ann Arbor; Arthur H. Vandenberg Jr, *The Private Papers of Senator Vandenberg* (Boston: Houghton Mifflin Co., 1952), 504. Hereafter cited as the Vandenberg Papers.

33. Letter to Mrs. Vandenberg, July 25, 1950, Vandenberg Papers, 503.

34. Letter from Vandenberg to Saunders, underlined, August 1, 1950, Bentley Historical Library; memorandum of conversation, Acheson with Senator Dulles, July 26, 1950, Box 65, Harry S. Truman Library.

35. Letter from Vandenberg to a constituent, August 1, 1949, Vandenberg Papers, 507; ibid., 503–4.

36. *New York Times,* July 26, 1949, 2.

37. Acheson, *Present at the Creation,* 311.

38. Ibid., 310; letter to Mrs. Vandenberg, Vandenberg Papers, August 2, 1949, 508.

39. Letter from Lippmann to Vandenberg, August 8, 1949, reel 5, Bentley Historical Library.

40. Letter from Vandenberg to Warburg, August 23, 1949, Vandenberg Papers, 511.

41. Letter to Mrs. Vandenberg, August 5, 1949, ibid., 508.

42. HR Committee on Foreign Affairs, 81st Cong., 1st sess., Mutual Defense Assistance Act, *Hearings,* July 28, 1949, 10.

43. Pach, *Arming the Free World,* 223; L. S. Kaplan, *Community of Interests: NATO and the Military Assistance Program, 1948–1951* (Washington, D.C.: Historical Office, Office of the Secretary of Defense, 1980), 189, fn85.

44. Senate Committees on Foreign Relations and Armed Services, Military Assistance Program, 81st Cong., 1st sess., *Hearings,* August 8–9, 1949, 51–52.

45. Policy paper approved by FACC, July 1, 1949, "Relationship between Military Assistance Program and U.S. Strategic Interests," *FRUS 1949,* I: 347–49.

46. Kenneth Condit, *The History of the Joint Chiefs of Staff: JCS and National Policy. 1947–1949* (Wilmington, Del.: Michael Glazier, Inc., 1979), II: 433.

47. *Congressional Record—Senate,* 81st Cong., 1st sess., vol. 95, pt. 9, August 15, 1949, 11408–9; ibid., pt. 10, September 21, 1949, 13083.

48. Ibid., pt. 10, September 16, 1949, 13109; quoted in *New York Times,* September 17, 1949, 3.

49. *Congressional Record-HR,* 81st Cong., 1st sess., vol. 95, pt. 9, August 17, 1949, 11662–63, 11674, 11688–89; ibid., August 18, 1949, 11761.

50. Public Law 329, Mutual Defense Assistance Act of 1949, October 6, 1949, 81st Cong., 1st sess., Title II, Sec. 201, Title III, Sec. 301, 303, Kaplan, *Community of Interests,* Title II, Sec. 201; Title III, Sec. 301, 303, 216.

51. Rearden, *Formative Years,* 506.

52. *Congressional Record—HR,* 81st Cong., 1st sess., vol. 95, pt. 10, September 22, 1949, 13168; see fn48.

53. Quoted in *The Times* (London), September 23, 1949, 4.

54. Statement by the President Announcing the First Atomic Explosion in the USSR, September 23, 1949, *Public Papers of the Presidents, 1949,* 485; Senator George quoted in *New York Times,* September 25, 1949, 4; Kee's denial in *New York Times,* September 27, 1949, 6.

55. Connally quotation in *Congressional Record—Senate,* 81st Cong., 1st sess., vol. 95, September 19, 1949, 13024–25; Kee quotation in *New York Times,* September 1949, 6.

56. Brookings Institution, *Current Developments in United States Foreign Policy* (September 1959), 22.

57. Quoted in *New York Times,* September 29, 1949, 14; *The Times* (London), November 11, 1949, 3.

58. Quoted in *New York Times,* September 22, 1949, 25.

59. Quoted in ibid., September 20, 1949, 16.

60. PL 216, The National Security Act of 1947, as amended by PL 216, August 10, 1949, Title II, Sec. 201(a).

61. Pach, *Arming the Free World,* 217.

62. Rearden, *Formative Years,* 510; the Foreign Assistance Correlation Committee (FACC) was supplemented but not replaced by the Foreign Military Assistance Committee (FMACC) in the summer of 1949.

63. Ibid., 511.

64. PL 329, Mutual Defense Assistance Act of 1949, October 6, 1949, Title IV, Sec. 402(d).

65. Vincent Auriol comments in *Journal du Septennat, 1947–1954* (Paris: A. Colin, 1974), 397–98; the allies, for the most part, expressed their resentment obliquely in their request for joint action with Western Union members rather than in explicit protests.

66. PL 472, Economic Cooperation Act of 1948, April 2, 1948, Article 2, Sec. 115 (4) (5).

67. Memo from Lemnitzer for Maj. Gen. James H. Burns, assistant to the secretary of defense for military affairs and military assistance, September 22, 1949, subject: French military budget, N7-1-(3)-A.2, RG 330, NARA, College Park, Md.

68. Tel. 1193, Robert D. Coe, chargé in Netherlands to the secretary of state, November 30, 1949, 840.20/11–30–49, RG 59, NARA.

69. PL329, Mutual Defense Assistance Act of 1949, October 6, 1949, Title IV, Sec. 402(d).

70. Quoted in 90th meeting of WU Permanent Commission, November 15, 1949, DG 1/2/5, WEU Archives, Brussels.

71. Tel. 4159, from the secretary of state to the embassy in the United Kingdom, November 18, 1949, *FRUS 1949,* IV: 351–52.

72. Letter from the secretary of defense to the secretary of state, April 15, 1949, CD6–2–46, RG 330 NARA; letter from the acting secretary of state to the secretary of defense, May 24, 1949, ibid.

73. Helen Leigh-Pippard, *Congress and U.S. Military Aid to Britain: Interdependence and Dependence, 1945–56* (London: St. Martin's Press, 1995; tel. 3814, ambassador to Italy (James C. Dunn) to the secretary of state, November 24, 1949, 840.20/11–2449, RG 59, NARA.

74. Tel. 4569, the ambassador to the United Kingdom (Douglas) to the secretary of state, November 22, 1949, N7–1-(1)-F.3, RG 330, NARA; memo from Francis T. Greene, special assistant to the secretary of defense, for Lemnitzer, December 5, 1949, subject: initial discussion with French, December 2, 1949, CD6–2–46, RG 330, NARA.

75. Achilles's memorandum of conversation with Frederick Hoyer-Millar, September 20, 1949, 840.20/19–2049, RG 59, NARA.

76. French pride was appeased by announcing that no agreements would be legally binding until approved by the National Assembly, tel. 4840, U.S. ambassador to France (Bruce) to the secretary of state, November 18, 1949, 840.20/11–1649, RG 59, NARA; memorandum of conversation, Acheson with Franks, December 17, 1949, Acheson Papers, Harry S. Truman Library.

77. Note *The Times* (London), December 22, 1949, 4; memorandum of conversation, Perkins to the secretary of state, December 16, 1949, 840.20/12–1649, RG 59, NARA.

78. Tel. 832, Edward J. Sparks, U.S. chargé in Denmark, to the secretary of state, November 28, 1949, N7–6-B8, RG 330, NARA; tel. 8818, Henry S. Villard, U.S. chargé in Norway, to the secretary of state, November 25, 1949, N7–1-(3)-B7, ibid.

79. Tel. 3806, U.S. ambassador to Italy (Dunn) to the secretary of state, October 30, 1949, N71-(3)-B.2, RG 330, NARA.

80. U.S. Department of State *Bulletin*, December 12, 1959, vol. 21, 909.

81. Summary record of a meeting of U.S. ambassadors in Paris, October 21 and 22, 1949, *FRUS 1949*, IV: 482.

82. Brookings Institution, *Current Developments in United States Foreign Policy*, November 1949, 3.

83. Jean-Jacques Servan-Schreiber, "Confusion Atlantique," *Le Monde*, November 11, 1949, 2; memo from Greene for Lemnitzer, November 23, 1949, subject: Norwegians, N7—1-1-(1)-F.3, RG 330, NARA; memo from Greene for Lemnitzer, December 5, 1949, CD6–2–46, RG 330, NARA.

84. Brookings Institution, *Current Developments in U.S Foreign Policy*, January 1950, 22; tel. 440, January 25, 1950, Julius C. Holmes, chargé in Britain, to the secretary of state, 740.5 MAP/1–2550, RG 59, NARA.

85. Pach, *Arming the Free World*, 225–26.

86. Senate Committee on Foreign Relations and Armed Services, 81st Cong., 1st sess., *Mutual Defense Assistance Act, Hearings*, August 10, 1949, 78.

4. The North Atlantic Council at Work

1. *Washington Post*, September 18, 1949, 3.

2. Introduction, *NATO Final Communiqués, 1949–1974* (Brussels: NATO Information Service, n.d.), 7.

3. Ibid., 39.

4. Ibid., 41; *New York Times*, September 18, 1949, 4.

5. *NATO Final Communiqués*, 43–44

6. Ibid., 43–46

7. Don Cook, *Forging the Alliance: NATO 1945–1950* (London: Secker & Warburg, 1989), 228.

8. Ibid.

9. Dean Acheson, *Present at the Creation: My Years in the State Department* (New York: W. W. Norton & Co., 1969), 329.

10. Memorandum of conversation, Erenel, counselor of the Turkish embassy with C. R. Moore, GT desk, September 22, 1949, subject: Defense Planning under the North Atlantic Treaty, 840.20/9–2249, RG 59, NARA.

11. Memorandum of conversation, Erkin, McGhee, and Moore, September 26, 1949, subject: Turkey and the North Atlantic Treaty, 840.20/9–2649, RG 59, NARA.

12. Memo from A. S. Fisher to McGhee, October 4, 1949, subject: Relationship of North Atlantic Treaty to the Treaty of Mutual Assistance between France, United Kingdom, and Turkey, 840.20/10–449, NARA.

13. See Lawrence S. Kaplan, *NATO 1948: The Birth of the Transatlantic Alliance* (Lanham, Md.: Rowman & Littlefield, 2007), 207–9.

14. L. S. Kaplan and S. B. Snyder, eds., *Fingerprints on History: The NATO Memoirs of Theodore C. Achilles* (Kent, Ohio: Center for NATO and European Community Affairs, Kent State University, 1992), 28.

15. Tel. A-900, Henry S. Villard, U.S. chargé d'affaires, Norway, to the secretary of state, November 2, 1949, 840.20/11–249, RG 59, NARA.

16. Tel. 1129, H. Freeman Matthews, U.S. ambassador to Sweden, to the secretary of state, November 10, 1949, 840.20/11–2049, RG 59, NARA.

17. Tel. 280, Edward J. Sparks, chargé d'affaires ad interim, to the secretary of state, November 18, 1949, 840.20/11–1949, NARA; tel. 158, Sparks to the secretary of state, December 2, 1949, 840.20/12–249, RG 59, NARA.

18. The Soviets would cite the terms of the Treaty of Peace with Italy in 1947, particularly Article 61, limiting the size of the Italian army, compromised by Italy's membership in NATO. Simultaneous notes were sent to the U.S., Britain, and France. See, for example, the Soviet note to Italy, in *New York Times*, July 20, 1949, 2.

19. Memo from George W. Perkins, Office of European Affairs, to Dean Rusk, deputy assistant secretary of state, October 7, 1949, subject: Repeated Soviet Charge of Violation of Italian Peace Treaty by Italy's Adherence to North Atlantic Treaty, 840.20/10–749, RG 59, NARA.

20. E. Timothy Smith, *The United States, Italy, and NATO, 1947–52* (New York: St. Martin's Press, 1991), 20–24.

21. Tel. 4006, U.S. ambassador to Italy (James C. Dunn) to the secretary of state, December 8, 1949, 840.20/12–849, RG 59, NARA.

22. Tel. 2240, ibid., September 16, 1949, 840.10/9–1649, RG 59, NARA.

23. Memorandum of conversation, Perkins, August 3, 1949, participants: Hume Wrong, ambassador of Canada, Perkins, Thompson, EUR, Galloway, EUR, *Foreign Relations of the United States* [hereafter cited as *FRUS 1949*], IV: 315; memorandum of conversation, September 16, 1949, subject: Portugal—Foreign Minister's Visit, Acheson Papers, Box 66, Harry S. Truman Library.

24. Memorandum of conversation, Perkins, August 3, 1949, *FRUS 1949*, III: 316; *NATO Final Communiqués*, 43.

25. Tel. 1813, the secretary of state to the embassy in Italy, August 12, 1949, *FRUS 1949*, IV: 319–20; memorandum of conversation, Acheson, September 14, 1949, participants: Bevin, Franks . . . Jessup, McGhee et al., ibid., 325–26.

26. Tel. 2240, the secretary of state to the embassy in Italy, September 16, 1949, 840.20/9–1649, NARA; Steven L. Rearden, *The Formative Years 1949–1950*, vol. 1 of *History of the Office of Secretary of Defense*, ed. Alfred Goldberg (Washington, D.C.: Historical Office, Office of the Secretary of Defense, 1984), 478.

27. Tel. 1769, David K. E. Bruce, chief of ECA Mission in France, to the secretary of state, November 16, 1949, subject: General de Gaulle's Statements on the Defense of Europe, 840.20/11–1649, RG 59, NARA.

28. *Le Monde,* November 12, 1949, 2.

29. Tel. 2240, the secretary of state to the embassy in Italy, August 12, 1949, *FRUS 1949*, IV: 319–20.

30. Tel. 2630, the secretary of state to the embassy in Italy, October 24, 1949, ibid., 345–46.

31. Walter Lipgens, *A History of European Integration, 1945–47*, trans. P. S. Falla and A. J. Ryder (Oxford: Clarendon Press, 1982).

32. Minister in the British embassy (Hoyer Millar) to the secretary of state, October 26, 1949, enclosure—personal message from Bevin, October 25, 1949, *FRUS 1949*, IV: 346–48.

33. *Council of Europe: The First Five Years* (Strasbourg: Directorate of Information, 1954).

34. *Parliamentary Debates (Hansard), House of Commons,* Fifth Series, vol. 470, 1948–49, November 17, 1949, 2208.

35. Tel. 4505, the embassy in France to the secretary of state, October 19, 1949, 840.00/10–2949, RG 59, NARA; tel. 3917, the secretary of state to the embassy in France, October 31, 1949, 840.10–3149, ibid.

36. *New York Times,* November 10, 1949, 1.

37. Tel. 5013, ambassador to France (Bruce) to the secretary of state, November 19, 1949, 840.20/11–2939, RG 59, NARA.

38. *Parliamentary Debates (Hansard), House of Commons,* Fifth Series, vol. 470, 1948–49, November 17, 1949, 2214–15.

39. *Assemblée Nationale,* Première Legislature, session de 1949, Comte Rendu in Extenso—215, 3rd séance, November 24, 1949, 3.

40. Tel. 5039, chargé in the UK (Holmes) to the secretary of state, December 19, 1949, *FRUS 1949*, IV: 364–65; tel. 3879, Holmes to the secretary of state, September 28, 1949, 840.00/9–2849, RG 59, NARA.

41. Meeting of United States ambassadors in Paris, October 21–22, to discuss major developments relating to Europe, *FRUS 1949*, IV: 492–93.

42. Ibid., 493; Bohlen to Kennan, October 29, 1949, 3–4, Box 140, George Kennan Papers, Seeley G. Mudd Library, Princeton University; George F. Kennan, *Memoirs, 1925–1950* (Boston: Little, Brown, 1967), 480.

43. Kennan to Bohlen, Kennan Papers, October 12, 1949,8, Box 140, Seeley G. Mudd Library, Princeton; note also that the letter is in 840.00/10–1249, RG 59, NARA.

44. The secretary of state to the acting secretary of state, September 26, 1949, *FRUS 1949*, IV: 338–39.

45. Ibid., Joseph Alsop and Stewart Alsop, "Boldness at Last," *Washington Post,* September 2, 1949, 21; Lippmann, "Wither Britain?" *Washington Post,* September 26, 1949, 7.

46. *Parliamentary Debates (Hansard), House of Commons,* Fifth Series, vol. 470, 948–49, November 23, 1949, 366–67; Pierre Billotte, *Le passe au future* (Paris: Editions Stock, 1979, 63).

47. The phrase, "planning as appropriate," appears in connection with three of the European regional planning groups, *NATO Final Communiqués,* 45.

48. Meeting of NAC, November 18, 1949, ibid., 47–48.

49. Ibid., 47–48; Assistant Secretary of State Perkins to the secretary of state, November 19, 1949, subject: U.S. Representation on the North Atlantic Defense and Financial and Economic Committee, 840.20/9–1949, RG 59, NARA; American embassy in Paris for Ambassador Harriman, November 30, 1949, draft guidance paper for U.S. members of permanent working staff, NATO-DFEC, 840.20/11–3049, ibid.

50. *NATO Final Communiqués,* 50.

51. Memo from Burke Knapp, Office of Finance and Development Policy, to Willard L. Thorpe, assistant secretary of state for economic affairs , October 14, 1949, 840.20/10–1449, RG 59, NARA.

52. Rearden, *The Formative Years,* 479; letter from Secretary of Defense Johnson to the president, April 16, 1949, White House Central Files, Confidential Files, Harry S. Truman Library.

53. *NATO Final Communiqués,* 50–1.

54. Tel. 156, Julius C. Holmes, chargé in the UK to Harriman, January 31, 1950, *FRUS 1950,* III: 13.

55. Kaplan, *NATO 1948,* 158–59.

56. Lawrence S. Kaplan, *The United States and NATO: The Formative Years* (Lexington: Univ. Press of Kentucky, 1984), 132–33.

57. Atlantic Union Resolution (S. Con. Res. 57), December 21, 1949, 840.20/12–2149, RG 59, NARA; memo from Kennan to the secretary of state, December 27, 1949, 840.20/12–2749, ibid.

58. Tel. 021919Z (army message), London to the secretary of state, transmitting Halaby's message to the secretary of defense, November 3, 1949, 840.20/11–349, ibid.

59. Tel. 4064, the embassy in the UK (FACC) to the secretary of state, November 9, 1949, 840.20/11–949, ibid.

60. Memo from Walter Surrey, deputy coordinator of the MAP, to the undersecretary of state, November 18, 1949, subject: Programming and Reporting Procedures on Military Assistance, enclosing memo from James Bruce and John H. Ohly, State, for Maj. Gen. James Burns, Defense, and Edward T. Dickinson, ECA, subject: MDAP, 840.20/11–1849, ibid.

61. Tel. 4714, Acheson to the American embassy, Paris (for Harriman), December 7, 1949, 4, 840.20/12–749, ibid.; tel. 5024, Holmes to the secretary of state, December 18, 1949, 2, 840/10.12–1849, ibid.

62. Tel. 5485, the American embassy in France (Bruce) to the secretary of state, December 30, 1949, 1, 840.20/12–3049, ibid.

63. Tel. 4539, Acheson to Harriman and Lt. Col. Charles H. Bonesteel, III, executive director, ECC, 840.20/12/2049.

64. Tel. 4714, Acheson to the American embassy, Paris (for Harriman), December 7, 1949, 1, 840.20/12–749, ibid.

65. Tel. A-1956, Douglas to Acheson, October 31, 1949, subject: Agenda for the Meeting of the Consultative Council of the Brussels Treaty Powers to be held November 5, 1949 in Paris, 2, 840.00/10–2469, ibid.

66. Tel. 1761, John H. Bruins, first secretary, the American embassy, London, to the secretary of state, November 4, 1949, subject: Meeting of North Atlantic MPSB, 2, 840.20/11–449, ibid.

67. Ibid.

68. Tel. 4023, chargé in the UK (Holmes) to the secretary of state, October 7, 1949, for FACC from ECA, *FRUS 1949*, IV: 341–42; FACC Memo 8, November 8, 1949, subject: Interim Additional Military Production Program Procedures, Assistant Secretary of Defense, ISA, Box 99, RG 330, NARA.

69. Tel. 4844, Bonesteel (ECC) to the secretary of state, December 5, 1949, subject: MDAP, 2, 840.20/12–549, RG 59, NARA.

70. Memo from Perkins to the secretary, undersecretary, November 29, 1949, subject: Comments on the agenda for the Defense Ministers' Meeting in Paris on December 1, 1949, 3, 840/20/11–2949, ibid.

71. *Le Monde*, November 20–21, 1949, 2; tel. 5013, the American embassy in France (Bruce) to the secretary of state, November 29, 1949, subject: Press Roundup (special on defense talks), 40.20/11–2049.

72. Memo from Perkins to Edwin M. Martin, director, Office of European Regional Affairs, December 19, 1949, subject: Forthcoming Meeting of the North Atlantic Council, 1, 840.20/12/1949, ibid.; *NATO's Final Communiqués*, 52.

73. The administration spokesmen were notably cautious about the future inclusion of West Germany into the Atlantic alliance at the April and May 1949 hearings of the Senate Foreign Relations Committee on the North Treaty; letter case to Acheson, August 18, 1949, 840.20/8–1849, RG 59, NARA.

74. Memo from Acheson, September 15, 1949 on Germany, Acheson Papers, Box 66, Harry S. Truman Library.

75. *Le Monde*, November 19, 1949, 2.

76. Occupation Statute Defining the Powers to Be Retained by the Occupation Authorities, April 9, 1949, *FRUS 1949*, III: 179–80; Norbert Wiggershaus, "The German Question and the Foundation of the Atlantic Pact," in *The Origins of NATO*, ed. Joseph Smith (Exeter: Univ. of Exeter Press, 1990), 123.

77. Robert D. Murphy, political adviser for Germany, to John D. Hickerson, director, Office of European Affairs, March 4, 1949, *FRUS 1949*, III: 211–21; Vincent Auriol, *Journal de Septennat*, 1949, III: November 25, 1949, 423.

78. Thomas A. Schwartz, *America's Germany: John J. McCloy and the Federal Republic of Germany* (Cambridge, Mass.: Harvard Univ. Press, 1991), 57; *The Times* (London), September 22, 1949, 4.

79. *New York Times*, October 11, 1949, 1.

80. Ibid., November 13, 1949, 43; *Parliamentary Debates (Hansard) House of Commons*, Fifth Series, vol. 469, November 17, 1949, 2219.

81. Quoted in *New York Times*, October 10, 1949, 2.

82. Ibid., November 23, 1949, 6; *Assemblée Nationale*, 3rd séance du November 25, 1949, Compte Rendu in Extenso, 6304; memorandum of conversation, December 1, 1949, subject: Acheson Meeting with Bonnet, Acheson Papers, Box 66, Harry S. Truman Library.

83. *Le Monde*, November 25, 1949, 1–2.

84. *New York Times*, November 29, 1949, 5.

85. Ibid., 5, 6; Konrad Adenauer, *Memoirs, 1945–1953*, trans. Beate Ruhm (Chicago: Henry Regnery Co., 1965), 267–68.

86. Auriol, *Journal de Septennat,* 1949, III, November 25, 1949, 422–23.

87. R. M. Cheseldine to Henry Byroade, director, Bureau of German Affairs, December 14, 1949, *FRUS 1949,* III: 356.

88. Ibid., 357.

89. The secretary of state to certain diplomatic officers, ibid., IV: 365–66.

90. Note by the secretary of the North Atlantic Defense Committee (C. H. Donnelly) to the committee, December 1, 1949, enclosing the approved revision of the "Strategic Concept for the Defense of the North Atlantic Area," ibid., quote 354.

91. Ibid., 355–56.

92. Ibid., 355.

93. D.C., Agenda for Second Meeting of Defense Committee, Paris, December 1, 1949, NATO Archives, Brussels; D.C.7, November 30, 1949, note by the secretary to the North Atlantic Defense Committee on proposal by the Italian delegate to send the directive from the Defense Committee to the Military Committee, with the D.C.'s recommendation, ibid.; D.C. 6/4, May 24, 1950, note by the secretary on Portuguese Objection for Paragraph 8g of the Strategic Concept, D.C. 6/1 (see paragraph 2, D.C. 6/3, ibid.).

94. Memorandum of conversation by the deputy director of the Office of European Affairs (MacArthur), December 3, 1949, participants: Halaby, Perkins, Achilles, MacArthur, *FRUS 1949,* IV, 357–58; memorandum of conversation by the secretary of state, with Johnson, ibid., 362–64; memorandum of conversation by the secretary of state, December 5, 1949, subject: Defense Committee Meeting in Paris on December 1, 1949, Acheson Papers, Box 66, Harry S. Truman Library.

95. Tel. 841, The Hague to the Department of State, December 14, 1949, subject: Press Comment on West European Defense, 840.20/12–1449, RG 59, NARA.

96. Ibid.

97. Kenneth W. Condit, *History of the Joint Chiefs of Staff: The Joint Chiefs of Staff and National Policy, 1947–1949* (Wilmington, Del.: Michael Glazier, Inc., 1979), 302–3.

98. S.G. 13/16, January 4, 1950 CCS 092, W. Europe (3–12–48), Sec. 40, RG 218, NARA.

99. Memorandum of conversation, Acheson to the president, January 3, 1950, *FRUS 1950,* III: 1.

5. Winter Uncertainties

1. Memo from the secretary of state to the president, January 3, 1950, subject: Strategic Concept for the Integrated Defense of the North Atlantic Area, *FRUS 1950,* III: 2.

2. See Chapter 3, fn72; tel. 5106, ambassador to France (Bruce) to the secretary of state, December 3, 1949, *FRUS1949,* IV: 681.

3. Tel. 4190, the secretary of state to the embassy in the United Kingdom, December 15, 1949, ibid., 360.

4. Quoted in Alex Danchev, *Oliver Franks, Founding Father* (Oxford: Clarendon Press, 1993), 99.

5. *New York Times,* January 7, 1950, 1; memorandum of conversation, Assistant Secretary of State George W. Perkins to the secretary of state, January 7, 1950, subject: Transmitting to the President the Strategic Concept, 740.5/1, Box 342, RG 59, NARA; Statement of the Presi-

dent Upon Issuing Order Providing for the Administration of the Mutual Defense Assistance Act, January 27, 1950, *Public Papers of the Presidents, Harry S. Truman, 1950*, 131–32.

6. See Chapter 4, 17.

7. Quoted in *New York Times*, January 15, 1950, 19.

8. Quoted in memorandum of conversation, January 18, 1950: Spaak and Acheson, Acheson Papers, Box 66, Harry S. Truman, Library.

9. Quoted in memorandum of conversation, January 19, 1950: Spaak, Silvercruys, Kennan Acheson, ibid.; memorandum of conversation, January 28, 1950, Spaak and Acheson, ibid.

10. Memorandum of conversation, January 23, 1950: Acheson, Harriman, William Foster (deputy administrator, ECA), Henry Labouisse (coordinator of foreign aid), subject: Mr. Hoffman's trip to Paris, ibid.; memorandum of conversation, January 24, 1950: Acheson, Labouisse, Franks, ibid; *New York Times*, January 31, 1950, 12; ibid., March 1, 1950, 1.

11. Tel. 1280, the ambassador in the UK (Douglas) to the secretary of state, August 30, 1950, *FRUS 1950*, III: 253.

12. FMACC, M-2, Foreign Military Assistance Coordinating Committee Minutes, February 10, 1950, Box 3425, RG59, NARA; L. S. Kaplan, *A Community of Interests: NATO and the Military Assistance Program, 1948–1951* (Washington, D.C.: Office of Secretary of Defense Historical Office, 1980), 95; quoted in Steven L. Rearden, *The Formative Years 1949–1950*, vol. 1 of *History of the Office of Secretary of Defense*, ed. Alfred Goldberg (Washington, D.C.: Historical Office, Office of the Secretary of Defense, 1984), 514.

13. Memo for files by deputy director of the MDAP (John H. Ohly), December 1, 1949, subject: Conference on the 1951 Budget Message, *FRUS 1949*, I: 411.

14. Ibid., 412.

15. Memo by the director of MDAP (Bruce) to the secretary of state, January 3, 1950, *FRUS 1950*, III: 3–5.

16. Statement by the president—Mutual Defense Assistance Agreements Signed, February 6, 1950, in Department of State *Bulletin* XXII, no. 553: 118–99.

17. Memorandum of conversation, Lemnitzer, director of Office of Military Assistance, for director, Mutual Defense Assistance, January 17, 1950, subject: Shipment of Assistance Prior to Ratification of Bilaterals in the Case of Countries Whose Constitutions Require Prior Parliamentary Approval, 740.5 Map/1–2550, Box 3493, RG59, NARA.

18. letter from Ambassador Bonnet to the secretary of state, March 20, 1950, T-6, Box 3843, RG 59, NARA; *New York Times*, March 21, 1950.

19. Tel. 478, the ambassador to Belgium (Murphy) to the secretary of state, March 23, 1950, 740.5 MAP/3–2350, Box 3483, RG 59, NARA; the secretary of state to the American embassy, Brussels, March 24, 1950, ibid.; tel. 518, Murphy to the secretary of state, March 29, 1950, ibid.

20. Tel. 548, the secretary of state to the American embassy, London, February 4, 1950, 740.5 MAP/2–450, ibid.; FMACC M-4, February 23, 1950, minutes of meeting—State, Defense, ECA, ibid.

21. Tel. 522, Julius C. Holmes (chargé in the UK) to the secretary of state, January 30, 1950, 740.5 MAP/1–3050, Box 3483, ibid.; FMACC M-4, February 23, 1950, Box 3483, ibid.

22. Tel. 439, the secretary of state for Harriman, January 25, 1950, 740.5 MAP/2–2550, ibid.; tel. 556, Richard Breithut, senior U.S. representative on the DFEC, Permanent Working Staff for Harriman, January 31, 1950, 740.5 MAP/1–3150, ibid.; tel. 664, Breithut for Harriman, February 6, 1950, 740.5 MAP/2–6550, ibid.

23. Tel. 758, ECC for Harriman, February 9, 1950, 740.5 MAP/2–950, ibid.

24. Letter from the secretary of defense to the secretary of state, March 22, 1950, MAP/3–2250, ibid.; Undersecretary of State James W. Webb to the secretary of defense, March 23, 1950, 740.5 MAP/3–2250, ibid.

25. Tel. 898, to MAP, for FMASC from ECC, February 16, 1950, *FRUS 1950*, III: 20–21.

26. *New York Times*, March 11, 1950, 1, 3; March 20, 1950, 3.

27. FMACC M-7, March 1950, Minutes: State, Defense, ECA representatives, John E. Ohly, acting chairman, Box 3493, RG 59, NARA; Ohly memo for Lemnitzer, March 1950, subject: Fiscal Year 1980 Department of Air Force Mutual Defense Assistance Materiel Program for Title I Countries, 740.5 MAP/3–750, ibid.

28. Ohly for the State Department and Lemnitzer for the Defense Department would attend the ceremony, quoted in *New York Times*, March 9, 1950, 3.

29. Tel. 268, the ambassador to the Soviet Union (Kirk) to the secretary of state, January 25, 1950, 740.5 MAP/1–2550, Box 3483, NARA.

30. Tel. 1351, the ambassador to Italy (Dunn) to the secretary of state, March 31, 1950, 740.5 MAP/3–3150, ibid.; tel. 1749, Ambassador Douglas (London) to the secretary of state, 740.5 MAP/3–2750, ibid.

31. Tel. 306, the ambassador to the Netherlands (Seldon Chapin) to the secretary of state, February 17, 1950, 740.5 MAP/2–1750, ibid.

32. Control 6363, the secretary of state to certain diplomatic officers, January 24, 1950, 740.5 MAP/ 1–2452; control 6855,the secretary of state to certain diplomatic officers, March 22, 1950, 740.5 MAP/3–2250.

33. *New York Times*, April 12, 1950, 1, 3; tel. 955, the secretary of state to the American embassy, London, March 2, 1950, 740.5 MAP/3–250, Box 3483, NARA.

34. Tel. 657, the ambassador to France (Bruce) to the secretary of state, February 10, 1950, *FRUS 1950*, III: 1359.

35. Quoted in tel. 1264, Bruce to the secretary of state, March 17, 1950, ibid., 1363.

36. Quoted in memorandum of conversation by the deputy director of the Office of European Regional Affairs (MacArthur), February 20, 1950, participants: Douglas MacArthur II and Jean Chauvel, permanent representative of France to the UN, ibid., 1362; Acheson's extemporaneous remarks at a press conference, February 6, 1950, quoted in Department State *Bulletin* 22 (January–March 1950): February 20, 1950, 272.

37. Tel. 933, London to the secretary of state (for FMASC from ECC), February 17, 1950, 740.5 MAP/2–1750, Box 3483, RG 59, NARA; memo from Walter E. Schwinn, Office of Public Affairs, to Edward W. Barrett, assistant secretary of defense, February 21, 1950, subject: Top Secret telegram no. 933 from London of February 17 concerning growing doubt in Western Europe about the value and effectiveness of NATO-MDAP, Box 3425, RG59, NARA.

38. Memo from Barrett to the secretary of state, March 1, 1950, subject: London cable 933, 740/5 MAP/2–1750, Box 3483, RG59, NARA; letter from John O. Bell, assistant director, MDAP, to Edwin M. Martin, director, Office of European Regional Affairs, March 3, 1950, 740.5 MAP/3–350, ibid.; a Belgian Gallup poll, conducted by the University of Brussels, reported that 63.6 percent of the people interviewed had only, at best, a knowledge of the Atlantic Pact, in tel. 164, Robert McClintock, first secretary of the embassy (Brussels) to the secretary of state, February 9, 1950, subject: Belgian public opinion on the Atlantic Pact, 740.5/2–950, Box 3425, RG59, NARA.

39. Memo from Schwinn to Barrett, February 21, 1950; tel. 292, Brussels to the secretary of state, February 25, 1950, 740.5/2–2550, Box 3425, RG59, NARA.

40. Quoted in statement by the minister in France (Bohlen) before the Voorhees Group, April 3, 1950, *FRUS 1950*, III: 1371. In April 1950 Secretary of the Army Gordon Gray had requested Undersecretary of the Army Tracy S. Voorhees to lead an intensive survey of what the army might do to increase the defensive capabilities of Western Europe, letter from Voorhees to the secretary of state, April 10, 1950, ibid., 43.

41. Vincent Auriol, *Journal de Septennat, 1950* IV (February 9, 1950): 139.

42. FMACC D-11, May 5, 1950, William E. Dietz, secretary, History of Bilateral Negotiations on Agreements under MDAA of 1949, 740.5 MAP/1–2750, Box 3583, RG 59, NARA.

43. Tel. 468, the secretary of state to the American embassy, London, February 1, 1950, 740.5 MAP/2–150, ibid.; tel. 574, the secretary of state to the American embassy, London, February 7, 1950, 740.5 MAP/2–750, ibid.

44. Tel. 98, the ambassador to Norway (Henry S. Villard) to the secretary of state, February 7, 1950, 740.5 MAP/2–750, ibid.; tel. 78, the secretary of state to the American embassy, Oslo, 740.5 MAP/2–950, ibid.

45. Quoted in tel. 209, Murphy (Brussels) to the secretary of state, February 9, 1950, 740.5 MAP/2–950, ibid.

46. Quoted in tel. 675, Bruce (Paris) to the secretary of state, February 10, 1950, 740.5 MAP/2–1050, ibid.

47. *New York Times*, February 18, 1950, 3.

48. Quoted in tel. 93, Bruce (Paris) to the secretary of state, April 4, 1950, 740.5/4–340, Box 3425, RG59, NARA.

49. J. J. Servan-Schreiber, "L'Avenir: la coalition atlantique," *Le Monde*, April 5, 1950, 3.

50. Tel. 33, Barrett to the secretary of state, March 1, 1950, 740.5 MAP/2–1750, Box 3425, RG 59, NARA.

51. Tel. 675, Bruce (Paris) to the secretary of state, February 10, 1950, 740.5 MAP/2–1050, Box 3483, RG59, NARA; *Le Monde*, February 10, 1950, 2; *New York Times*, February 15, 1950, 3.

52. Of the many excellent secondary accounts of the H-bomb controversy, Rearden's *The Formative Years*, 446–56 stands out as succinct as it was perceptive. Richard G. Hewlett and Francis Duncan, *A History of the United States Atomic Energy Commission: The Atomic Shield 1947–1962* (University Park: Pennsylvania State Univ. Press, 1969), 362–409, have written an authoritative official study of the H-bomb decision. For the views of key participants, see Harry S. Truman, *Memoirs II: Years of Trial and Hope* (New York: Signet Books,1956), 352–54; Dean Acheson, *Present at the Creation: My Years in the State Department* (New York: W. W. Norton & Co., Inc., 1969), 345–49; Paul H. Nitze, *From Hiroshima to Glasnost: At the Center of Decision: A Memoir* (New York: Grove Weidenfeld, 1989), *The Journals of David Lilienthal: The Atomic Energy Years 1945–1950* (New York: Harper & Row, 1964), II: 613–33; Lewis L. Strauss, *Men and Decisions* (London: Macmillan & Co, 1963), 214–30.

53. Acheson, *Present at the Creation*, 345–46; letters from Truman to Sen. Brien W. McMahon, chairman, Joint Committee on Atomic Energy, November 2, 1949 and January 5, 1949, Papers of Harry S. Truman, Box 175, Harry S. Truman Library; Joseph Alsop and Stewart Alsop, "Pandora's Box," *Washington Post*, January 2, 1950, 8.

54. Strauss, *Men and Decisions*, 217, 219, quote.

55. McMahon to the president, November 1, 1949, Box 175, Papers of Harry S. Truman; memo from Symington to Secretary Johnson, November 8, 1949, ibid.

56. Lilienthal, *Journals*, II: 629; memo of telephone conversation, Souers and Acheson, January 19, 1950, Papers of Dean Acheson, Box 175, Harry S. Truman Library.

57. On January 13 Bradley sent the Joint Chiefs' study to Johnson, who in turn sent it directly to the president. See Helwett and Duncan, *Atomic Shield*, II: 400; Lilienthal, *Journals*, II: 632–33; Acheson, *Present at the Creation*, 348–49; statement by the president on the hydrogen bomb, January 31, 1950, *Public Papers of the Presidents, Harry S. Truman, 1950*, 138.

58. Acheson, *Present at the Creation*, 373.

59. Samuel F. Huntington, *The Common Defense: Strategic Programs in National Politics* (New York: Columbia Univ. Press, 1961), 48–49.

60. Johnson was quoted in comments to Adm. Richard L. Connally: "Admiral, the Navy is on the way out. There is no reason for having a Navy and Marine Corps," in Lt. Gen. Victor H. Krulak, *First to Fight: An Inside View of the U.S. Marine Corps* (Annapolis, Md.: Naval Institute Press, 1999), 120.

61. Memo from the secretary of defense to the president, April 16, 1949, Confidential Files, White House Central Files, Papers of Harry S. Truman, Harry S. Truman Library.

62. Acheson, *Present at the Creation*, 373–74; the flare-up between Acheson and Johnson is well documented. See Nitze, *From Hiroshima to Glasnost*, 94–95; Paul H. Nitze, "The Development of NSC 68," *International Security* (Spring 1980): 170–76.

63. See Rearden, *Formative Years*, 526–27.

64. NSC 68, the president to the executive secretary of the National Security Council, April 12, 1950, with enclosure: A Report to the President Pursuant to the President's Directive of 31 January 1950, *FRUS 1950*, I: 234–35, 237, 267.

65. Ibid., 279, 280, 281; see also memo by assistant secretary of state for UN affairs (John D. Hickerson), April 5, 1950, ibid., 217, who thought advantages in using the UN to negotiate with the Kremlin were outweighed by disadvantages.

66. NSC 68, ibid., 250, 286.

67. Ibid., 235, 292.

68. Quoted in Rearden, *The Formative Years*, 532, quoted in Princeton Conference—10/10/53— Reel 3, Track 2, p1, Papers of Dean Acheson, Box 80, Harry S. Truman Library.

69. Auriol, *Journal du Septennat, 1950*, 138.

70. Ibid.

71. Tel. 1264, the ambassador to France (Bruce) to the secretary of state, March 17, 1950, *FRUS 1950*, III: 1363–64.

72. Memorandum of conversation by U.S. high commissioner for Germany (John J. McCloy), January 20, 1950, participants: Harriman, Bruce, McCloy, ibid., 1608–9; Tel. 308, Chapin (The Hague) to the secretary of state, March 30, 1950, 740.5/3–3050, Box 3425, RG 59, NARA.

73. Memo from Donald P. Downs, Office of British Commonwealth and Northern European Affairs (BNA) to Henry R. Labouisse, director (BNA), February 20, 1950, subject: Article 43 Forces, 740.5/2–2050, ibid.

74. Memo from Martin, director, Office of European Regional Affairs (RA) to Hayden Raynor (EUR), February 23, 1950, subject: Article 43 forces, 740.5/2–2350, ibid.

75. Memo from Martin (EUR) to George W. Perkins, assistant secretary of defense for European affairs (EUR), January 13, 1950, subject: Possible Items for Discussion with Representatives of the Joint Chiefs, 740.5/1–1350, ibid.

76. Documents Relating to the Exchange of Classified Military Information between the United States and the United Kingdom, January 27, 1950, *FRUS 1950*, III: 1617; Col. T. W. Hammond, Intelligence Division, CSGID assistant executive for planning and coordination to JAMAG London, February 10, 1950, 940.5/-1650, Box 3425, RG59, NARA. Memo from J. H. Burns, Office of the Secretary of Defense (OSD), February 13, 1950, 740.5/2–1350, ibid.

77. Summary of Discussion between the British Chief of Staff and the U.S. Joint Chiefs of Staff in London, August 2, 1949, CCS 092 Western Europe, Box 95, Box 95, RG218, NARA.

78. Memo from the deputy director, Office of European Regional Affairs (Douglas MacArthur II) to Perkins, February 16, 1950, subject: Communication from Secretary Johnson to Defense Minister Pleven on Standardization, 740.5/2–1650, Box 3425, RG 59, NARA.

79. Memo from Martin to the deputy assistant secretary of state for European affairs (Llewellyn E. Thompson), March 14, 1950, subject: Requests for Technical Military Information, 740.5/3–1450, ibid.

80. Martin to Najeeb E. Halaby (OSD), March 17, 1950, 740.5/3–1760, ibid.

81. Lord Ismay, NATO: The First Five Years, 1949–1954 (Paris: NATO Information Service, 1954), 29.

82. Tel. 1246, the secretary of state to the American embassy (Paris) for Harriman, March 22, 1950, 740.5/3–2250, Box 3425, RG59, NARA; Wallace J. Thies, Friendly Rivals: Bargaining and Burden-Shifting in NATO (Armonk, N.Y.: M. E. Sharpe, 2003), 63.

83. Interview with General Lemnitzer by Alfred Goldberg, Lawrence Kaplan, Doris Condit, March 4, 1976, 8, Office of the Historian, Secretary of Defense, Washington, D.C.

84. Tel. 1172, Webb to the American embassy (London), March 15, 1950, 740.5/3 MAP/3–1350, Box 3483, RG59, NARA.

85. Control 4861, the secretary of state to certain American diplomatic officers, February 16, 1950, 740.5/1–1650, ibid.; Communiqué of the Military Committee of the North Atlantic Treaty Organization, The Hague, March 28, 1950, FRUS 1950, III: 35; the secretary of state to certain diplomatic officers, March 27, 1950, ibid., 34.

86. Bradley memo for the NATO Standing Group, March 22, 1950, subject: NATO Medium-Term Defense Plan, July 1, 1954, parts I and III, CCS 092 Western Europe, Box 99, RG 218, NARA.

87. Tel. 289, the ambassador to the Netherlands (Chapin) to the secretary of state, February 10, 1950, FRUS1950, III: 29.

88. Bonesteel's comments at a meeting of United States ambassadors in Rome, March 22–24, 1950, Summary Record, undated, ibid., 820, quoted in Bonesteel's letter to Ohly, March 29, 1950, ibid., 37.

89. Parliamentary Debates (Hansard), House of Commons, Fifth Series, vol. 473, April 5, 1950, 1199. It is worth noting that no member of the U.S. Congress or of the French Assemblée Nationale commented on the proceedings of the NATO Defense Committee.

90. Ibid., 1196–99, quoted in Facts on File X, no. 492 (March 31–April 6, 1950): 106.

91. Memo from Assistant Secretary of State Perkins to Deputy Undersecretary of State Dean Rusk, March 7, 1950, subject: Proposed Meeting of the North Atlantic Council, 740.5/3–750 CS/E, Box 3425, RG59, NARA.

6. To London

1. Wallace J. Thies, Friendly Rivals: Bargaining and Burden-Shifting in NATO (Armonk, N.Y.: M. E. Sharpe, 2003), 61–62.

2. Memo from Ridgeway B. Knight, Office of European Regional Affairs (RA), to Assistant Secretary of State for European Affairs George W. Perkins, April 7, 1950, subject: Highlights of Recent NATO Meetings, quote 1, 740.5-4-750, Box 3425, RG 59, NARA.

3. Ibid., quotes 1, 3.

4. Tel. 400, the American embassy, the Hague, to the secretary of state, March 31, 1950, 740.5 MAP/3, Box 2483, RG 59, NARA.

5. Ambassador to the UK Lewis P. Douglas to Acheson, April 11, 1950, "a very private" handwritten note, Dean Acheson Papers, Box 67, Harry S. Truman Library, Independence, Mo.

6. FMACC, M-13, April 13, 1950, Minutes, quote 5–6, Box 104, RG 330, NARA.

7. FMACC, D-12, April 17, 1950, subject: Accomplishments of the North Atlantic Treaty, quote 6–7, Box 194, RG 330, NARA.

8. FMACC, D-3/6, April 29, 1950, subject: proposed Fiscal Year 1952 Budget—Program Presentation Book to the Bureau of the Budget, quotes in 62, Box 103, RG 330, NARA.

9. Office of European Regional Affairs Paper, May 3, 1950, subject: May Foreign Ministers' Meeting, quotes 1–2, FM D A-21/, Box 1467, RG 59, NARA.

10. Charles S. Maier, "Finance and Defense: Implications of Military Integration 1950–1952," in *NATO: The Founding of the Atlantic Alliance and the Integration of Europe,* ed. Francis H. Heller and John R. Gillingham (New York: St. Martin's Press, 1992), 337–38.

11. Draft Report on Implementing the North Atlantic Treaty, prepared in the Office of European Regional Affairs, *Foreign Relations of the United States* [hereafter cited as *FRUS 1950*], III: 73.

12. Memo from the Joint American Military Advisory Group—Europe (JAMAG) to the JCS, May 18, 1950, subject: Estimate of Effectiveness of Armed Forces of the United Kingdom, France, and Italy, Records of the Geographic File, quote 25, 092 Western Europe, Box 103, RG 218, NARA. This estimate originated in MAAG's suggestion to the ECC on April 21, 1950, for congressional hearings on the proposed fiscal year1951 MDAP.

13. Lord Ismay, *NATO: The First Five Years 1949–1954* (Paris: NATO Information Service, 1956), quote 29.

14. Senate Committee on Foreign Relations, Committee on Armed Services, June 6, 1950, *Hearings,* Mutual Defense Assistance Program, quote 30.

15. The secretary of state to the acting secretary of state, May 16, 1950, *FRUS 1950,* III: quote 109, summary of NATO council meeting.

16. Ibid., 109.

17. Ibid., 110–11.

18. Ibid., 111; Dean Acheson, *Present at the Creation: My Years in the State Department* (New York: W. W. Norton & Co., 1969), 398–99.

19. Transcript of questions by members of Congress to the secretary of state and his answers at the special session in the Coolidge Auditorium, Library of Congress, May 31, 1950, Dean Acheson Papers, Box 76, Harry S. Truman Library.

20. Thies, *Friendly Rivals,* 62–64.

21. See L. S. Kaplan, *NATO 1948: Birth of the Transatlantic Alliance* (Lanham, Md.: Rowman & Littlefield, 2007), Chapter 6.

22. Don Cook, *Forging the Alliance: NATO, 1945–1950* (London: Secker and Warburg, 1969), quote 235; Douglas to Acheson, May 18, 1950, Dean Acheson Papers, Box 67, Harry S. Truman Library.

23. Cook, *Forging the Alliance,* quote 235.

24. *New York Times,* May 16, 1950, quote 23.

25. Letter from Douglas to Acheson, May 18, 1950, quote 1, Dean Acheson Papers, Box 67, Harry S. Truman Library.

26. The ambassador to the UK (Douglas) to the secretary of state, June 10, 1950, for Lt.

Col. Charles H. Bonesteel, executive director of the ECC, and Richard C. Breithut, senior U.S. representative on Permanent Working Staff of DFEC, *FRUS 1950*, III: 127–28.

27. Tel. 1840, Frances E. Willis, first secretary, the American embassy in the UK, to the secretary of state, April 12, 1950, subject: Meeting of the Consultative Council at Brussels, April 16 and 17, 1950, an analysis by *The Times*' diplomatic correspondent, 740.5/4–1250, Box 3425, RG 59, NARA.

28. Tel. 1999, Douglas to Acheson, April 13, 1950, personal, 1, 740.5/4–1350, Box 3426, RG 59, NARA.

29. Ibid., 1–2.

30. The ambassador to the UK (Douglas) to the secretary of state, April 18, 1950, personal, *FRUS 1950*, III: 55–57.

31. The secretary of state to the embassy in the UK, April 15, 1950, *FRUS 1950*, III: 53.

32. Tel. 189, the embassy in the UK (Douglas) to the secretary of state, May 6, 1950, 396.1-LO/5–650, Box 149, RG 59, NARA.

33. The secretary of state to the embassy in the UK, April 15, 1950, *FRUS 1950*, III: 53.

34. The ambassador to the UK (Douglas) to the secretary of state, April 18, 1950, *FRUS 1950*, III: 56–57.

35. Letter from Douglas to Acheson, May 18, 1950, 4, Acheson Papers, Box 67, Harry S. Truman Library.

36. Memorandum of conversation, Acheson, Spaak, Silvercruys, January 19, 1950, ibid., Box 66, ibid.

37. Memorandum of conversation, Theodore C. Achilles, director, Office of Western European Affairs (WE), and Edwin M. Martin, director, Office of European Regional Affairs (RA) to Lt. Gen. Alfred N. Gruenther, army deputy chief of staff, and Maj. Gen. Lyman L. Lemnitzer, director, Office of Military Assistance, March 22, 1950, quote 1–2, 750.5/3–2250, Box 3425, RG 59, NARA.

38. Jean-Jacques Servan-Schreiber, "L'Avenir de la Coalition Atlantique," April 5, 1950, *Le Monde*, 1, 3.

39. *Resistance: The Political Autobiography of Georges Bidault*, trans. Marianne Sinclair (New York: Frederick A. Praeger, 1969), 177.

40. See Kaplan, *NATO 1948*, Chapter 1.

41. The ambassador in France (Bruce) to the secretary of state, April 15, 1950, *FRUS 1950*, III: 54–55; Jean-Jacques Servan-Schreiber, "La Troisième Etape," *Le Monde*, April 15, 1950, 1, 3.

42. Tel. 85, Horatio Mooers, American consul in Lyon, to the State Department, April 18, 1950, subject: First Reaction in Lyon Consular District to Bidault's Proposal Regarding Establishment of a "High Atlantic Council," 740.5/14–1850, Box 3425, RG 59, NARA; the ambassador in France (Bruce) to the secretary of state, April 22, 1950, *FRUS 1950*, III: 60–1.

43. The ambassador in France (Bruce) to the secretary of state, April 22, 1950, *FRUS 1950*: 61.

44. The secretary of state to the embassy in France (Bruce), April 21, 1950, ibid., quote 59–60; memo from John Foster Dulles, consultant to the secretary of state, to undersecretary of state, April 21, 1961, ibid., 60.

45. Tel. 383, the American embassy in Norway (Villard) to the secretary of state, April 27, 1950, 740.5/4–2750, Box 3425, RG 59, NARA; tel. 85, Mooers to the State Department, April 18, 1950, subject: Press Reaction . . . 3, 740.5/4–1859, Box 3425, RG 59, NARA.

46. Tel. 1829, the American embassy in France (Bruce) to the secretary of state, April 20, 1950, 740.5/4–205, Box 3425, RG 59, NARA.

47. Tel. 561, the American embassy in the Netherlands (Chapin) to the secretary of state, May 9, 1950, 740.5/5–950, Box 3425, RG 59, NARA; tel. 383, the American embassy in Norway (Villard) to the secretary of state, April 27, 1950, ibid.

48. Tel. 1792, the American embassy in France (Bruce) to the secretary of state, April 19, 1950, 740.5/3–1950, ibid.

49. Acheson described him sympathetically as "slender, stooped, bald, with long nose, surprised and shy eyes and smile, might have been a painter, musician scholar rather than a lawyer, member of parliament, former Premier of France who had put the Communists out of the Government," *Present at the Creation,* 271.

50. Vincent Auriol, *Journal du Septennat,* April 20, 1950, 182–83.

51. The secretary of state to certain diplomatic offices, April 11, 1950, *FRUS 1950,* III: 49.

52. Memo from Bernhard G. Bechhoefer, Office of UN Political and Security Affairs (UNP), to John D. Hickerson, assistant secretary of state for UN Affairs, May 2, 1950, subject: Tentative Draft Agenda for North Atlantic Council, 740.5/5–450, Box 3415, RG 59, NARA.

53. Tel. 404, Julian F. Harrington, chargé d'affaires, the American embassy in Canada, April 5, 1950, to the secretary of state, subject: CCP Leaders Reference to Article 2 of NAT, 1–2, 740.5/4–550, RG 59, NARA; tel. 551, Harrington to the secretary of state, May 4, 1950, subject: External Affairs Minister Reiterates Support of NAT Article II . . . , 1–2, 740.5/5–450, ibid.

54. Tel. 406, the American embassy in Norway (Villard) to the secretary of state, May 4, 1950, 740.5/5–450, Box 3425, NARA; the American embassy in Italy (Dunn) to the secretary of state, May 5, 1950, 740.5–550, ibid.

55. Fourth session of NAC, London, May 12–18, 1950, in *Texts of Final Communiqués, 1949–1974* (Brussels: NATO Information Service, n.d.), quote 56.

56. Letter from Acting Secretary of Defense Stephen T. Early to the secretary of state, February 3, 1950, 740.5 MAP/2–350, Box 3483, NARA; memo from Undersecretary of State James W. Webb to the secretary of defense, February 17, 1950, 740.5 MAP/2–350 CS/N, ibid.

57. Tel. 939, the secretary of state to the American embassy in the UK, March 1, 1950, 740.5/3–150, Box 3425, NARA.

58. FM D B-32, May Foreign Ministers' Meetings: Background Paper on the Agenda Item: Report of the IWG on the Establishment of a North Atlantic Planning Board for Ocean Shipping. Paper prepared in the State Department's Office of European Regional Affairs. It outlines the issues and solutions agreed upon by the IWG and recommends that the U.S. move that the NAC approve the directive, 396.1-LO/5–450, Box 1467, NARA.

59. *Texts of Final Communiqué,* 55.

60. Memo from the chairman, Joint Chiefs of Staff, to the secretary of defense, April 27, 1950, subject: Spain, 395.1-LO/5–350, Box 1467, NARA.

61. Memo from Assistant Secretary of State George McGhee for Near Eastern, South Asian, and African Affairs to the undersecretary of state, May 1, 1950, subject: Continuing Desire of Turkey to be Included in a Formal Security Arrangement, *FRUS 1950,* III: 79–80. Tel. 85, Acheson to the American embassy in the UK, with information to Ankara and Paris, May 3, 1950, 396.1-LO/5–350, Box 1467, RG 59, NARA.

62. Tel. 66, the American embassy in the UK (Douglas) to the secretary of state, May 1, 1950, 396.1-LO/5–150, Box 1467, NARA. From Ambassador at Large Philip C. Jessup, head of the advance party of U.S. negotiators at the London preparatory talks. He was subsequently the alternate U.S. member at the NAC meeting.

63. Tel. 74, the American embassy in the UK to the secretary of state, May 1, 1950, 396.1-

LO/5–150, Box 1467, NARA; tel. 112, the American embassy in the UK to the secretary of state, May 3, 1950, 396.1-LO/5- 350, ibid. Both messages were from Jessup to Acheson.

64. Tel. 123, the American embassy in the UK to the secretary of state, May 4, 4 P.M., 1950; tel. 736 to Paris, from Jessup for David K. E. Bruce, ambassador in France, 396.1-LO/5–450, Box 1467, NARA; tel. 133, repeated to Paris tel. 743, the American embassy in London to the secretary of state, May 4, midnight, 1950, ibid.

65. Tel. 736, quote, ibid.; U.S. delegation to the tripartite foreign ministers' meeting to the acting secretary of state, May 9, 1950, *FRUS 1950*, III: 1021.

66. Memorandum of conversation, Oliver Franks and George Perkins, April 6, 1950,740.5/4–550, Box 3425, RG 59, NARA.

67. Tel. 80, the secretary of state to the American embassy in the UK, May 3, 1950, 395.1 LO/5–350, Box 1467, RG 59, NARA; note the article by influential military correspondent Drew Middleton, "Arming the Germans: Asset or Liability?" *New York Times*, April 2, 1950, 4E.

68. Tel. 145, the American embassy in the UK to the secretary of state, May 4, 1950 396/1 LO/5–450, Box 1467, RG 59, NARA.

69. Tel. 115, the American embassy in the UK to the secretary of state, May 3, 1950, 36.1 LO/5–350, ibid.; memo from Byroade to the secretary of state, May 6, 1950, quote 2, 396.1 LO/5–650 TSF, ibid.

70. MIN/TRI/P/7—Ministerial Talks: United States/United Kingdom/France, May 6, 1950: Policy towards Germany, 376.1-2-/5–650 SF, Box 1467, RG 59, NARA; United States delegation at the tripartite foreign ministers' meeting to the acting secretary of state, May 12, 1950, quote, *FRUS 1950:* III, 1044.

71. Jean Monnet, *Memoirs,* trans. Richard Mayne (New York: Doubleday & Co., 1978), 308; René Massigli, *Une comedie des erreurs, 1943–1946* (Paris: Plon, 1978), 196–97.

72. Acheson, *Present at the Creation,* 382–83; Alan Bullock, *The Life of Ernest Bevin: Foreign Secretary, 1945–1951* (London: Heinemann, 1983), 771–74.

73. Quoted in the Princeton Conference, 10/10/53—Reel 3, Track 2, p. 10, Acheson Papers, Box 80, Harry S. Truman Library; Acheson, *Present at the Creation,* quote 384); tel. 157, Webb to the American embassy in the UK (Dulles personal Acheson), May 10, 1950, 740.5/5–1050, Box 3425, RG 59, NARA.

74. Acheson, *Present at the Creation,* 385–86; Monnet, *Memoirs,* 300.

75. United States delegation at the tripartite foreign ministers' meeting to the acting secretary of state, May 12, 1950, *FRUS1950*, III: 1045; Monnet, *Memoirs,* 304; Konrad Adenauer, *Briefe, 1949–1951* (Berlin: Seidler Verlag, 1985), 212–15.

76. Tel. 1924, ECC (Bonesteel) to Kibler, Breithut, April 11, 1950, 740.5/4–1150, Box 3425, RG 59, NARA.

77. Tel. 82968, army message to the secretary of state, May 15, 1950, quote 2, 740.5/5–1550, ibid.

78. Letter from the secretary of defense to the secretary of state, May 6, 1950, 740.5/5–650, ibid.

79. Tel. 135, the acting secretary of state (Webb) to the American embassy in the UK (for Martin), May 8, 1950, quote 2, 740.5/5–850, ibid.

80. Tel. 1860, Secretary of State Acheson to the American embassy in France (for Harriman), April 27, 1950, 740.5/4–2750, ibid., tel. A-100, the secretary of state to the American embassy in Canada, May 8, 1950, subject: Proposed U.S. resolution in North Atlantic Council, quote, 740.5/5–850 A/UT, ibid.

81. Tel. 64, the American embassy in the UK (from Jessup) to the secretary of state, quote, May 1, 1950, 396.I-LO/5–150, Box 1467, RG 59, NARA.

82. Tel. 138, the secretary of state to the American embassy in the UK, May 3, 1950, 396.1-LO/5–650, ibid., for an example of U.S. frustration over resolutions for the May summit; PRI/P/11, May 2, 1950, United States, United Kingdom, France Tripartite Talks: French Delegation Draft, quote, 396.I-LO/5–250, ibid.

83. *Texts of Final Communiqués,* par. 54–55; Ismay, *NATO,* quote 28; the italics were noted in Steven L. Rearden, *The Formative Years: 1947–1950,* vol. 1 of *History of the Office of Secretary of Defense,* ed. Alfred Goldberg (Washington, D.C.: Historical Office, Office of the Secretary of Defense, 1984), 486.

84. Memorandum of conversation, William Munthe de Morgenstierne, Webb, Charles E. Rogers, BNA, May 26, 1950, subject: Norwegian Ambassador Discusses London Conference of Foreign Ministers, quote, 740.5/5–2660, Box 3425, RG 59, NARA; from the secretary of state to the acting secretary of state, May 16, 1950, *FRUS 1950,* III: 105–8. Acheson's summary of high points of meeting of foreign ministers.

85. Tel. 63, the American embassy in the UK (Douglas) to the secretary of state, May 1, 1950, 396.1-LO/5–150, Box 1467, RG 59, NARA; tel. 87, the secretary of state to the American embassy in the UK, May 3, 1950, 396.I-LO/5–250, ibid.; memorandum of conversation, Hickerson, United Nations Affairs (UNA); Durward V. Sandifer, deputy assistant secretary of state, UNA; Bechhoefer, UNP, May 4, 1949, subject: Meeting of International Working Group, 740.5–5/5–450, Box 3485, RG 59, NARA.

86. Tel. 125, Acting Secretary of State Webb to the American embassy in the UK, May 6, 1950, 396-I-LO/5–650, Box 1467, RG 59, NARA; tel. 84, the American embassy in the UK (from Jessup) to the secretary of state, 396.I-LO/5–250, ibid.; TRI/P/17, May 3, 1950, United States, United Kingdom, France Tripartite Talks, Item 2 (a): NATO, Provisional Proposal with amendments from the British delegation, omitting the word "executive," 396.I-LO/5–350 ibid.

87. Tel. 71, the secretary of state to the American embassy in the UK, May 3, 1950, 396.I-LO/5–350, ibid.

88. Tel. 2367, the American embassy in the UK to the State Department (for Perkins), May 17, 1950, quote 396.I-LO/5–1450, noting military implications of the French resolutions; Memo . . . by Office of European Regional Affairs (Knight) and deputy director of that office (MacArthur), May 24, 1950, *FRUS 1950:* III, 126.

89. TRI/P/19, May 4, 1950, United States, United Kingdom, France Tripartite Talks, Item 2 (a); Draft Prepared by Sub- Committee "A," quote, 1, 396.I-LO/5–450, Box 1467, NARA.

90. *Texts of Final Communiqués,* quote par. 3, 54.

91. Tel. 159, the American ambassador in the UK (Douglas) to the secretary of state, May 5, 1950, quote, 396.I-LO/5–550, Box 1467, RG 59, NARA; tel. 187, Douglas to the secretary of state, May 6, 1950, 396.I-LO/5–650, ibid.

92. Tel. 138, Acting Secretary of State Webb to the American embassy in the UK, May 8, 1950, 396.I LO/5–650, ibid.

93. Department of State, Division of European Affairs, June 1, 1950, subject: North Atlantic Council Meeting, 740.5/6–150, Box 3425, RG 59, NARA.

94. *New York Times,* May 21, 1950, E-30; Acheson, *Present at the Creation,* quote, 399.

7. The Shock of June 25, 1950

1. Mutual Defense Assistance Program, Supplement, *Hearings,* Senate Committee on Foreign Relations and Committee on the Armed Services, 81st Cong., 2 sess., June 6, 1950, editor's note, 401; Special Message to the Congress on Military Aid, June 1, 1950, *Public Papers of the President, Harry S. Truman,* 405.

2. Mutual Defense Assistance Program, 1950, *Hearings,* June 5, 1950, Committees on Foreign Relations and Foreign Relations, 81st Cong., 2nd sess., 12; ibid., 38.

3. Ibid., June 16, 1950, 91; *Facts on File Yearbook, 1950,* v. 10, August 25–31, 276.

4. Mutual Defense Assistance Program, Supplement, *Hearings,* Senate Committee on Foreign Relations, June 6, 1950, 410; ibid., 412.

5. Memo from Harding F. Bancroft, UNP, to Bernhard Bechhoefer, UNP, June 9, 1950, subject: United States Deputy to NAT Central Organization, 740.5/6–950, Box 3425, RG 59, NARA.

6. Memo from Lucius D. Battle, special assistant to the secretary of state, to Acheson, June 9, 1950, Acheson Papers, Box 67, Harry S. Truman Library.

7. Memo from Perkins to the secretary of state, June 2, 1950, subject: North Atlantic Council of Deputies, 740.5/6–850, Box 3425, RG 59, NARA; Perkins to the Secretary of State, June 8, 1950, subject: Canadian Views on North Atlantic Council of Deputies, 740.5/6–850, ibid.

8. Franks's memo to Acheson, June 19, 1950, delivering a telegram from Bevin, June 19, 1950, *FRUS 1950,* III: 128–29; *New York Times,* June 24, 1950, 6.

9. Memorandum of conversation, Sir Derek Hoyer Miller and George W. Perkins, June 13, 1950, subject: NATO Deputy, 740.5/6–1350, Box 3425, RG 59, NARA; tel. 760, The Hague (Chapin) to the secretary of state, June 23, 1950, 740.5/6–2350, ibid.; *New York Times,* June 24, 1950, quote on 6.

10. North Atlantic Council Deputies, D-R/1, July 25, Summary Record of the First Meeting Held at Lancaster House on the 25th of July at 10:30 A.M., NATO Archives, Brussels; D-R/2, Summary Record of the Second Meeting, ibid.

11. The secretary of state to the United States delegation at the tripartite preparatory meetings at London, May 2, 1950, *FRUS 1950,* III: 914; the secretary of state to the embassy in the United Kingdom, March 23, 1950, ibid., quote on 33–34.

12. The secretary of state to the United States delegation at the tripartite meetings in London, April 25, 1950, ibid., 861.

13. FMACC, N 18, Minutes of Combined Meetings of May 25 and 26, Box 102, RG 330, NARA.

14. *New York Times,* June 3, 1950, 1; ibid., April 6, 1950, 4.

15. Ibid., April 12, 1950, 1; ibid., April 17, 1950, 4.

16. Ibid., June 17, 1950, quote on 4.

17. Ibid., May 7, 1950, quote on 1.

18. Draft Declaration for the Three Foreign Ministers on Germany, May 7, 1950, *FRUS 1950,* III: quote on 1087; Paper Agreed Upon by the Foreign Ministers, May 22, 1950, ibid., 1089–91.

19. *New York Times,* June 9, 1950, 1.

20. Adenauer's speech on May 21, 1950 in *New York Times,* June 3, 1950, 3.

21. Letter to Speaker Transmitting Supplemental Estimate of Appropriations for Military Assistance, August 1, 1950, *Public Papers of the Presidents, Harry S. Truman,* 564.

22. Mutual Defense Assistance Program, 1950, *Hearings,* June 5, 1950, quote on 20 and 40.

8. Conclusion

1. John Keegan, "60 Years on: NATO Has Become the Victim of Its Own Success," April 2, 2009, excerpted from *London Daily Telegraph,* April 3, 2009, 5.

2. "NATO at 60: Towards a New Strategic Concept," January 15, 2009, Wilton Park Conference.

3. Harlan Cleveland, *NATO: The Transatlantic Bargain* (New York: Harper & Row, 1970).

4. *Texts of Final Communiqués,* London, May 18, 1950, 54–55.

5. Dean Acheson, *Present at the Creation: My Years in the State Department* (New York: W. W. Norton & Co., 1969), 399.

Select Bibliography

The documents and books listed are, for the most part, those included in the text.

Primary Sources

ARCHIVES

Arthur H. Vandenberg Papers, Bentley Historical Library, University of Michigan
Dean Acheson Papers, Harry S. Truman Library
J. William Fulbright Papers, University of Arkansas
John Foster Dulles Papers, Princeton University
Liddell Hart Centre for Military Archives, King's College, London
NATO Archives, Brussels
U.K. National Archives, Kew
U.S. National Archives and Records Administration, College Park, Md.
Western European Union Archives, Brussels

PUBLISHED DOCUMENTS

Bulletin, Department of State
Congressional Daily Digest
Congressional Record
Council of Europe: The First Five Years (Strasbourg: Directorate of Information, 1954)
Current Developments in United States Foreign Policy, Brookings Institution
Débats parlementaires (France)
Documents on Establishment and Organization, Department of Defense
Foreign Relations of the United States
Hearings, Committee on Foreign Relations, U.S. House of Representatives
Hearings, Committees on Foreign Relations and Armed Services, U.S. Senate
House of Commons, Parliamentary Debates (Great Britain)
NATO: The First Five Years, Lord Ismay
Public Papers of the Presidents of the United States, Harry S. Truman

Texts of Final Communiqués, NATO
Yearbook of the United Nations, United Nations

NEWSPAPERS AND INDEXES

Algemeen Handelsblad (Amsterdam)
Current Digest of the Soviet Press
Daily Worker (London)
Facts-on-File
Figaro (Paris)
Index to the Proceedings of the Security Council
Keesing's Contemporary Archives
Le Monde (Paris)
Newsweek
New York Times
Verdens Gang (Oslo)
The Times (London)
United Nations: Index to Proceedings of the General Assembly
Washington Post

MEMOIRS, DIARIES, CORRESPONDENCE

Acheson, Dean. *Present at the Creation: My Years in the State Department.* New York: W. W. Norton, 1969.

Achilles, Theodore. *Fingerprints on History: The NATO Memoirs of Theodore Achilles.* Edited by L. S. Kaplan and S. R. Snyder. Kent, Okla.: Lemnitzer Center for NATO European Community Studies, 1992.

Adenauer, Konrad. *Briefe 1948–1951.* Berlin: Seidler Verlag, 1985.

Alphand, Hervé. *L'Etonnement d'être: Journal,1939–1973.* Paris: Fayard, 1977.

Auriol, Vincent. *Journal du Septennat,* vol. 3. Paris: Armand Colin, 1974.

Bonnet, Georges. *Le Quai d'Orsay sous trois républiques.* Paris: Fayard, 1961.

Bérard, Armand. *Une ambassadeur se souvient: Washington et Bonn, 1945–1955,* 5 vols. Paris: Plon, 1976–82.

Bidault, Georges. *Resistance: The Political Autobiography of Georges Bidault.* Translated by Marianne Sinclair. New York: Frederick A. Praeger, 1969.

Bohlen, Charles E. *Witness to History.* New York: W. W. Norton, 1969.

Chauvel, Jean. *Commentaire: d'Alger à Berne, 1944–1952.* Paris: Fayard, 1971.

De Staercke, André, ed. *NATO's Anxious Birth: The Prophetic Vision of the 1940s.* New York: St. Martin's Press, 1985.

Forrestal, James V. *The Forrestal Diaries.* Edited by Walter Millis. New York: The Viking Press, 1951.

Ismay, Hastings. *NATO: The First Five Years, 1949–1954.* Paris: NATO Information Service, 1954.

Jebb, Gladwyn. *The Memoirs of Lord Gladwyn.* New York: Weybridge and Talley, 1972.

Kennan, George F. *Memoirs, 1925–1950.* New York: Bantam Books, 1969.

Lie, Trygve. *In the Cause of Peace: Seven Years with the United Nations.* New York: Macmillan, 1954.

Lilienthal, David E. *The Journals of David Lilienthal: The Atomic Energy Years 1945–1950.* New York: Harper & Row, 1964.

Massigli, René. *Une comédie des erreurs, 1943–1956.* Paris: Fayard, 1972.

Monnet, Jean. *Memoirs.* Translated by Richard Mayne. Garden City, N.Y.: Doubleday, 1978.

Montgomery, Bernard Law. *Memoirs of Field-Marshal the Viscount Montgomery of Alamein.* Cleveland: World Publishing Co., 1958.

Nitze, Paul H., with Anne M. Smith and Steven L. Rearden. *From Hiroshima to Glasnost: At the Center of Decision: A Memoir.* New York: Grove Weidenfeld, 1989.

Spaak, Paul-Henri. *The Continuing Battle: Memoirs of a European, 1933–1966.* Translated by Henry Fox. Boston: Little, Brown, 1971.

Stikker, Dirk U. *Men of Responsibility: A Memoir.* New York: Harper & Row, 1966.

Strauss, Lewis L. *Men and Decisions.* London: Macmillan Co., 1963.

Taft, Robert A. *The Papers of Robert A. Taft,* vol. 4. Edited by Clarence E. Wunderlin Jr. Kent, Ohio: Kent State Univ. Press, 2006.

Truman, Harry S. *Memoirs, 1946–1952: Years of Trial and Hope.* New York: New American Library, 1965.

Vandenberg, Arthur H. Jr., ed. *The Private Papers of Senator Vandenberg.* Boston: Houghton Mifflin Co., 1952.

MONOGRAPHS

Bland, Douglas L. *The Military Committee of the North Atlantic Alliance: A Study of Structure and Strategy.* New York: Praeger, 1991.

Bozo, Frederic. *La France et l'Otan: de la guerre froide au nouvel ordre européen.* Paris: Masson, 1991.

Bullock, Alan. *The Life of Ernest Bevin: Foreign Secretary, 1945–1951.* London: Heinemann, 1983.

Condit, Kenneth W. *The History of the JCS: The Joint Chiefs of Staff and National Policy, 1947–1949.* Wilmington, Del.: Michael Glazier, Inc., 1979.

Cook, Don. *Forging the Alliance: NATO, 1945 to 1950.* London: Secker & Warburg, 1989.

Danchev, Alex. *Oliver Franks: Founding Father.* Oxford: The Clarendon Press, 1993.

Donovan, Robert J. *Tumultuous Years: The Presidency of Harry S. Truman 1949–1953.* New York: W. W. Norton & Co., 1982.

Heller, F. H., and J. R. Gillingham. *NATO: The Founding of the Atlantic Alliance and the Integration of Europe.* New York: St. Martin's Press, 1992.

Hitchcock, William H. *France Restored: Cold War Diplomacy and the Quest for Leadership in Europe, 1944–1954.* Chapel Hill: Univ. of North Carolina Press, 1998.

Huntington, Samuel P. *The Common Defense: Strategic Programs in National Policy.* New York: Columbia Univ. Press, 1961.

Ireland, Timothy P. *Creating the Atlantic Alliance: The Origins of the North Atlantic Treaty Organization.* Westport, Conn.: Greenwood Press, 1981.

Kaplan, L. S. *A Community of Interests: NATO and the Military Assistance Program, 1948–1951.* Washington, D.C.: Historical Office, Office of the Secretary of Defense, 1980.

———. *NATO 1948: The Birth of the Transatlantic Alliance.* Lanham, Md.: Rowman & Littlefield, 2007.

———. *The United States and NATO: The Formative Years.* Lexington, Ky.: Univ. Press of Kentucky, 1984.

Knorr, Klaus, ed. *NATO and American Security.* Princeton, N.J.: Princeton Univ. Press, 1959.

Leffler, Melvyn P. *A Preponderance of Power: National Security, the Truman Administration, and the Cold War.* Stanford, Calif.: Stanford Univ. Press, 1992.

Leigh-Pippard, Helen. *Congress and U.S. Military Aid to Britain: Interdependence and Dependence.* London: St. Martin's Press, 1995.

Mazuzan, George T. *Warren R. Austin at the UN, 1946–1953.* Kent, Ohio: Kent State Univ. Press, 1977.

Osgood, Robert E. *NATO: The Entangling Alliance.* Chicago: Univ. of Chicago Press, 1962.

Pach, Chester J. Jr. *Arming the Free World: The Origins of the United States Military Assistance Program, 1945–1950.* Chapel Hill: Univ. of North Carolina Press, 1991.

Rearden, Steven L. *History of the Office of the Secretary of Defense: The Formative Years 1947–1950.* Washington, D.C.: Historical Office, Office of the Secretary of Defense, 1984.

———. *The Evolution of American Strategic Doctrine: Paul H. Nitze and the Soviet Challenge.* Boulder, Colo.: Westview Press, 1984.

Riste, Olav. *Western Security: The Formative Years European and Atlantic Defence, 1947–1953.* New York: Columbia Univ. Press, 1985.

Ruddy, T. Michael. *The Cautious Diplomat: Charles E. Bohlen and the Soviet Union, 1929–1969.* Kent, Ohio: Kent State Univ. Press, 1986.

Schwartz, Thomas A. *America's Germany: John J. McCloy and the Federal Republic of Germany.* Cambridge, Mass.: Harvard Univ. Press, 1991.

Smith, E. Timothy. *Opposition Beyond the Water's Edge: Liberal Internationalists, Pacifists, and Containment, 1945–1953.* Westport, Conn.: Greenwood Press, 1999.

———. *The United States, Italy, and NATO, 1947–1952.* New York: St. Martin's Press, 1991.

Smith, Joseph, ed. *The Origins of NATO.* Exeter: Univ. of Exeter Press, 1990.

Thies, Wallace J. *Friendly Rivals: Bargaining and Burden-Shifting in NATO.* Armonk, N.Y.: M. E. Sharpe, 2003.

Wiggershaus, N., and R. G. Foerster. *The Western Security Community: Common Problems and Conflicting National Interests During the Foundation Phase of the North Atlantic Alliance.* Providence, R.I.: Berg, 1993.

Williamson, D. R., and S. L. Rearden. *The Origins of U.S. Nuclear Strategy, 1945–1953.* New York: St. Martin's Press, 1993.

Wunderlin, Clarence E. Jr. *Robert A. Taft: Ideas, Tradition, and Party in U.S. Foreign Policy.* Lanham, Md.: Rowman & Littlefield, 2005.

Index

Acheson, Dean: Additional Military Production Program and, 74; Anglo-French tensions and, 68–69; Atlantic High Council for Peace and, 126; balanced collective forces *vs.* balanced national forces and, 119; bilateral agreements and, 52–53; Britain *vs.* Europe and, 86–88; Brussels Pact and, 20–21; dismantling German industry and, 78; Foreign Relations Committee and, 23; German Question and, 26, 145; HR 5748 and, 41; MAP bill and, 35–36, 151; Medium-Term Defense Plan and, 135–36; military development of Europe and, 84–85; Mutual Defense Assistance Act and, 41–44, 47–48, 141–44; Mutual Defense Assistance Program and, 91, 94–95; National Security Council committee and, 100–103; NATO's pre-integration organization, 60; NSC 68 and, 105; Regional Planning Groups and, 64–66; Schuman Plan and, 128, 132–33; United Nations and, 14–17

Achilles, Theodore A., 2, 40, 52

Additional Military Production (AMP) Program, 74–75, 89, 91, 108, 112, 116, 123

Adenauer, Konrad, 79, 81–82, 133–34, 145–47

Ad Hoc Political Committee, 13

aircraft, 77, 114, 117–18

air forces, 84, 92

air operations, enemy, 82–83

air power, 83, 151

Algemeen Handelsblad, 84

Allied High Commission, 24

Alphand, Hervé, 25

Alsop, Joseph, 69

Alsop, Stewart, 69

America (Jesuit magazine), 2

American imperialism, 4, 16, 50, 53

American neocolonialism, 50

Anglo-American harmony, 120

Anglo-French tension, 66–70

anti-aircraft weaponry, 36, 114

anti-Communism, 27, 28, 94

anti-tank weapons, 77

armed forces, 7, 117

Armed Services, Committee of, 41

Armed Services Committee, 38, 43

Aron, Raymond, 98

Asian crisis, 148

Atlantic alliance, 31, 38, 43, 49, 55

Atlantic Cominform, 124

Atlantic High Council for Peace, 124–27, 134, 137, 144

Atlantic Pact: absence of Spain from the, 27; Arthur Vandenberg and the, 18; expansion of Article 2 and the, 128; implementation of the, 34, 68–69; machinery of, 36, 44, 75; military assistance and the, 23; Soviet aggression and, 43; UN Charter and, 7, 14–16

atom bombs, 7, 47, 84, 99, 106, 108, 136

Atomic Energy Commission, 101–2

Auriol, Vincent, 78–79, 81, 95–96, 106, 127

Austin, Warren R., 11, 13, 16–18

balanced collective forces *vs.* balanced national forces, 118–19

balance-of-power structures, 14

Barrett, Edward W., 99

Basic Law, 25, 78, 81

Battle, Lucius, 143

Belgium, 89, 92–93, 121, 129, 143

Bell, John O., 115

Bender, Mrs. Clifford A., 17

Berkeley Radiation Laboratory, 101